FROM AN ORDINARY EXTRAORDINARY
AFRICAN AMERICAN ELDER

It was such an honor to have my story included in *Ordinary Extraordinary African American Women: The Elders.* It is important that the voices of the Elders be heard; and now, thanks to the author, Stephana Colbert, we will hear the stories and learn from some of the special Black women in the next generation.

—NORMA JUNE WILSON DAVIS

ALSO BY STEPHANA COLBERT

Color Him Father: Stories of Love & Rediscovery of Black Men, Edited by Stephana I. Colbert & Valerie Harrison (2006)

"My Favorite Green Dress" in *Color Him Father: Stories of Love & Rediscovery of Black Men (2006)*

"Race & Racism: Inequities in the Criminal Justice System." In *Black Culture & Experience: Contemporary Issues,* Vol. 71, (eds.) Venise T. Berry, Anita Fleming-Rife and ayo dayo. Peter: New York (2015)

Ordinary Extraordinary African American Women: The Elders (2017)

ALSO BY JEWELL JORDAN PUBLISHING, LLC

Color Him Father: Stories of Love & Rediscovery of Black Men (2006)

Ordinary Extraordinary African American Women: The Elders (2017)

Bishop Morris Brown: The Invisible Man of the African Methodist Episcopal Church (2019)

ORDINARY
EXTRAORDINARY
AFRICAN AMERICAN WOMEN:
AS WE MATURE

STEPHANA I. COLBERT

JEWELL JORDAN PUBLISHING LLC
OKLAHOMA

For information address Jewell Jordan Publishing, LLC, 1205 South Air Depot Blvd, Suite 153, Midwest City, Oklahoma 73110

Interior Design and Cover Design by The Roberts Group

Photographs: Back flap photograph by Butch Neece. Other photographs in this book were supplied by the story subjects.

Library of Congress Control Number: 2020949613

Hardcover ISBN: 978-0-9778418-4-4
Paperback ISBN: 978-0-9778418-5-1
eBook ISBN: 978-1-7360906-0-2

First edition

Printed in the United States of America

The paper in this book meets the guidelines for permanence and durability of the Committee on Production Guidelines for Book Longevity of the Council of Library Resources

For Wynell Marie Neece & Jordiene Jewell Petitt
My sisters & My sheroes
Love you to the moon!

CONTENTS

FOREWORD

I recently watched a program that was a conversation with a group of Black women. It was such a pleasure to hear the voices of this group of women discussing our journey and our obstacle of invisibility in a world where we play such an important role. One of the most powerful comments made during the course of this conversation was, "Black women specialize in the wholly impossible." Wow . . . that's it, that's what we do and that is why telling our stories is so important. In this second book in the series, *Ordinary Extraordinary African American Woman: As We Mature*, there are twelve stories about women who have thrived and survived through successes and disappointments.

These stories are examples of the 16 million Black woman of America. Mostly they are stories about women quietly putting one foot in front of the other and getting the job done all while raising children, caring for parents, supporting brothers, sisters, grandchildren, and friends. Often, they work in environments that are oppressive, sometimes hostile, and generally provided with pay that is less than most all others.

In this edition of *Ordinary Extraordinary African American Woman: As We Mature*, the women are between the ages of 45 and 69 and work in a variety of fields including accounting, social work, and psychology. There is a travel writer, two women of the cloth, with very different approaches to ministry, and finally, a career postal worker.

Reading these real-life stories reminds me of the fictional stories J. California Cooper often told. They all have elements of struggle, joy, hardship, and success. Many have turned trials into opportunities and learning. The theme of learning and growth was always at the heart of the stories told by J. California Cooper.

This book celebrates the light we Black women bring into the world. Light like that of my grandmother. She was a domestic worker for most of her life and she lived until she was 98 years old in her own little house, cooking her own breakfast until 97. Her life was very ordinary: she loved a man and divorced him, raised two children, worked for one White family for 30 plus years. She was an extremely great cook who drove until she was 90, only stopping when she realized she could not remember what pedal she needed to use to stop the car. And here's the thing, she knew at that point to stop driving. No one needed to tell her to stop, she did it on her own. She had a grand sense of humor that remained through her 97th year. She went to church, loved the Lord, and lived what many may call a very small life, but at sixty-three, I pray for the peace she seemed to radiate most days.

I so appreciate my sister's desire to tell the stories of ordinary, everyday Black women. Most of the stories have no glamour, special awards, or any form of high recognition but they are about real-life. These stories reveal how one overcomes childhood abuse, disappointments in marriages, with children, family, and in one's career, but also celebrate the strength and self-preservation of the Black woman. We indeed specialize in the "wholly impossible."

Jordiene J. Colbert Petitt
MSW, MBA
Retired
November 2020

FROM THE AUTHOR

In 2006 in the middle of the night, three armed men broke into my apartment, held a sawed-off shotgun to my head, tied me up, ransacked my apartment, and raided my bank account. The good news was that other than a split lip received from the butt of the gun, I was physically unharmed.

Nonetheless, I was not in a good place. A friend gave me the name of a therapist—Stephanie Brooks—one of the women we celebrate in these pages. My therapy sessions were not always productive because for a long time I wouldn't talk about what happened. However, they were my safe haven while I worked through my night of terror. I tell you this primarily because our community needs to embrace taking care of our mental health. It is important and can be lifesaving. In addition to shedding a light on this need, Stephanie's journey is that of a woman of commitment, brilliance, perseverance, and ultimately joy.

That is one of my takeaways from all of these ladies' journeys—Joy! There are some difficult circumstances with which each woman is faced and which she must overcome—physical, mental, and sexual abuse, divorce, racism, self-image, blindness, single parenting, raising an autistic child, glass ceilings, being the "only", teen pregnancy, illness, abandonment, caring for family, the murder of a parent, loss of a child, finding her place—but overcome they do, all ending in a place of joy, loving themselves and where they are in life.

These are women in my age group—my peers—with whom I share a common bond based upon when we grew up—the 50s & 60s—the still revolutionary times when we went to college—70s & 80s—and most particularly the fact that although there is still much to learn and accomplish we have all matured from our younger selves based upon our life experiences. There are so many of my peers—friends, relatives, and colleagues—who are extraordinary in the way in which they have led what many of them would characterize as ordinary lives. Their journeys could fill the pages of hundreds of books like this one—and perhaps we will have others. But for now, the twelve women in this volume must represent the thousands of African American sheroes between the ages of 45 and 69 whose stories go untold. It is, therefore, my honor and pleasure to share the journey of each of them.

Stephana I. Colbert
November 2, 2020

RENÉE STEPHANIE GORDON

DARE TO BE DIFFERENT

When children (and adults) are exposed to what is bad and hurtful, especially when the hurt and bad emanates from someone who is close—like a parent—that child may emulate the parent—sometimes spreading even more hurt and evil.[1] But . . . that is not always the result—the abused do not always become the abuser. Rather, with the hurt and

---

1. *Sad Legacy Of Abuse: The Search For Remedies*, New York Times, Science, By Daniel Goleman, January 24, 1989 *Long-term effects of child abuse and neglect on emotion processing in adulthood*, Joanna Cahall Young & Cathy Spatz Widom, Journal of Child Abuse and Neglect, Volume 38, Issue 8, August 2014, Pages 1369–1381)

pain deeply etched into our youthful memories, we can and do some-times become kind and thoughtful adults. Such is the case with Renée Stephanie Williams Gordon—rising above her father's inexplicable mis-treatment to become a wonderfully good person—daring to be different.

Born in Philadelphia, Pennsylvania, Renée Stephanie Gordon is the only child of Bessie and James Williams. Although her parents had siblings, none of them had children; therefore, Renée had no cousins and was the only grandchild on either side of the family. Essentially, she grew up with adults who adored her—including her father—who was a musician.

I clearly remember every night before he went to the club—I had a practice piano in my room—he would come into my room and play my piano and sing "Daddy's Little Girl" to me so that I could go to sleep. We went EVERY-WHERE together! I thought I was the apple of his eye.

Renée's parents divorced when she was five, initially sharing joint custody. At first, that arrangement seemed to work. As time passed, however, it did not—at least not for her father. Renée describes it this way . . .

Then one day . . . boom! It went from sugar to shit! All of a sudden, he didn't want to talk to me or have anything to do with me. I came to understand that my father was not happy about being divorced.

Her father's discontent over the divorce manifested in hurtful and seemingly mean-spirited interactions with Renée when he had custody of her on the weekends.

He would say to me, "I'm not sure you are my daughter; you are too ugly to be my little girl." Really hurtful things. Interestingly I did not know about verbal abuse until Oprah; and when I heard it being discussed on her show, I said, 'Oh my God! I was abused!' As an adult I reflected on my father's behavior towards me and decided that was his issue; but at six years old you cannot make those distinctions; so it was very hurtful.

Although divorce seemed to trigger her father's cruelties, remarriage did not assuage his anger or moderate his abuses of Renée. In fact, that Mr. Williams' new wife had a child the same age as Renée seemed to exacerbate his bad behavior.

At the end of each visit, my father would take us to a toy store and tell us to pick out a toy—"whatever you want" we were told. Being little girls we would settle on the same thing. When we got to the cash register, he would take mine and say, "You are not a good little girl so you do not deserve a toy." Beverly [Renee's stepsister] would get her toy and I would get nothing. He never let me keep mine because he said I didn't deserve it. That happened three times.

When Renée had enough of this weekly ritual, she determined that it would not happen a fourth time.

I was clever—not bright, but clever. I decided I didn't like that. So [the next time] we went to the store and he said, "You can get anything you want," I said, 'I don't want anything.' He grabbed me and took me up and down the aisles insisting that I get something. I resisted; so he bought me the 45 record "I Saw Mommy Kissing Santa Claus". I used to think I wanted to beat him with it.

There was a "last straw" in these interactions between Renee and her father. Although Renée did not like vegetables (*my grandmother didn't make me eat them*), whenever she visited her father, he had her stepmother make only vegetables for Renée—*not meat or anything else.* She arrived for her visit on Friday evenings. If she did not eat the vegetables on her plate on Friday, they would be back on Saturday and then again on Sunday afternoon.

On one of the last Sundays Renée ever spent with her father, when he placed the plate of vegetables before her, Renée recalls she began to cry. She says he first taunted her—*He told me, "You are so tough I can't believe you are crying!"*

Then, in an ultimate fit of anger, Renée's father took scissors and cut off her two long braids. Placing a tam on her head, he took Renée home. (Actually, because the relationship between her mother and father was so difficult, her parents had no contact and Renee's father would always take Renée to her grandmother's at the end of each weekend visit where Renée's mother was there awaiting her return.)

When my mother saw me, she said, "There's my baby!" and hugged me. She then pulled off my tam and asked, "What happened to your hair?" I told her 'Daddy cut it off.' She took off running down the street trying to catch my father's car. When my grandfather came out of the house, he asked me what my mother was doing. I told him, and he and my uncle jumped in the car going after my mother and father.

Renée's mother had her father arrested for assault, although he was ultimately not prosecuted. However, after a subsequent court hearing during which the judge talked to seven-year-old Renée, her father's visitation rights were limited. Thereafter, Renée's contact with her father was virtually non-existent.

My father took the position that if he was going to have his visitations limited, he never wanted to see me again, which is pretty much what happened.

The remainder of her father's family—including her grandmother—followed suit and refused any relationship with Renée—except for her grandfather. Until his death, Renée's grandfather surreptitiously remained a constant in Renée's life by visiting Renée at her school—at each visit making her promise not to tell anyone he had been there.

He would come to my school and have them bring me down to the office where he would sit and talk to me. At the end of each visit, as he was leaving, he made me promise not to tell anybody, including my grandmother (his wife). "Don't tell anybody that I came to visit," he would caution.

Her grandfather died when Renée was 13; and although her mother acquiesced to Renée's pleas to let her go to the funeral, the two were escorted from the funeral home when Renée's father saw them.

Even without physical contact, her father persisted in his anger against Renée and her mother.

Every birthday he would send me an orthopedic shoe with a metal leg brace suggesting that my legs were crooked. My mother called and told him to stop sending them, but he continued. He also sent telegrams to my school that just said, "You're still ugly." or "I know that you're failing everything because you are stupid." He may have continued to send the notes; however, once my mother found out she stopped the school from giving me the telegrams.

Renée did not see her father again until she was 17 when she was ready for college and her mother wanted child support extended to help pay for college. Her father had paid minimal child support to that point (every dollar of which Renée's mother put into a bank account for her).

My father stood up and said my mother had forged the papers. The judge asked how he knew. My father said, "Because that girl is too stupid to go to any college."

The judge ordered Renée's father to continue child support until she graduated from college.

At 21 when Renée was about to get married, she sent her father an invitation to the wedding (*Somehow you always want that person's love and acknowledgment*). Although her father opened the invitation, he shredded it and put the bits of paper from the invitation inside an envelope, which he sent back to her.

Despite all of this, Renée says her mother never said anything bad about her father. As an adult, Renée asked her mother why she *did not tell me my father was crazy*. Her mother told her, "That was for you to find out. I didn't need to bad-mouth him. I didn't need to say a word. Why would I run him down; then you would dislike me? So I just let him behave the way he behaved and it would be clear."

Although her father was out of her life, his influence on Renée has persisted. Because her father was always late to pick her up for his weekends, Renée is never late. And when others are late to meet her, she is *a mess—a basket case—because I assume you have no intention of meeting me because I am ugly or stupid*—words her father often used to describe Renée after the divorce. Even today, having let much of the negativity she experienced from her father go (*I realized it was more about him than it was about me*), she describes herself as *so insecure.*

Influences

Would the sins of her father define Renée?

No. The world got better for Renée, in part because people who came into her life—family and friends, male and female—through her mother counterbalanced the negativity of her father, leaving Renée with the distinct impression that she could do anything, and harboring no ill-will towards anybody. She is quite simply a beautiful, good person.

Who were these influences?

Mr. Horace Revis: You can do anything!

My mother met a man—Mr. Revis—who was with her until she passed away 40 years after they met. She dated him but said she did not marry him because she did not want me to have a stepfather. She did not want another man in my life that might hurt me the way my father hurt me.

From Mr. Revis Renée learned those things her mother could not teach her . . .

My mother was a reader, polite with good manners and all of that. On the other hand, Mr. Revis could shoot pool, and play pinochle; and so I learned from him all those 'other' things. I can shoot pool, play pinochle, and listen to jazz with an intelligent ear as he taught me how to listen to music and appreciate it.

. . . and that she too was special.

I was a tomboy and wanted to ride the bike with the boys. Boys would not let me ride with them. I came home whining to my mother that they wouldn't let me ride. Mr. Revis asked why and I'd say 'Because I am not a boy.' He'd tell me that I could ride as good as any boy. He was the person who let me know that I could do anything I wanted to do. He taught me this by saying, "I don't care what anybody else is doing, you can do it," whether that was riding a bicycle or getting good grades in school. He said, "If they got it, you can get it."

Aunt Myrtle . . . Travel

Renée developed a love of travel as a teen and young adult because of an aunt. It would ultimately become a second career for her when she retired.

My aunt Myrtle—appropriate name—traveled all the time; she kept a suitcase packed. I probably continue to travel because she would take me sometimes. When I was 21, and had just gotten married, she was going to Morocco. My new husband Barry and I went along. At one point we thought we lost her and began running around trying to find her. We found her in the back of a store smoking a hookah, having a grand old time.

From Aunt Myrtle I learned that people are just people. They may dress differently; but basically, the vast majority of people are not out to harm you. And if you have a genuine interest, they will pick up on that. She would ask serious questions—questions indicating her genuine desire for knowledge. She/you/anyone can go just about any place with that attitude—especially if your interest is in others as human beings.

From another of her mother's friends Renée learned how to get along with anybody and everybody.

I live by something told to me by a friend of my mother: She said, "You can make anybody like you. Find out what they like and give them plenty of it." I never forgot that. And that is true. So in the worst situations, I am able to turn it back to something of interest to that antagonistic person. So those things enabled me to go anywhere.

Renée's uncle . . .

My uncle was an engineer and liked the army, building, construction, and the zoo. If I wanted to go to the zoo and didn't want to go alone, he would take me. And we would go to airshows and he'd explain everything about planes. As a travel writer today I can use that to do research and get people to talk.

Mr. Benjamin . . .

My grandmother was such a missionary—she was part of the church mission to help the sick. Because I was with her all the time, I had to be a little missionary as well. So I would go with her to Mr. Benjamin's home—he was blind and he liked me to read the Bible to him. The next time we went to Mr. Benjamin's home we found out he had died, but he left me something: a little white bible. That moved me on somehow in my journey. He didn't talk much; he was in a wheelchair. Maybe I thought then that people can die; this person can mean a lot to you and then they are not there anymore, but there are ways that you can remember them. That Bible is always somewhere that I can get it in a minute. It is very precious to me because Mr.

Benjamin thought enough of me to leave it for me. I think it has to do with the fact that he's gone; but not really.

So it was all of these 'others' in her life that allowed Renée to overcome her father's cruelties; and even, according to Renée, her father.

Even though my father was not in the picture after I was six, he taught me about being nice to people (he was not) and bullying (he was a bully).

The last time Renée saw her father she was about 35 years old. He knocked on her door. Unbeknownst to Renée, her father was living in an apartment building near her, having temporarily separated from his wife.

So there was a person at the door. I opened the door and recognized him but didn't say anything. He said, "Oh I guess you don't know who I am. I'm your father." I said, 'I know exactly who you are. Can I help you?' He said, "Well, I thought maybe we could go to dinner." I said, 'Dinner? For 30 years, I have been having dinner and you never cared whether I ate or didn't eat. Why would you care today?' He said, "Well I just want to make up." I said, 'I'm very sorry, but I just can't do that right now; maybe later, but I can't do that right now. Thank you for coming.' And I closed the door. And I don't think I ever saw him again because he had a massive heart attack when he was 56 and died. My mother called to tell me because his wife called her. The first thing I thought was, 'He can never say he is sorry.' That's the first thing that I thought; then I went on back to sleep. I never regretted turning him away; there was just too much stuff with him.

Before Renée's father died, in the ultimate irony, her mother and her father's second wife found themselves working at the same business in adjoining cubicles.

Both had the last name of Williams. One day, a man came and stood between two cubicles and said, "I am looking for the wife of James Williams." They both acknowledged that she was the person he was looking for (My mother never remarried). Turns out the other woman was the wife of my father. They did not know of their connection because they did not discuss personal stuff. However, since they had already been friends of sorts that did not change.

In fact, Renée's mother continued the friendship with her father's second wife—Ms. Arneatha—because she *felt sorry for her being married to my father*. While they never physically visited each other, they developed a long-standing telephone friendship—particularly after Renée's father died. And when Renée's mother died, because they were friends, Renée sent Ms. Arneatha a card advising her of her mother's passing.

She called me on the phone and said she couldn't make it to the funeral. She had some issues, but she said, "I want you to know I'm very sorry; and that I really loved your mother like a sister." And we talked and she said she didn't really have anybody. She said she wasn't close to her daughter Beverly and that my half-brother Brian (he's a doctor) was his father's child (I was not sure what that meant). And she said that "your mother used to send me postcards." So now, wherever I go in my travels (Ms. Arneatha must be in her 80s) I send her a postcard.

One has to ask why Renée goes out of her way, even today, for a woman who she believes could have stopped some of her father's bad behaviors?

My mother used to say be nice to everybody because you never know who's going to give you your last cup of water. So here I am with that cup

Without the distractions of her father, and because she was the only child among so many adults, Renée had a rich, full childhood surrounded with good people who taught her about life, books, school, and an empathy for those with difficulties that she perceived to be far worse than her own.

My Grandmother . . . Books & the World

Renée read a lot and always had books. Her grandmother was an English teacher. Early in their marriage Renée's grandparents moved north from the Carolinas to Philadelphia. In Philadelphia, her grandmother could only teach in segregated schools, of which there were very few at the time. So she had trouble finding a job. Fortunately, because Renée's grandfather had his own business, this presented no financial difficulty for the family. Shortly after Renée turned four, her aunt fell down a flight of steps and broke her leg, putting her in traction.

So we (my aunt and grandmother and I) would read and write (my aunt taught me how to write) all day. My grandmother would teach me poems and literary works like "Hiawatha" and "the Village Blacksmith" and "The Midnight Ride of Paul Revere". So I'm reciting these things that high school students knew, but it was because of my grandmother. Because of her, I developed a love of books and how books could take you places and expose you to things to which you otherwise would not be exposed. So all day long, I would be with people who taught me things. We would have real, adult conversations.

Starting School . . . Missing Home

Her world of reading and writing with her aunt and grandmother was Renée's normal—and not a circumstance she expected or wanted to end. At some point, however, age caught up with her and Renée's mother enrolled her in kindergarten. Renée was not happy.

On the first day of kindergarten, (five blocks from home), my grandmother walked me to school. She barely got home and turned around and I was standing there. I told her I walked home. She told me that I was supposed to stay all day. I said, 'Nana they are going to play all day long and I don't wanna play with them; I would rather play with you!'

Renée's mother took her back to school, where Renée stayed. And although she started school when she was four, because of time spent reading and learning with her grandmother, Renée was ahead of her class. Her teacher tried to convince Renée's mother to allow Renée to skip to the next grade, but Renée's mother—wanting her to stay with children closer to her age—refused. Nonetheless, she had to figure out a way to keep Renée at school.

My mother didn't hit me; she had a conversation with me. She said, "I have a job and you have a job. Your job is to go over to school and stay there all day and do as you are told. My job is to go to work, stay all day and do what I am told. Now, if I don't do my job you don't eat, we don't have lights. If you don't do your job then I have to put you on punishment and you will have to stay in your room. These are the things that happen when people don't do their jobs." I said, 'Oh, a job.' That made sense to me. So I went to school and never missed a day.

Challenging Authority

I was supposed to write a report on the Little Big Horn. I worked hard on it. I did all of the research and pointed out that Custer attacked the Indians, so when Custer and his soldiers were wiped out, they deserved that. (I probably said it just like that). The teacher went ballistic and gave me an F. I told them to read history. The teacher called my mother, who asked, "Well what is the truth? Show me what is inaccurate about her report that resulted in you giving her an F." The teacher backed off after that and eventually gave me a B.

All the people around me made me a thinker because each of them was eccentric.

Growing up in an adult world . . . Still being a child
Whether the eccentricities of the people surrounding Renée were real or imagined, she delighted in the world they lived in and created for her.

I enjoyed growing up in a world of adults, and as a result, I don't like small talk—that inconsequential gossip.

However, Renée's adult companions—particularly her mother—were ever mindful that she was a child.

On Saturdays and Sundays I did not go to my grandmother's. On those days I would go outside and my mother taught me how to jump rope and ride bikes and play games like other children. It made me compassionate.

Particularly compassionate perhaps as a result of a childhood friendship.

My best friend when I was six or seven years old was a severely retarded girl. Nobody else would play with her. We would sit and we would play. I don't know how retardation plays out; but as she grew older, she became increasingly more violent. She would pull my hair or hit me. One day my mother saw her punch me in the face. She called me inside and said, "Honey, why do you just sit there? You don't have to sit there and let that happen. You can come inside." I said, 'Mama, she doesn't know what she is doing and nobody else will play with her.' I played with her until her mother could no longer handle her and she was finally placed in an institution. But I still remember her; and she's the best friend I remember.

Renée says that she was also not lonesome for other kids.

Sometimes my mother's friends who had children would have sleepovers and say, "Bring Stevie' (what they called me). I said, 'I don't want to go. I have my own room; why would I want to go somewhere else?'

Generally her mother would respect Renée's wishes. However, all of this seeming freedom for Renée did not mean that she did not understand consequences if she misbehaved or did something wrong.

Crime and punishment

If I did anything bad . . .

I stole a book once from the library. I could only get five and I read a book a day—still do—and 5 just wasn't enough books. So I put one in my book bag and checked out 5. I don't know that I processed that it was theft; and I don't know if I planned to return it. My mother checked my book bag that day, including counting the number of books, and called me on the carpet. I said, 'Mama, I wanted to read the book and there is a limit.' And she said, "Yes, but you are now a thief. That's theft; I don't care what you wanted, you stole a book. Now we have to take it back to the library and give it to your friends and explain that you took the book." I asked if I could say it was an accident. She asked, "Was it an accident?" When I said no, she told me, "Then you can't say that because then you would be a liar and a thief."

Renée was shaken because her mother was saying she stole from her friends.

One summer I went every week to the library reading program. I missed a week when I was sick and the librarians called the house. They were concerned. That is when I realized they were my friends. So I stole from friends, and that was horrible, and I was a thief and I would never, ever do that again. My mother made me see that it was theft—she was not going to call it anything nice; you stole the book; and you have to own up to what it was.

Higher Education . . . A Many and Varied Experience

Renée completed grade school, middle school, and high school and was ready for college. Her decision about post-secondary education was based on Renée's love of learning and *this thing about paying for* *education. I would never pay. If **you** pay, then I will go.* Her choices for college were based upon these principles. She first attended Temple University in Philadelphia, Pennsylvania, as an undergraduate majoring in English—intending to go to graduate school at Temple for a degree in Library Science. Renée wanted to be a librarian. However, after realizing that she did not want to take six years to get that degree, she transferred to Cheyney State, an HBCU (Historically Black Colleges and Universities), about thirty miles outside Philadelphia, enrolling in Cheyney's new English Master's program.

They had a brand-new English Master's program, which was free—they gave me a stipend, and I got teaching experience. I taught Shakespeare I and II. I loved Shakespeare but did not like teaching college students. I was very young and the students were the same age as I was. Every day I had to meet the challenge of teaching people who were my age. I just didn't want to do that. I enjoyed the curriculum and it eventually smoothed out. But the students were constantly challenging me.

Despite these challenges, Renée's mentors at Cheyney made her experience there rich and wonderful.

I worked with the most brilliant educators that I ever met, and they are still my models for teaching. I had teachers who were old! I had people who were actually there at the Harlem Renaissance. I had Dr. Fletcher—who has to be one of my favorite people—as a professor. He knew Alain Locke and James Baldwin. Often, he would say, "Alain said this" or "James was doing that." The man was brilliant!

Graduating with a Bachelor's degree from Cheyney State, Renée subsequently received a degree in Conflict Resolution from American University, a degree in Philosophy from St. John College in New Mexico, and a certificate from Indiana University.

I guess the degree of which I am most thankful is my degree in Philosophy from St. John's in New Mexico; and then I have a certificate in the "Bible as Literature" from Indiana University. Those two have made me better understand the world around me.

She obtained the degree from American while a teacher at an inner-city high school in Philadelphia—Bartram High School—believing that the conflict she saw in her classroom was a microcosm of the greater conflict in the world.

The same methods that we used to solve conflicts in the larger world incubate in high schools. If you don't have any skills to take into the world how are you going to solve bigger conflicts? You go from "Somebody stole my pencil and I'm going to punch them in the mouth." to "Somebody stole my country, and I'm going to invade them."

Being married

Shortly after graduating from Cheyney State, Renée got married. She and her future husband, Barry, met at a mutual friend's house while both were still in college. Barry had a *great job* working as one of the first Black employee's hired by Philly based Breyer's Ice Cream. As a result, finding a job after college was not a priority for Renée. That changed, however, when Renée's desire to buy her new husband a birthday present with money she earned set her looking for gainful employment—if only for as long as it took to earn enough money for pay for his gift. She thought the perfect job would be as a substitute teacher—so she called the school board.

Beginning to work

The day I called the school board, I was talking to the lady on the other end, and she asked my name. As we are talking, we discovered that I was talking to Mrs. Jones, my old Girl Scout leader. She said, "Honey you can work as long as you want. I have this school, Bartram High School, and this teacher will be out the rest of year, so you can work until summer (Barry's birthday was May 17th)." I told her I just really wanted to work about a week. So she said, "Well it's a very good school so work as long as you want and then on the last day you want to work just tell them you will not be able to return after that day, and they will need to get somebody else."

Once Renée began to work, she enjoyed the work and the people—eventually working through the end of the school year. On her last day, the principal asked Renée if she wanted a permanent job. She wanted the position but had not taken the test required for permanent employment. Despite some initial push back, because Renée's test results placed her at number two on the list to teach high school English (there was only one other Black English teacher in that Philadelphia public high school at the time), *for the next 33 years I taught at Bartram High School.*

Renée never taught anywhere else.

Bartram High School . . . First and Last Job

In those 33 years Renée had *nearly every job at that high school.*

I think the principal—Louis B. Antonio—knew something about me that I did not know about myself—I could not continue to do the same job over and over again. Thus, he allowed me to have every other job that it was possible to have. I never obtained a principal's certificate—I didn't want to be a principal. I do not like telling adults what to do. I do not understand needing to tell adults what to do.

Running a charter school

If they said, "we want to start this new program," I would step in. I was the trouble shooter throughout the school. At one point the district moved to charter schools. So the principal said, "We want you to run a charter school." I did.

Charter School Newsletter

As if running the charter school was not enough, Renee initiated and managed the school newsletter for the new charter faculty and staff.

And at one point Renée was *school disciplinarian*. She learned her approach to this position from her mother.

I disciplined them the way I was disciplined—we had a conversation. I never had a student go off on me or had a kid want to hit me. A student might come to the office kicking and screaming; but I would say, 'I really can't understand what you are saying.' Then they would calm down and we could talk. I did that for two years until they got rid of the position all together. They brought in someone from the District who was more punitive and did not have time to sit down and talk and diffuse the situation—refusing to get to the deeper issues.

The Students

The students were Renée's life blood while at Bartram—regardless of the hat she wore.

I always had my own office because I ran all the activities in school that were not sports—all the proms, dances, anything like that. I had a wonderful time! Those were some of the best years of my life because of the diversity of what I was doing. I enjoyed the students. I enjoyed watching them learn—all of them. Of course people say some of them didn't learn anything, but to me, the beauty of teaching is that you don't really know what they learn. Someone used to say to me that teaching is like watering a plant. Plant the seed and water it and you never know what will happen.

Bartram . . . the history

By the time Renée left Bartram High School what had once been a predominantly White (85%) populated high school had become a high school that was 99 % Black. The neighborhood had changed from Irish Catholic to a predominantly Black population once the Catholics fled the neighborhood.

It was in a solidly White Irish Catholic neighborhood but surrounded by the projects. Lots of the children in the neighborhood went to Catholic rather than public school; so gradually Black kids came to Bartram—having to fight their way to school in that neighborhood in the morning and fight their way home at night.

Renée recalls a number of incidents that reflected the racism within the community directed towards the Black kids at Bartram, including, unbelievably, an announcement that June 6th was 'kill a nigga day.'

One year it was so horrible that they closed the school and told the kids not to come back until September. In that instance, the teachers had to come every day and just sit.

Despite these setbacks, Renée remained at Bartram—hoping to make a difference—because she continued to enjoy what she was doing, the students, and the people with whom she worked, until a staff change.

A new principal & time to retire

A new principal came to Bartram just after Renée completed her 30th year working at the school. The new principal—a 55-year-old African American woman who had moved up through the ranks—was assuming her first job in that capacity in the Philadelphia school system. After 33 years, perhaps it was time for Renée to move on to a new challenge. In any event, there was an immediate disconnect between the two. The reason did not ultimately matter after the new principal—who rarely spoke to Renée—smacked Renée with a yard stick one morning.

She hit me! We are walking down the school hall in opposite directions. She had a yard stick. Some days she would speak; some days she did not. I always spoke; because I didn't want her to say otherwise. This morning I said,

'Good morning.' I passed her and I felt a whack across my butt. I stood there and thought, 'What the hell was that?' I turned around and she's standing there laughing. "I got you Ms. Gordon; I got you." I thought, 'I could mash this woman into the wall.' I said, 'You certainly did.' And I continued around to the office and put in for my retirement. I later found out that she sent out a memo—which I never set eyes on—which commanded that under no circumstances was anybody to give me a party for my retirement.

But they did anyway

It was splendid! I came to work as usual. At 9 am, a friend, Rita Nelson, came around with a big punch bowl and spread it all out in my office. In my office, I could, of course, have a party. The first group came with gifts to my office at 9:15 for my retirement party. A friend of mine brought luggage tags and each person who came by filled one out. Another group came at 9:30, and so forth. There was never a crowd; you would never know a party was going on. At the end of the day my friend brought a trunk into which I put all the luggage tags.

You never know what you have 'til it's gone

A month after Renée retired, the principal called her offering to pay Renée $300 a day as a consultant. Renée declined the offer initially; however, she ultimately agreed.

She said, "We really need you." Finally, I told her I'd come in the next week and come in for free but admonished her not to ask me again. I told her to have a list of things she wanted me to do. I did it for free because I didn't want her to say, "that hussy charged me!"

Travel writing . . . her mother/her students

In retirement Renée is a successful, travel writer—going all over the world and then sharing her travel stories in her own travel column in the *Philadelphia Sun* newspaper. Her hope is that those who read her stories—even if they are never able to travel outside their basic boundaries—can have the 'experience' of travel.

Renée's love of traveling began with her Aunt Myrtle as a child and continued throughout her life—often with her mother as her travel companion. She frequently travels with Barry.

I always traveled. I often spent part of the summer out of country and part of the summer in the country. One summer I wanted to go to Hong Kong but couldn't find anybody to go with me. I went by Mom's for my daily visit, telling her of my dilemma. Her response: "You didn't ask me." She said, "Of course I want to go!" I told her that I didn't think she was such an adventurous person. She said, "Where do you think you got it from?" So we went to Hong Kong and from then on, we would go to a particular place in or out of the country, and we would spend two or three weeks traveling the entire state or country to see the sites. Those were the best times because my mother and I got to know each other in new and different ways.

While still at Bartram, Renée found ways to make her travels special for her students.

When I traveled, I wanted to open the world to my students. After a while, I didn't teach many classes, but I had to teach one. I would bring back t-shirts from my trips, and I'd have a raffle, and the kids would be excited. When I started the raffle, I intended to give the shirt to the student with the highest grade, but I said 'no, because that kid always gets prizes.'

Sometimes my students would say, "'You don't have any kids Ms. Gordon so your influence will die." And I'd say, 'That's not true, because at some point you will pass along some information, and it will be something I said, that you get from me; so I will live on.'

*I would talk to my students about different aspects of where I went—the state or country. I would always say 'and when **you** travel **you** will see this or be sure to go and see this.' I never said, 'when I travel . . . ' One day a male student said, "Ms. Gordon we are never going to go anywhere or do anything. We're gonna be right here." My heart broke. I said, 'That is not true. I can show you the world, but you can live it—you can go out and do this. There is so much more.'*

So, I began to write and bring it back to them—making it more historical

and more educational. I gave out certificates to students for each education-
al achievement weekly. I began to write in a manner to let the students
know that these people in other places were no different from them. There
are young people, poor people, Native Americans. My articles are 60 percent
history. That was deliberate because I was writing for a specific audience. So
I had started writing and we would discuss my articles and I would show
pictures.

Unfortunately, Renée's mother developed diabetes and had her leg
amputated. Thereafter, she refused to travel with Renée.

She was used to being a princess; so she could never wrap her head
around not having a leg. I bought three prosthesis but she always said they
didn't work. She was in a wheelchair. I told her we could still travel and go
places that I could push her in her wheelchair. But she refused. She said,
"I'm not going to have people looking down on me!" So I began to journal
on the places I went. I would tell her about sites so she could visualize being
there. I never put my journal in my suitcase, always in my handbag. When
they picked me up from the airport, I would hand my mom the journal.

It was Renée's mother who brought her writing to the attention of the
Philadelphia Sun.

One day I was going off on a trip and Mommie said, "I read this piece
and it was wonderful, and I really think you should send it to the newspa-
per." I said, 'Everybody's mother thinks she can do something worthwhile.' So
I disregarded her suggestion.

When I returned home from my trip there was a message on my an-
swering machine from the editor at the Philadelphia Sun newspaper, Teresa
Emerson, saying that she received this piece in the mail and wanted to talk
to Renée Gordon. My mother sent in her favorite piece!

Taken aback, but curious, Renée agreed to meet Ms. Emerson to talk
about her writing. She was told the newspaper would publish the article,
pay her, and wanted her to sign a contract to provide other articles. Renée
responded that she could not accept pay because she had a job.

Ms. Emerson said, "Well why did you send [the article] to me?" I told
her my mother sent the article. The whole office burst out laughing.

Renée and the newspaper ultimately agreed that Renée would write an article every two weeks. That was more than 20 years ago, and Renée is still going strong. You can read her articles at: www.philasun.com.[2]

Why Renée writes:

I have a goal: to educate people. My travel is paid for, and I can continue to achieve my goal. I often run into kids to whom I gave paper certificates while at Bartram during our travel discussions, and they tell me they still have my certificate and how much that meant to them. One of the kids brought by roses.

My mother and my other Sheroes

Renée identifies '*the triumvirate: my grandmother, my aunt, my mother* as having the greatest influence in her life; however, her mother takes the top spot.

My mother was my greatest influence. At first, I didn't think so. First it was my grandmother—reading, and singing songs (Oh Shenandoah, La Marseillaise [the French National Anthem]. Who knows those songs as a kid? She was the one who laid the foundation. Then my aunt with travel. She was my 'Auntie Mame.' We would go to New York to see the Rockettes or plays. She was not married and had no children and was unencumbered. She'd say, "You know what Puddin', we are going to go to New York to see a play. We are going tomorrow so you have to ask your mother can you go." So that's what we did.

My mother was not necessarily a good mother for small kids, but she was excellent for a teenager. She was the kind of mother I would have been. I read the book about what makes a good mother, and I'd check them off. She would do extraordinary things. When I was eight, I had this thing for Ramsey Lewis and his "In Crowd" album recorded Live at Bohemian Caverns in DC. For my birthday that year my mother got us an airplane ride (I'd never been on a plane) and told me, "We are going to go to the Bohemian Caverns, and then we're going to spend the night and come back home the next day." When I was 17, I had this Motown thing. So my mother knew this older girl who was a nurse. She talked to her parents and paid for us to both fly to

---

2. In addition to the Philadelphia Sun Newspaper Renee is a contributing editor of *Tango Diva*. She is also the recipient of the African Diaspora World Tourism American Roads Award.

Detroit and see Motown. It wasn't a museum at the time so we could just walk by and then go see the sights of Detroit.

My mother had one of those gypsy hearts like I do—if there was something adventurous I wanted to do, and she could achieve it, she would.

On the loss of her mother . . .
On the day of our interview, it had been thirteen years since Renée lost her mother to diabetes. Even now, the pain of her loss is palpable . . .

These chairs [in her kitchen] were my mother's chairs. I had perfectly good leather chairs—in the attic. However, these chairs will be with me forever because they were my mother's chairs. My mother passed in 2001— thirteen years today. I blank the anniversary out as much as I can. Everything is painful. I was most afraid that I would forget what she looked like. That has not even been an issue. I was particularly down years ago (after Mr. Revis also died). I came into the kitchen and right here in the middle of the kitchen table was a picture of them. They were smiling and waving. It was not a picture I had ever seen before. Somehow, I knew I was at a level of sadness that they wanted to lift me up by sending the picture. I still never have really felt she is gone in that way. I can't go put flowers on her grave; and I haven't been back there since she died. The thought of it makes me hyperventilate.

No Need to Go Back
Renée Stephanie Gordon is happy with her age and where she is in life— not wanting now to go back and repeat any age.

I made a vow that whatever age I am I'm glad to be that age. I've earned being who I am. I worked very hard for the white hairs. This is too much awareness for somebody 22. There are too many years to synthesize all that you learned in the past. By extension, I don't mind being this age; I wish people around me would change. They are the ones with the problem. I'm ok with me; I'm just having a problem with you.

In light of, and perhaps in spite of the effects of her father's treatment of her at such a young age, Renée's expression of her greatest triumph is not a surprise.

I think my greatest triumph is that I am a good person. That sounds crazy; but that was my grandmother's wish for me. That was how I was guided by my family. They said, "Money and all of that is fine, but the crux of it is that at the end of your life you have lived a good life." And while you cannot tell if you lived a good life until the moment of your death because that's the sum total of everything, I would venture to say that I have lived a good life in as much as it was possible; by not hurting people; by trying to uplift people; by presenting them with options. I have never deliberately caused anybody any pain; and my recognition of the importance of that fact is my greatest triumph.

Another triumph is my cognizance of the fact that we need to be moral upstanding people—in spite of religion, in spite of upbringing, and everything else. It's our awareness of that. And then you can act upon it. Because if you are not aware, you cannot act. So I think I've reached a level of awareness so I can say, 'I'm not going to do that because that would hurt that person.' Rather than stumbling into something and saying, 'Oops, let me stop.' So many people don't stop and take that second to ask, "Well what are the ramifications?" So it goes back to being a kid and understanding consequences. In life, the greatest thing anybody can know and understand is consequences.

Finally, on being 'Different' . . .

I've been different all my life. We're not supposed to be different. Differences are not rewarded or talked about in our society. So if you dare to be different or a little eccentric and you're not quiet about it, then you are censored. And the biggest takeaway at this age, after looking back, is that it's ok; it's ok to be different.

YVETTE ANNETTE STEVENSON

Taking Care of My Family

Yvette Stevenson is an African American woman who fiercely loves her family, goes to work every day to provide for her family, takes care of her family when they are sick and in need, and when faced with challenges, duties and responsibilities, and the hard knocks of a sometimes unkind world, with strength, faith, courage, and perseverance overcomes them all and always, without question or regret. She does not talk of being burdened by these twists and turns of her journey, but rather with pride of meeting the challenges head on and overcoming them—seizing the moment for her family.

Born in Oklahoma City, Oklahoma in 1959 and raised in Spencer, Oklahoma—a sprawling farming community just outside of Oklahoma City—Yvette Annette Stevenson, the oldest of six—four girls and two boys—grew up spending summers and holidays in the historically all-Black town of Clearview, Oklahoma, which is about 80 miles from Oklahoma City. She says they referred to it *as going to the country.*

Today at 61 years old and unexpectedly retired from her 30-year career at the US Postal Service because of an illness of her own, Yvette manifests neither regret nor angst for assuming caretaking responsibilities throughout her life. There have certainly been challenges—money and time for herself—but none so overwhelming that she was defeated or prevented from doing what she needed to do—take care of family. This latter sentiment—taking care of family—has provided Yvette with the determination to overcome whatever obstacles might have been placed in her path because she says . . .

All you have is your family . . .

This heartfelt belief has guided and sustained Yvette during good times and bad.

The good times were summers with her five siblings and family reunions in Clearview, Oklahoma, where her grandmother—104-year-old Marguerite Rich ("Aunt Mac"), the family matriarch—lived and still does. The reunions—or "Golden Treasures" as Yvette and her extended family called them—were joyous occasions but also kept the Rich family together and committed to each other—through hard times, celebrations, feuds, births, and deaths. And although Aunt Mac suggested she was embarking on her last reunion in 2016 when she was 100, her 22 children, grandchildren, great grandchildren, nieces, and nephews know that she will continue to enjoy their reunions as long as she is able.

Thus, the family togetherness emanating from these reunions and her own love of family, likely made Yvette's role as caregiver both natural and inevitable. This role started when she was young.

Although her mother remarried after her parents' divorce, her stepfather's military service and her mother working nights meant that Yvette was in charge, making sure that the tasks of the day for she and her five siblings—including cooking, cleaning, washing and ironing—were properly completed.

I am the oldest; so it was like I was a mom. My mom worked nights. My stepfather was in the military. He worked at Tinker, so he was always TDY (Temporary Duty Travel), which meant he traveled away from home a lot. So, in the morning my job was to get up, get the kids up, make breakfast, and get them ready for school or daycare (buses picked up for both). After school, I would come home and make dinner. On Saturday mornings we didn't get to sleep until ten. Instead, Mom got up early and started to wash. We were up at seven with beds made. Once our beds were made, we couldn't get back in them. We had lots of chores: cleaning the refrigerator and oven, waxing the floors, hanging the clothes outside on the line, bringing them in, and ironing them.

Notably, these additional duties of care did not keep Yvette from enjoying her childhood. There was just structure, which included making sure she and her siblings followed her mother's rules.

My childhood was fun. We played all day until the streetlights came on—so long as the beds were made, and chores were done before we began whatever adventures we got into on a given day. The only thing I didn't like is that we had to be in earlier than the rest of the kids on the street. We had no restrictions about where we could go and what we could do, but we had to be in by a certain time. So, on Saturdays after our work was done in the house we would be outside all day.

This routine—both the joy of being young and the responsibility of taking care of her siblings—interspersed with summer visits to her father in Kansas City—defined Yvette's childhood.

Then at 17, Yvette's journey took a turn—she was pregnant. Because she had good grades, Yvette graduated a year early allowing her to both tend to her new son Royce and decide on her future. Tragically, three months after he was born, Royce died.

Grieving for her son, Yvette needed some changes.

Desiring to be a nurse like her mother, and also wanting to experience life on her own, with a scholarship to the University of Oklahoma, Yvette moved out of her mother's home and started her college career as a commuter student. Her mother was supportive.

When I was ready to move out of my mama's house, my mom took me shopping and opened a charge account so I could buy furniture. I moved into one of the rent houses my family owned. I wanted to get away. I wanted to live alone. At that time when you got out of school it was time to move out. Now they want to stay until they are 25!

While Yvette enjoyed this new experience of living on her own, college was another matter . . .

[As a college student] I was a nerd. I just went to class—I didn't do anything else. I went for a semester but didn't like school. I wanted to be a nurse like my mother; but when a patient in a nursing home where I worked died, I didn't want to be a nurse anymore. I don't think it would have mattered if I had lived on campus because I just didn't want to be in school anymore. When I graduated from high school, I really had the idea that I would get a job . . . Perhaps I should have left the state to go to college. But . . . school is not for everybody. I'm family-oriented and that's all I wanted to do.

So she started a family. In the ensuing years, Yvette and her significant other had two sons—Kynton and Royce (named after her first born). For the first few years the four of them seemed the idyllic family Yvette desired. For whatever reason however, the relationship did not last, and the couple broke up. While Yvette remained friends with her sons' father and he helped financially when able, Yvette as the custodial parent had a myriad of challenges, which she had to meet head on, just as she had done as the oldest child. She got a job, and with the help of her mother and aunts, she raised her kids.

In the midst of this part of her journey Yvette's 34-year-old mother, Maine Gibbs, was diagnosed with colon cancer requiring surgery. Although Yvette no longer lived with her mother, after her mom's release from the hospital, she daily tended to her mother's needs until she was well enough to take care of herself. Although her mom's recovery was long and tedious, Yvette was there—*without regret or distress*—and her mother got well.

Finding Love

Yvette found love—or thought she had—for a second time; and at the age of 28 she got married. Yvette's daughter Ashley was the gift of their union, although she and her husband would ultimately divorce after five years of marriage. After the divorce Yvette moved forward raising two pre-teen sons and her daughter as a single parent, now working part-time at the Post Office.

There are obstacles and challenges based on life. There was a time I had to live payday to payday until I got things situated. That's when I started working more because I had people depending on me. I had been working part time at the Post Office and then I realized that I had to work full time—get a full paycheck—in order to make ends meet.

Once she was able to make ends meet for her family, Yvette was determined to provide some of her children's' wants, while also making sure they were safe and cared for.

My daughter wanted to play soccer, which cost extra money; so, then I said I need to get on the overtime list so I can work more. I was working the evening shift in order to work a 40-hour week and so I could be home when my children came in from school. I got my sister to come live with me so she would be there when I was working in the evening. Two of my children were 13 and 14 years old and they needed supervision.

Grandmother

The role of grandmothers has changed—expanded—reminiscent of the days of the extended family. Today, whether because our parents are busy working or not available, grandparents have become surrogate parents in many households. It is not unusual to find grandparents—especially grandmothers—raising their grandchildren, having sole responsibility for their care and comfort. They have raised their children, and now at an age when they might expect their focus to be on retirement, rest, and relaxation—with only responsibility for themselves—they are raising their grandchildren. If nobody else can or will take care of their grandchildren, they will. Such has been part of Yvette's journey. She has raised four of her five grandchildren—all girls—somehow finding time to also look out for her fifth grandchild, her first grandson.

Ten and eleven years older than their sister, Yvette's sons grew up and left home while her daughter Ashley was still in high school. Both started families of their own—Kynton had five girls and a son. Royce had one son. A variety of circumstances caused Yvette to assume the responsibility of raising her granddaughters. She took custody of three of her granddaughters before Ashley went to college. Eventually, a fourth granddaughter would also come to live with her. Yvette was embarking on the task of raising a second set of children—this time, her grandchildren.

At just about the same time her mother got sick again.

Taking Care of Mama . . . A Second Illness
Twenty years after overcoming colon cancer, Yvette's mother required minor surgery to repair a tear in her bladder. Unfortunately after eleven hours of surgery, she was in intensive care with a punctured intestine. A few days later she had a serious infection resulting in a seven-month hospital stay. What was minor had turned into a devastating illness. Even after her lengthy hospital stay, Yvette's mother needed regular care. Yvette would provide it.

When she got home, I was not living there but my brothers were. It seemed that every day or every other day something was wrong, and Mama needed attention. So, I would go over to tend to her. It reached the point that we eventually had to take her back to the hospital.

When finally released from the hospital a second time, Yvette's mother moved in with Yvette. Her family helped.

My aunt and her husband would come and take my mom to the doctor for me—she was going three days a week—and I would pick her up. My youngest granddaughter who was seven would make sure Mama had her bowl of cereal by her bed before she went to school. That was her job; and then she would go out and catch the bus. All my aunts helped. On the days that my one aunt could not come to the house the other two would come in and watch my mother, clean up around the house, and talk about how my kids had too many shoes.

Ashley was in college by now, and while obviously very busy, Yvette successfully juggled the needs of her mother and her granddaughters, all the while continuing to encourage her daughter to finish college. It wasn't a cakewalk. There were money problems because her mother had no insurance and was too young to qualify for Medicare. And there were family squabbles about her mother's care and other things about which families disagree in such circumstances. But through it all, Yvette's focus and resolve never changed: caring for her mother in the best way possible—while also raising her grandchildren.

Yvette is proud of her mother's survival and the quality of care she and her family were able to provide. After the second surgery and its complications, doctors advised Yvette and her siblings that they did not expect their mother to last more than a few weeks. She lived almost three years.

We never had home health care services for my mother; it was just family taking care of her. We eventually had hospice, but until hospice it was just us. If I had to take the girls out of town for a cheerleading convention or whatever, then my sister, who is now deceased, or my brother would come over and stay with Mama.

My brother stayed with her on the weekends because I worked on the weekends. His presence made my mom's day because she could get up and take care of him! She would wait on him hand and foot. I wouldn't let her do it for me. I'd make her go sit down; but my brother would say, "you want to fix me a steak?" and of course my mother was happy to do so. She would go in there and start cooking just for him.

Despite the quality of care she received, Yvette's mother never fully recovered from the surgery. And as her light began to dim, she had a last wish—to live in her own home for the final months of her life. Despite some unforeseen circumstances, Yvette and her family fulfilled her mom's wishes.

In the last six months of her life Mama said she wanted to go home to her house. She was steady losing weight. I told her that I would make that happen. But when we got to her house, we saw that somebody had been in the house and stolen all her appliances—stove, refrigerator, washer/dryer—all of it! And with her particular illness she had to have a washer and dryer. So, I bought her a washer and dryer, a refrigerator, a cook stove, and microwave. I brought the TV from my house and took it to her so she would have TV. I also had to buy a hospital bed because Mama was in hospice by this time and needed a hospital bed. Hospice would come every day, but she needed around the clock care.

Reminiscent of her responsibilities as a child, Yvette established a routine for her mom's care.

So, my routine was that I would get up and get my granddaughters off to school. Then I would go over to my mom's house, taking my work clothes— [by this time Yvette was a full-time employee of the U.S. Postal Service]— and stay with her till about 2. My aunt would come at 2:30; so my mom was only there by herself for about 30 minutes. My aunt was there till about 6 and then my brother would come when he got off work. He was staying with her nights and weekends. But if something happened, he would call me and say, "You need to come out here and change Mama because you know I can't do that." I would go home from work, check the girls, then I would go back to check on Mama and then go back home, and we would start the process all over again the next morning.

This was our schedule for six months—until she died. Mama died on November 3rd, 2007 at 11 p.m.

When Yvette's mother died, the void was felt by the entire family. Yvette felt the void of losing her mother; but was otherwise at peace.

I didn't have any regrets. I understood my mother. All I did was pray that she would be comfortable. I didn't want her to suffer. Whenever my mother asked for something, I got it for her if I could—one way or another. She never had to go without much of anything. When she passed, I said my goodbyes and had done all I could do.

❦

Perhaps because she abandoned her college career, Yvette has encouraged her children and grandchildren to get a college education. She is proud that her daughter Ashley succeeded in graduating from college. Additionally, in 2018 granddaughter Kylina graduated from high school and enrolled in college at Texas Southern University in Houston, Texas.

My granddaughter is doing great at Texas Southern! She came home for the Christmas break [her freshman year] for two weeks and worked the whole time she was here! But she was ready to go back to school. She said, 'it's time for me to go back Grandma.' She booked her flight home and back. I gave her the credit card. She said she had to be there so she could get started for next semester. The school opened and she was there.

Yvette is delighted that her youngest granddaughter, Kyeiah, is now also a college student at Drury University in Springfield Missouri.

As her granddaughters navigate college classes, and campus life Yvette is always there to listen, advise, encourage, and even scold when necessary—to be there for family. And while her children and grandchildren may not always follow her advice, they have each moved forward with their lives in large part because of Yvette's determination and perseverance despite the difficulties; despite the obstacles.

Significant Moments

The good . . .

After six decades on earth, Yvette Stevenson has *"had a life!—much of which has been* life-changing. As the primary caregiver for her granddaughters, many of their milestones—graduations, childbirth, acceptance, and successes in college—are some of the most important, life changing moments in Yvette's life. But she says . . .

Everything I do I consider to be a life-changing moment. When my oldest granddaughter graduated from high school, I was proud. I bought JC Penney out! When I had this great grandbaby, I was excited; but my excitement was tempered because I almost lost my granddaughter having my great grandbaby. So, I was happy that they both survived. They get on my last nerve, but I would do anything for them!

So yes, now she spends much of her free time helping to care for her great-granddaughter, whom she admittedly spoils, but says *I spoil her with discipline.* That means that her great granddaughter has rules she is expected to follow when she is with Yvette—just as Yvette had rules during her own childhood—and if she follows the rules, she gets *whatever she wants!*

Some bad . . .

When asked about a significant moment that was a negative Yvette pauses, pensive. Eventually . . .

*Yes, there was . . . when my son went to prison for 20 years . . . he is still there . . . It's something that I don't discuss with other people. I talk to **him**; we talk about it. It's not something I'm proud of—he's not proud of it. He says he's sorry every time I go to see him. He finally got in his head—although too late—what I had been telling him: 'Everybody ain't your friend . . .'*

He won't be out for another five years; and Yvette says that *when he gets out, he's on his own, and he understands that.*

. . . But I have to keep moving forward when there are obstacles like this. I have other children. I can't stop. I can't stop living for that. I had to keep moving forward. When my mother got sick, I had sisters who couldn't deal with it. I had to; it was not an option; and I still had two kids when he went to prison. He had a son; and while I didn't raise his son I still have to keep up with his son.

In addition to her son's imprisonment, the death of her first-born when he was three months old, and the death of her mother, the slow death of her companion of many years in 2011 left Yvette devastated.

He began stumbling without cause. An MRI revealed a mass on the brain.

After his release from the hospital, for the remaining two months of his life, Yvette stayed with him on weekends when she got off work so his daughter could be with her children. Her memories of this time are movingly clear and specific . . .

He died on November 15, 2011—two months after his diagnosis—September to November. It was something that had apparently been in the back of his head for over 20 years. His sister passed away a year later from the same thing. That was horrific. Five years passed before I got involved with anybody else.

❦

There's Always Work at the Post Office and Dealing with Racism

Until an unexpected illness in May 2019 Yvette was a window supervisor for the US Postal Service. She had worked for the post office for over 34 years. Historically the USPS has been a place that provided employment to Black people when other places did not. For those who remember Robert Townsend's movie, *Hollywood Shuffle*, there is a line in the movie that resonates with many Black folk who were denied employment at other places before, during and after segregation, and/or who were faced with doing domestic work even when armed with a college education: *there's always work at the Post Office.*

However, while it was a good job—when Yvette really needed it—as with any job, working at the Post Office was not always the panacea. As anyone working in the public service industry can attest dealing with the public has its challenges, and for many African American women—and men—racism and sexism are often lurking around the corner. Yvette says . . .

Racism exists in Oklahoma; I've been called the n-word and overlooked [in my job] because I'm Black and because I'm a woman.

Yvette recalls being called into her supervisor's office and being told that someone else was promoted over her. The news was delivered with an admission that the promotion was a mistake. Yvette believes the admission was simply designed to make her supervisor feel better—it certainly did not justify the decision.

As for working with the public . . .

On the window I've been called the n-word, I've had packages and money thrown at me and a complaint filed accusing me of being rude when I did not provide the answer the customer was looking for. I wasn't rude. Fortunately, there were cameras; because when they rolled the camera the film confirmed that I was not rude.

These challenges neither defined her time at the Post Office nor kept her from providing for her family.

Takeaways from Her Journey thus far . . .

Yvette says she has done just about everything she wanted to do in her life, and . . .

I've learned to love me; take care of me; do what I want to do because nobody else will do it for me if I don't do it for myself. I can't expect anybody else to do it for me.

Some of Yvette's advice reflects her life and her belief that 'it's about family.'

I tell my grandkids: family is all you got. If you can't love and trust your family and depend on them, you have nothing. Friends are okay—they come and go. But your family is always going to be there. That's what I always told my own kids: you can't love and depend on anybody else; it's just the four of us and we have to depend on each other. So, if one needs, the other needs to help.

For anyone facing obstacles Yvette has some tried and true advice . . .

When you meet obstacles you just have to stand strong; you have to meet them head-on, figuring it out, looking at what you are going into, and thinking about what your options can be. If you go this way what would the outcome be? If you do it the other way what would the outcome be?

Most importantly, don't just sit there and focus on "I can't do it." Get "I can't" out of your mouth!

In May 2019 after experiencing unusual physical challenges (severe headaches, nausea, fainting), Yvette had brain surgery. As a result, she was unexpectedly retired from the US Postal Service (she had planned to do so in 2020). She nonetheless perseveres—caring for her great granddaughter and going through a home renovation to make life more comfortable for she and any family who might need a place to stay.

Yvette makes clear that none of her caretaking responsibilities have prevented her from doing the things she wanted to do. Rather, she has simply always found ways to enjoy life while also taking on whatever responsibilities she faced.

Yvette Annette Stevenson helped raise her siblings, lost one son as a baby, raised three children mostly as a single parent, cared for her mother through two major illnesses while also raising her four granddaughters and keeping tabs on her two grandsons, saw her significant other through his terminal illness, and is now helping to care for her great granddaughter. Any one of these responsibilities could be daunting. To successfully navigate all of them requires phenomenal patience, perseverance, and grace.

In the words of Maya Angelou, Yvette is a 'phenomenal woman.'[3]

---

3. See Maya Angelou, "Phenomenal Woman" from *And Still I Rise*. Copyright © 1978 by Maya Angelou @ https://www.poetryfoundation.org/poems/48985/phenomenal-woman

TYNA THERESA PRICE
The Meaning of Sisterhood

African American women like Tyna Price live extraordinary lives because of their impact on their communities and how they influence and interact with others. There is often a driving force—a motivation— behind the contributions of these women. That catalyst for Tyna is two-fold: her mother and the Delta Sigma Theta Sorority.

Tyna's mother taught her to "treat people the way you want to be treated. If you want to be treated nice, then you treat people nice; and hopefully, that comes back to you." She said, "do the best that you can, never say you can't." For Tyna that meant *always try*.

These guiding principles have directed the life and journey of Tyna Theresa Price, creating in her one of the most giving people in this world. And her mother's legacy is an Ordinary Extraordinary African American woman, Tyna Price, who at sixty something is vibrant, happy, and living her best life.

As is true for many of us, Tyna's "happy" has not been without trials, tribulations, and pain, as she lost her stepdad before she graduated high school, while her mother was murdered some thirty years later. These have been devastating losses, which are difficult, if not impossible from which to recover. But Tyna has done so—relying on the nurturing, loving foundation of her childhood—pushing forward in spite of tragedy, while continuing to focus on the needs of others. One of the ways she has been able to do so is by embracing the traditions and ideals of the Delta Sigma Theta Sorority, particularly that of "service to the community." With effort, leadership, and hard work Tyna has had a positive impact on the lives of young African American women seeking guidance and direction in a world where their worth and value has never been fully acknowledged.

Raised in Des Moines, Iowa as part of an extended family that included her mother, brother, grandparents, aunt, and her aunt's two children, Tyna remembers a time when neighborhoods were communities, filled with young children, and families who cared about and looked out for each other.

I think back when we were growing up, you helped other people, whether it was something that happened to your house or yard or kids, everybody in the neighborhood would look after each other. You didn't think twice about doing it.

When Tyna's parents married, her father was in the military, requiring him to be away from home quite a bit. Tyna saw him summers when he took his annual leave from the service and remembers visiting her paternal grandmother with him. When Tyna was two years old, her parents divorced. Thereafter, it was her mother and her extended family—particularly her grandparents—with whom Tyna was close growing up.

Of the adults in my life when I was a child, I was closest to my mother, my aunt, my grandma, and grandpa. My grandparents and my aunt went to work while my mother stayed home, cooking, cleaning, and watching us kids. My grandmother was an elevator operator in a building downtown. When we would go downtown, she would let us run the elevator—only if unoccupied of course—even though we never could stop it on floors.

Tyna had a definitive role in her extended family.

I was the big sister to three other people at least. There was my brother and then my two cousins, who were more like sisters and brothers than cousins. We hung out together because we were in the same house. We played in the yard together. When one had to go, everybody had to go.

When Tyna's mother remarried, her family—mother, stepfather, and Tyna and her siblings—moved to a new home across town. Although they missed their friends, Tyna and her siblings were simply happy that their mother had remarried. Although her stepfather was the biological father of her two youngest siblings, he had no favorites.

I had a good childhood. I was never hungry, and always had a place to live. I had most of the things I wanted and everything that I needed. My parents would make me go to school and do well in school so that I could be what I wanted to be. I liked school, especially English and Art. I wasn't the best artist, but I loved arts and crafts kinds of things. And even though I didn't like science and history, I did well in all of my subjects.

My stepfather treated all of us the same. When I say 'my Dad' that's who I am talking about. He was the family disciplinarian, but he also taught me how to ride a bike and how to do different things. So from the age of eight until 17 he was there.

Having gone back to school to get his degree in mechanical engineering, Tyna's stepfather used his degree to teach mechanical drafting in junior and senior high schools in Des Moines.

That was in the last six or seven years of his life. He died when I was a senior in high school. He was complaining about his arm hurting. My mother told him to go to the doctor, which he did. They figured out he had a blood clot. He was hospitalized, but they were never able to dissolve the clot, and it eventually went to his lung and he died.

Her dad's death was emotionally draining (*that was the first time someone really close to me died*) and changed their household dynamic. Prior to her stepfather's death, Tyna's mother had worked part time. She now had to go to work full time, leaving Tyna, as the oldest, responsible for the household chores and looking after her younger siblings. Tyna did not mind the increase in household chores; but the loss of her stepfather was palpable. It was a difficult time.

It was devastating because here's the only dad that's been in your life and now, he's not there. We missed him. When you are young you know your parents won't live forever—but at that age you never imagine that something like that will happen.

The new financial burden was also difficult.

My mother stayed at home until I went into 9th grade. She had started working, but it was different after my stepfather died. We went from a household with two incomes to only one with four kids to support. And my brother was in college. He and I both had jobs in the summer; but I'm sure all of this created financial stress for my mother—stress she never showed to us. We still had everything we needed and most of what we wanted.

In the midst of losing her stepfather, Tyna had to think about graduating from high school and deciding what college she would attend. She was attending a technical high school because she *didn't want to go to the same school that my brother went to* and *I figured I can also learn a trade or learn how to do something else.* She chose Business as her trade, which encompassed, typing, shorthand and the like. That decision would later pay big dividends.

Even in his absence, she felt her stepfather's influence when she began to consider college.

A friend and I were considering going to an HBCU rather than a majority school. My stepfather had gone to Langston University in Oklahoma, so I applied there. I also considered Spelman College in Atlanta. But I did not know whether I wanted to be so far away from home. The other schools on my list were Morningside College in Sioux City, Iowa and the major state school, the University of Iowa (UI). When the UI's representatives came to our high school to recruit, I decided on the UI—they were offering me a full ride scholarship! Also, a lot of my friends were going there and I figured the UI was just far enough away from home.

College

Although Tyna went to college expecting to get a degree in Elementary Education, believing that she wanted to be an elementary school teacher, she changed her mind after her first work-study job.

I was a study hall monitor at a high school. And I said, 'no way; I can't be bothered with these crazy kids all day long.' That's when I changed my major to fashion merchandising.

Fashion merchandising was a good fit for Tyna—one which utilized skills she had developed growing up.

Fashion merchandising required taking what was called at the time 'home economics' courses like cooking and sewing (by the time I finished college they stopped calling it home economics). I enjoyed taking home economics because I already knew how to cook and sew, but that taught me a lot more.

Growing up Tyna learned how to cook and sew out of both curiosity and necessity.

At Christmas we would always make cookies and candy. I started learning how to cook probably when I was in fourth or fifth grade baking with my mom. Then, being the oldest girl, I would always have to start dinner before my mom got home from work. So that's how I learned how to cook.

Tyna learned how to sew at the community center in 7th third grade...

... because I was short and tubby, and I couldn't find any clothes that fit me. I could find tops—blouses or whatever—but it was always hard to find skirts and pants and dresses. And going school shopping I was out of the girl's size 14, and back then what was considered women's clothes were too old looking. My mother had started sewing. She called herself trying to learn how to sew so she would make all these clothes for us—my sister Sheila and me—from this ugly material! The style was ok, but the material was ugly—at least ugly in a 12-year old's mind. So that's when I learned how to sew. My mom would take me to buy fabric and I would take it to a basic home economic development class at the Community Center where I learned how to sew. The first thing I made was a wraparound dress, then a jumper. I learned a bit more on the basics of sewing by taking home economics in high school and made a lot of my clothes from seventh grade until well into college.

In college, having soured on a career in teaching, majoring in Fashion Merchandising was a natural next choice for Tyna, allowing her to *do something I know how to do*. She liked clothes, fashion, and shopping—all necessary for a fashion buyer. But the requirements of the major were certainly more rigorous than just shopping.

To do fashion merchandising, I had to take chemistry, which I hated, but it was a prerequisite for food classes and textile and dyeing class. With food classes you had to learn the science behind food; then we had to cook food. But we also had to learn the science behind ingredients, your multiplication and all that stuff.

To both confirm her interest and enhance her opportunities in the Fashion Merchandising industry as a Buyer, Tyna got a job at JC Penney. By the time she graduated from college she was interviewing for jobs in fashion merchandising.

Disappointment ... Perhaps

Tyna initially interviewed with JC Penney for a management training position, and had several interviews as a Buyer, but was not the successful candidate.

I was disappointed that I didn't get a job as a fashion buyer. And even after my first year working for the City, I still was interviewing for jobs as a buyer—to no avail. At first, I thought it was because I didn't really have any experience, which is why I took the job at JC Penney. I thought well maybe I need to get some retail experience. But even after that, I didn't get a job. So I don't know at that time those decisions could have been racially motivated; I'm not sure. I guess I didn't give it much thought. I just went ahead and did what I had to do so I would be able to live.

Deciding what she had to do did not include a move back to Des Moines.

I knew I could move back home if I had to, but I never really thought about moving back to Des Moines. I liked being away from home and I think Des Moines was just far enough away. If I had to get there, I could. And I thought about whether moving back home would mean that I was going to move back home with my Mom or what.

One thing was clear, Tyna had to decide on an alternative to Fashion Merchandising.

So I said, 'You're about to graduate, you have got to have a job doing something.' So I focused on my clerical skills, developed in high school. And that's when I got the job working for the City of Iowa City. Back then—in the 70s—computers were just beginning to come into important existence. In my new job with the City, I was doing data entry with the cards and big old machines. So, that job allowed me to learn some different skills—computer skills.

The glass is always half full for Tyna.

I felt lucky I had gone to a vocational school that gave me good typing and transcription skills.

Tyna retired from her position at the City after more than 33 years in 2012—never using her Fashion Merchandising degree the way she intended, which was disappointing."

If I had a disappointment, I would say that it was not getting the job that I had hoped I would get [in fashion merchandising]; but I wasn't disappointed in that I knew I had skills that would allow me to get a job enabling me to live comfortably. We always want more, but I'm thankful that I had skills that permitted me to always be able to get a job so that I could take care of myself.

But before her adult work life . . .

In her first year of college Tyna—who had always done well in school—
was surprised to find that she was struggling academically.

*When I first started college, I wasn't as prepared as I should have been. I
don't know if that was due to having gone to a technical high school or not.
Whatever the cause, when I arrived at the UI, I realized that I did not have
the strongest study skills. In high school, once I got past my required courses, it wasn't like I had to study a lot. So I did struggle my freshman year in
college. It wasn't that I couldn't do the work, but I just didn't study the way
I needed to. Once I came to that realization, I knew I had to do some things
differently—I had to study more than I had been to do well in my classes.*

At least part of her incentive to do so was Tyna's decision to seek
membership in the sisterhood of the Delta Sigma Theta Sorority. It was
a decision that would contribute to her life's direction of service to her
community.

Delta Sigma Theta . . . The Sisterhood

When Tyna arrived at the UI for freshman orientation, her orientation
counselor was in the process of re-chartering the Delta Sigma Theta Sorority, Inc., chapter in Iowa City, which had been inactive for twenty years.
A group of African American young women attending the UI expressed
an interest in becoming Deltas. Tyna was impressed with those engaged
in the effort and interested in joining the chapter.

*Back then, the Black students were a more cohesive group. All of us were
involved in the Black Student Union or the Black Gospel Choir, or both.
So everybody knew everybody. And I looked up to that particular group of
women who were part of the Delta Sigma Theta sorority—they were leaders
on campus. Prior to college I knew women in the community—some of my
neighbors—who were members of the organization, but I didn't really know
that much about the Deltas and what they did. All I really knew about them
was they would always have this big ball to raise money for scholarships.
And that's how I developed my initial interest in the organization from the
things they were doing. When I arrived at college I said, 'Let me figure out
how I'm going to do this.'*

There were a few obstacles in the way of Tyna joining the group: there was a monetary fee to join, and the criteria to become a Delta included maintaining a certain grade point average and doing service in the community.

I had to figure out how to gather the money required to join—it was maybe a hundred dollars, which back then was a lot of money for me—and there were criteria as far as grades. That was the end of my freshman year and my grades were not that good; so that was one of my motivating factors for working hard to bring my grades up. You also had to get letters of recommendation from people.

Tyna was only interested in joining the Delta Sigma Theta Sorority—*I never thought about joining any other sorority.* Nearly 45 years later, she remains a very active member of the Deltas—particularly the Iowa City chapter—where she has held all the major offices of the chapter, as well as regional offices, and received a number of awards—both from the Delta organization and others for her leadership in Delta and the community.

What has held her interest and sustained her level of commitment?

My Mission

Delta is a service organization whose members are women dedicated to service and scholarship. I enjoy that I am doing service for others. Most people know that I'll do anything I can for you if it's in my realm of talents or within my knowledge base. As I said, the idea of helping others came from my mother and the neighborhood and community in which I grew up. Thus, having been raised in that environment, helping others in need was just something that you did, and you didn't really think twice about doing it.

Recently, as part of its Juneteenth celebration[4], the Iowa City Juneteenth Committee awarded Tyna its Juneteenth Trailblazer's Award as Outstanding Community Leader in Iowa City. Tyna had no idea who nominated her for the award.

When I gave my speech, I said, 'I don't even know who nominated me, but the things I do, I don't do for recognition.' That said, I guess it's nice to know that somebody notices. After the ceremony ended, this young woman

---

4. Juneteenth is a celebration of the day enslaved Black folk in Texas were told of the abolition of slavery—June 19, 1865—some 2½ years after the Emancipation Proclamation and six months after the passage of the 13th Amendment.

came up and told me that she was the one who nominated me. When I met her, she was a student at the UI who worked at the Women's Resource and Action Center here in Iowa City. And she and I had been a part of a girls' mentoring program together. So she knew that I was a Delta and that our chapter had been volunteering a lot at the Women's Resource Center. She told me that she and several others had nominated me for the award.

The award reflects Tyna's impact within her Iowa City community, and importantly, the impact she has had on young women. It speaks to how important it is for young women, particularly young African American women, to have people—mentors—to look up to, whether they are a couple of years older, or 10 or 20 years older. Tyna recognizes the value of what she does because of the impact that other women within and without the Delta organization have had on her.

Every time I go to a convention, I'm struck by the number of women who are part of the organization and by having the opportunity to meet notable women. I have been on several committees where I've met the presidents of the organization, and women who are for lack of a better term, 'big whigs' in the organization, members who are chairs of committees, particularly the membership committee.

She was particularly influenced by one of her Delta sisters.

Barbara Curtis was one of these women—an ordinary woman who was extraordinary in what she did. As chair of membership she believed that members needed to get something for their membership and the time and effort that they put into the organization. So she always made sure that there were activities where people could just come and have a good time. You might get some type of token—a recognition pen or some other prize— while you were there. I believe she would sometimes spend her own money; but, she always said that she just wanted to make sure that the members knew that they were appreciated and received some type of recognition for their service and their longstanding membership in the organization. So that impressed me.

And by being appointed to or volunteering to work on several different committees, I've had the opportunity to meet most of the national presidents and be in their presence. There are just some dynamic Black women in the world—who are a part of the Deltas, but also those involved in other organizations! I think about Frankie Freeman who recently died. She was one hundred years old. She was the first Black woman appointed to the Civil

Rights Commission. And that lady was something! And just to meet women like that makes a great impression on anyone—whether you are a Delta or not.

Being a Mentor

An aspect of the Delta Sigma Theta Sorority service objective in mentoring young girls and women is to guide them in a way that lifts their self-esteem and offers positive alternatives, which they may have been unable to see for themselves. Tyna embraces these objectives as part of her personal responsibility and hopes those who benefit will pay it forward. Thus, following in the footsteps of her Delta mentors and the many women she has met while a Delta member, Tyna has welcomed the opportunity to mentor girls and young women—*who didn't have the type of upbringing that we had back in a time when we were probably much poorer than they are.* As a result, Tyna and her Delta sisters have developed programs designed to allow these young women to freely discuss self-esteem and other issues important to them. They listen as well as instruct and guide. Particularly useful has been an activity called, "if you really knew me." The responses are sometimes funny, but often sobering . . .

Sometimes the young women choose to talk about very surface things such as "I like to wear a weave" or "I like to get my nails done." After they become members we go back and visit some of the things that they said and give them the opportunity to go deeper if they choose to about what people should know about them. And sometimes when I talk to these girls and those girls who come to our programs, I listen to their stories and I'm thinking to myself, 'I feel like I lived a fairy tale life.' We didn't have any of the worries they have. Like I said, we never went hungry; we always had shoes and clothes and a place to live. We never had to worry about our parents not being there. I told this one group of kids that it makes me sad that in the year of 2018, [when this interview was conducted] that in some areas of the country, in these United States of America, which is supposed to be the wealthiest country in the world, that as a Black community we still suffer injustice. In addition, I think the structure of the Black family has just gone to hell. It's falling apart. When you listen to these kids, fortunately, a number of them have been able to thrive in school and get into a college and away from home, but they're struggling because they don't have the support. They certainly don't have financial support. If they didn't get a full ride they are probably really struggling. But as I said, it makes me sad. I feel like I lived a fairy tale. I feel like I was rich in all ways compared to some of these stories I hear.

And hearing and observing their struggles, Tyna puts into motion her mother's words:

I just try to do my best. If somebody calls me—one of my sorors or friends—and says, "I have somebody from my church who is coming to The University of Iowa, can you meet them, meet their parents?" if I am able I will do so. I've met several people and their parents when they came to the UI for the first time. I tell them if they need to go to the grocery store or whatever to call me—or to go to the airport, whatever. I think it just makes a world of difference.

Some of these young women just need some guidance. Lots of times they just need somebody to talk to, somebody to listen to them. And I don't know, it's sad that many of the people who are younger than us have not had those people—I don't know what happened with their family life.

Thus, part of Tyna's mission is to turn some of the negative she observes into positive. .

The key to turning this around is to have more people who have been able to succeed in whatever they define as success—whether it's graduating from college or having your dream career or whatever—to give back. I think that's one of the reasons why our generation was able to do a lot of things that we were able to do—because people took an interest in us, people cared about what we did and how we succeeded, whether it was school—you always had a teacher—Black or White, who took an interest in you—through church, or your neighborhood, there was somebody who invested in you in some type of way. And I think more of us—our generation and those 35 and 45 year olds who were able to attain more than their parents probably have—need to give back in whatever way we/they can—volunteering somewhere or whatever they/we can do.

My most important contribution is my time; trying to mentor the new members to know what the organization is about and how to make it a part of their everyday living as they move forward—transitioning from college to the work world or going to graduate school or whatever they choose to do. I just tell them, somebody invested in you; somebody took the time to try to help you and you have to continue to do that.

A life changing moment . . .

Tyna's dedication to her mission of helping others, investing in the lives of young African American women through her sorority has been a constant in her life—before and after her most challenging, life changing moment in 1997: the death of her mother.

Tyna's mother had managed to successfully raise her four children after her husband died, giving them what they needed to meet the world. Tyna identifies her mom as the most influential person in her life.

My mother taught me most of what I know to be the woman I am. She taught me to value me; she taught me to look out for me; not to let people, male or female, run over me. She always taught us that even if you have a husband, you have your own, because you never know what might happen. He could die. You might decide you don't want to be with him anymore, but at least you have a foundation for yourself. She taught me to treat people the

way you want to be treated. If you want to be treated nice, then you treat people nice; and hopefully, that comes back to you. She taught us to just do your best. Do the best that you can. Never say you can't. Always try.

There it is—that wisdom—again. The words Tyna lives by.

Tyna's mother was also a breast cancer survivor . . .

And then she was murdered.

It was an unexpected, horrific, random act of violence—perhaps making it all the more painful. It remains difficult for Tyna to talk about . . .

The most life changing thing is when my mother died. One, how she died; two, because she was my everything. You always know that

they won't be here forever, but it's still painful. I think it changed me just to *know you should appreciate people who are there for you; and you never take anything or anyone for granted, because you never know what's going to happen. Nowadays you hear people complaining about their mom and I say, 'You need to stop that complaining right now because when she's not here you are going to wish she was!'*

Spirituality

Tyna continues to work through the loss of her mother. It is at best an uneven process—and although it has been more than twenty years, there are good days and there are bad. Tyna has not, however, given up on life or her mission in life. She remains committed to helping others, mentoring, doing her best. Her belief in a higher power—her spirituality—has helped.

I have always gone to church, and I think religion is one of those things that a lot of people struggle with. I believe there is a higher being and that you just have to believe in something. I guess I believe there are angels in heaven, wherever they are, who watch over us because sometimes you do things and you have to say, 'somebody must be watching out for me.' I believe there is some type of spiritual being that guides you. It can be a song—we used to say, "Either preaching has to be good or the music has to be good." So it's a song or message that's going to make me think about something—that lets me know the point of me being in church today. It has to be something, although it doesn't necessarily have to be that deep for me anyway. But fortunately, I haven't had a lot of traumatic things in my life. I know some of the things that go on with other parents and kids and I'm like, 'Oh my God, that would drive me crazy!'

Words of Wisdom

Tyna's words of wisdom reflect her journey . . .

I would tell people to first and foremost always do your best. If you do your best nobody can take that from you. Do your best in school to get the education that you need to do the things you want to do. Don't let anyone— within your power—keep you from trying to reach your goals—you have to at least try. What's the saying, 'Nothing beats a failure like a try.' If you don't try, you'll never know if you can succeed. You will never know whether you can do it or not. If there's something you really want to do, try it. And just be the best person you can be! I don't think people are always the best people they can be.

Imagine a world where everybody in it tried to be the best person they can be!

Tyna's other piece of advice is to *surround yourself with positive, like-minded people, and to have some type of spiritual grounding.*

The Future: What's Next?

Tyna hopes to continue to do the things that she has been doing—

. . . to help people, to have my health and my right mind—just to let me live life one day at a time and do as much as I can and what I am able to do.

Traveling to places within the U.S. to which she has never been—*there are a few states I have not been to and I would still like to go to them*—is also in her plan; although places outside the United States—*except maybe London and South Africa*—are not particularly compelling.

I thought I wanted to go on a hot air balloon ride; but I don't know if I still want to do that anymore. Maybe parasailing . . .

Tyna's journey thus far *has been slow and steady; a few twists and turns. Not too rocky, slow and steady, that's how I would describe it along the way.*

At 65, Tyna sees herself as . . .

. . . a strong, independent, proud, Black woman. Happy and proud to be a Black woman. I don't think I would want to be anyone else. I think I'm happy and happy with me. I'm happy with the choices that I've made in life. No regrets. There are always things that you say, maybe I should've done this or done that. I wouldn't say that I regret not doing it. It's never too late, I guess.

And if somebody asked Tyna to respond to the question: if you really knew me, what would you say?

If you really knew me . . .you would know that I am a loyal and honest friend; and if you become my friend, you will probably be my friend for life. But I also tell people that if you do something to undermine me or let me know you don't value my friendship, then you don't ever have to worry about being my friend. I tell people, 'I'll do anything for anyone but don't try to use me, don't try to take advantage of me, don't take me for granted.' Most people who really know me will say, 'that is so true.'

It is not surprising then that Tyna's greatest triumph is . . .

. . . just being able to be me; being able to be the person I want to be, and to be able to do most of the things I want to do in life. I think my greatest triumph is just being happy. Being happy that I'm able to be here and at this age to not have any major illnesses, just to be.

Tyna Theresa Price, vibrant, happy, and living her best life!

TARA BRADLEY

Embracing Myself

When *Hair Love*—one of the few movies about people of color that was recognized in 2020—won an academy award for Best Animated Short Film, communities of color—but particularly the African American community—rejoiced. It was affirming of who we are and how we look. It was important because our view of ourselves is often shaped by others—whether we are teased or bullied, praised or complemented. What others think of us or say to us about our appearance will sometimes morph into what we think about ourselves.

It's interesting to hear people say that you are a pretty dark-skinned sister. I can remember when I would pick my daughters up from school the teachers thought that the two sisters who were closer to my skin color were my daughters—not my twin daughters Jennifer and Jillian. Black women come in a rainbow of skin colors and we are all beautiful. Unfortunately, some people still consider skin color to determine whether you are pretty or not. That's one of the reasons why I respect my friend Donkor, because he embraces natural beauty.

In a society so taken with physical appearance, for a child, especially an African American child, navigating all of this—issues of skin color, hair texture, etc.—and reaching the conclusion that you are beautiful can be a challenge. Sometimes it takes time—a little or a lot. But as Tara Patmon Ravnell Bradley discovered, after some time we appreciate and embrace ourselves and our beauty—we celebrate!

Guthrie to Oklahoma City

Tara was born in Guthrie, Oklahoma while her parents were students at Langston University, an HBCU located in Langston, Oklahoma. After her parents graduated, they moved with Tara to Oklahoma City. Tara does not remember these early years. Her memories begin at five.

I don't remember Guthrie at all. I know I was born there because it was the hospital closest to Langston. And I don't remember moving to Oklahoma City. But I know that my parents built their first home—three bedrooms with a water cooler air conditioner—in Oklahoma City on the corner of 26th and Rhode Island. At five years old—when my memory really begins—I went to Creston Hills Elementary School. Kindergarten was only half a day at that time, so after school I stayed with a neighbor until my parents got home from work. She fed me crackers with grape jelly for lunch.

Catholic Schools

After moving to Oklahoma City, Tara's parents—who were Catholic—began attending Corpus Christi Catholic Church. Oklahoma City was still largely segregated, and there were few African American families attending the church or its grade school. Nonetheless, Tara attended Corpus Christi Catholic School from first through eighth grade.

Our teachers were nuns. We went to mass every morning before school. At the time, women and girls had to cover their heads when entering the church, so we wore beanies during mass.

The learning experience for Tara and her classmates was much the same as other grade-schoolers—reading was fundamental.

I learned how to read in grade school. We had to stand at our desks and read those See Spot Run books, the Dick and Jane Reader, and our catechism [book of faith] books.

The award-winning book and movie *Hair Love* was not yet even a thought in the 1960s, and Tara remembers being teased.

Bullying and Hair

I've always had issues with my hair . . . I mean forever! I have never really liked the way my hair looked. So, in the 5th grade my mother bought me a pretty fall [a partial wig designed to add to your hair], which she had cut into a youthful style. It had little bangs with a flip in the back. I even took my 5th grade picture with my cute fall!

I also remember some of the eighth-grade girls coming up behind me in the lunch line and pulling my fall, trying to pull it off.

I was chubby at that time and they teased me about that as well. I guess I told my mother about how they were treating me, so the summer before the 8th grade she put me on a diet. I couldn't eat bread or sugar—I couldn't eat anything! But I probably lost about 15 pounds and I was glad about it, so I didn't mind the diet. I guess they were just being girls; but it hurt my feelings.

High School and Boys . . .

When Tara entered high school, the teasing and bullying did not stop—it just came from a different source.

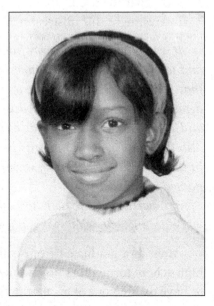

It was crazy because when I arrived at Bishop McGuinness as a 9th grade freshman, the girls who had bullied me were so nice to me. It was the boys I went to grade school with who were now teasing me mercilessly.

So much so that Tara expresses surprise that the wounds from high school did not more permanently affect her self-esteem. Like most teenagers her age she was noticing boys, extremely self-conscious about her appearance, and looking for approval. At her high school at least, she was receiving anything but the approval she sought and needed.

When I started 9th grade, I was wearing braces, extremely skinny, and very self-conscious about the way I looked. I still didn't like my hair, so I was wearing afro puffs—which were fashionable at that time. Nonetheless some of the boys who were my classmates in grade school who joined me in high school teased and bullied me about the way I looked. I was really hurt and surprised when one of my classmates call me ugly.

Tara did not tell her mother about what the boys were saying because *I didn't want her to worry.* Instead, she stopped going to the cafeteria where her classmates—including the bullying boys—tended to congregate during their free time.

What bothered me the most was that at Corpus Christi we grew up as a family; so for them to treat me like that in high school . . . I don't know why. The older guys in high school were nice; it was the ones in my class who hurt my feelings.

However, Tara did not let the bullying and teasing at Bishop McGuinness prevent her from engaging in activities in which she was interested. She ran for freshman class secretary; and although she did not win, it was a victory that she tried.

Interestingly, this mistreatment did not exist outside of high school.

It was totally different away from my high school. I didn't let the bullying and teasing at Bishop McGuinness prevent me from engaging in activities that I was interested in outside of school. A friend and I applied to a local department store to be teen models. The local newspaper covered the event, and I was selected to represent Bishop McGuiness as a teen model. I was also first runner up in the Miss Black Teenage Oklahoma Pageant. I was in the first Miss Fashionetta, which show-cased teenage students, and was named best model.

So I participated in activities that helped me to appreciate and like me while dealing with what was going on at McGuinness.

After Tara graduated from college and returned home, some of her high school tormentors now wanted to date her, one of whom professed to have no memory of his part in the harassment and bullying.

Years later—by then I had choices—I remember telling one high school classmate whom I was dating about being hurt and how they teased me and said I was ugly. He said, "I don't remember that." I don't know how I felt about the fact that he didn't remember, but I recall telling my daughters when they were very young not to allow others to hurt them with their words. I would recite the well-known adage, "Sticks and Stones may break your bones but words will never hurt you".

Family

My parents

Tara characterizes herself as *the obedient child;* so she got along with both her parents, always trying to do the right thing. Although, she believes that she was not the favorite child of either parent, it was never a worry or concern, just a fact.

Parents have favorites. I don't think that I was the favorite of my mother—my brother was her favorite; and I think my sister was my dad's favorite. I was just right there. I never felt left out because I was a pleaser. I always wanted to please my parents, so I was always favored but not the favorite.

My mother and Mark had a bond. My brother was working from home when my mom got sick. Mark decided to work from my mother's house while she was ill. This was a special time for them before my mom passed away).

Tara describes her father as *just a jolly good-natured, fun-loving* person whom *EVERYBODY loved!*

They called him Big John. He had this huge, big laugh. He was a big man—he wasn't fat, he was just big and tall. He was about like 6'4 or 6'5 and people just loved being around him. They just actually loved my dad.

And I would notice that my father would go the extra mile for my sister and get more emotional when things happened with her. My sister and dad really enjoyed their time together when my dad became ill. My sister remembers lighting his cigarettes because he was blind. They would sit around the table and chat and drink cocktails.

Tara was close to her mother and delighted in whatever time they spent together. As a result, whatever her mother would ask her to do, Tara would do.

I really really enjoyed being with my mother. The first time I ever remember my mother hugging me though is when my daughters were in the hospital. I went to church and I saw her, and I started crying. And so I think that was the first time she hugged me. She wasn't openly affectionate.

Nonetheless, Tara's bond with her mother was impenetrable; and both of her parents were a significant influence. Tara recalls her parents' support for each other—even when their roles were seemingly reversed.

My mother always said that it was very rare that Black women had the option to stay home and not work. She felt it took incomes from the husband and the wife to make a decent living. However I remember when my father decided to enroll in the first Physician Assistant Class at the University of Oklahoma. My mother was the breadwinner for the family while my dad was enrolled in the PA program. My brother and sister didn't notice anything different except for the fact that my dad was away from home more while he was going to school.

Siblings

Tara has a different relationship with each of her siblings—Marc and Tracy. The bond with Marc seemed inevitable as they shared a birthday.

Marc—Little Brother for My Birthday

Marc came into the world on Tara's birthday—exactly four years after she was born. That event coupled with the fact that she has lived with him for one reason or another for a good part of her adult life has made for a very close relationship with her only brother.

We were living on Rhode Island Street. I told my parents that I wanted a rocking chair for my birthday. I got a brother—I got Marc—instead.

Tara eventually got that rocking chair—*it was a little black iron rocking chair*—but not right away. Her parents had other concerns.

Because my mother was a librarian at St Anthony's Hospital and the nuns didn't want their employees to be pregnant, we kind of had to hide Marc—I'm serious! For about a year after he was born, Marc stayed in Lawton, OK—a 20-minute ride from Oklahoma City—with Momma Florence, my great-grandmother. We would visit him on the weekends.

By Marc's second birthday, Tara's mother left St Anthony's and was working for the Library for the Blind—where no such requirements about pregnancy or children existed—and Marc joined the family for good. For the next several decades Tara and Marc would develop their life-long bond as siblings and friends.

Marc and I are very close. When Marc decided to go to Hampton, a high school friend and I drove him to Hampton his freshman year. I remember when we dropped him off, I started crying. Our close relationship has continued into adulthood.

Tara loves her sister Tracy just as she loves her brother; and there are childhood memories of their relationship that she holds dear. However, Tracy was born nearly four years after Marc. Thus, the seven-year age difference—Tracy was still in middle school when Tara entered college—hindered their ability to develop a close relationship until they reached adulthood. Moreover, Tara was always in charge and Tracy always had to take her direction from Tara.

I was more or less she and Marc's babysitter. When Tracy came home from the hospital to our house on Rhode Island I remember that Marc and I would just sit and hold her and look at her.

Tracy and I are also totally different in the things that we like. I love working with organizations like my sorority and the Links.[5] On the other hand, Tracy has vowed never to join the Links and and although in the family tradition she pledged the Delta Sigma Theta sorority, she has not been a particularly active member. She says, "That's just not me."

Today, distance is responsible for keeping the two sisters apart. Tracy lives in Texas; therefore the opportunity to do the things they jointly enjoy or just hang out is very often limited.

---

5. The Links, Incorporated is an international, not-for-profit corporation established in 1946 consisting of more than 16000 professional women of African descent. It is one of the nation's oldest and largest volunteer service organizations. The Oklahoma City chapter of The Links, Incorporated was established in 1957, the same year Tara was born.

As in most families, my siblings and I were different; however, those differences were celebrated rather than disparaged. Thus, Marc, Tracy and I have all matured, secure about who we are while developing into productive and successful citizens. That is something that would please my parents. Before our mom passed away, she told me that she just wanted to make sure that we would all be okay, and we are.

Being the Oldest

A few years after Tracy was born when Tara was headed into her teens, she more completely assumed her duties as the oldest child—becoming primarily responsible for her siblings when her parents were not home.

As the oldest, of course I had to do the babysitting—during the summer and school vacations at Thanksgiving and Christmas. I was the person in charge.

Rather than resenting these 'oldest' duties, Tara found that it allowed her to do things she wanted to do—and her siblings were willing participants.

Being in charge allowed my passions to come out. I loved to cook; so in the summers I would give my brother and sister Monopoly money. They would come into the kitchen and sit down and order food from the menus that I created. They were like, "okay, I'm gonna have such and such today." And I would cook what they ordered like I was a chef at a restaurant. I would serve them their order and they would pay with Monopoly money. So I lived out my fantasies through them during the summer. They cooperated because they didn't know any better—and I think I made it fun.

Obviously creative as a youngster, with a personality to match, 'Tara's Kitchen' was really a precursor to the Food Network!

Then there were other duties Tara had to assume as the oldest and first to drive—like carpooling. While she was thrilled when her mother bought her a brand new gold Chevy Malibu when she entered high school, the consequence of that wonderful gift was that she had to transport her brother and sister—and some of the neighborhood kids—to school every day.

My parents were building a new home. They sold our home before our new home was completed. Thus, we moved to an apartment complex while our new home was being built. During this time I had to drop them all off—my siblings and the kids in the neighborhood—at Corpus Christi Catholic School before I went to Bishop McGuinness High School. But it was not a burden. I did not want to change roles with my younger siblings. I noticed that my younger sister and brother didn't have to do some of the things that I had to do; but that was okay. I didn't care. I loved the responsibility and felt grown-up.

Then it was time for college. There was never a question that going to college was the next step and it would be a time when growing up would become more of a reality for Tara.

College

My siblings and I always knew that we would go to college. My mother and father always told us that they could never make enough money to take care of us forever; however, they said, "What we can give you is a good education that will allow you to take care of yourself."

Tara's classmates in high school were mostly White. Her high school was less than 10% people of color. Both her parents had gone to Langston University, the only HBCU in the state of Oklahoma. And Tara's mother wanted her to have the "Black experience" in college, and in a new environment.

My mother always wanted to go to Dillard University in New Orleans. She talked about the beautiful buildings on their campus and everything that attracted her to Dillard. But her dream of going there was not possible; so she went to Langston. As a result, she wanted her children to have the experience of going away to college. She said, "this will give you an opportunity to grow up." The ground rules were that it had to be a HBCU out of the state of Oklahoma; but there were only certain places we could go. She said "no" to Howard University because she didn't like the idea of her daughter being in a metropolitan city like Washington DC. She wanted us to go to small colleges.

It came down to Hampton Institute in Virginia, or Tuskegee Institute in Alabama. Back then it wasn't a matter of going to visit a college; we just had to choose. So I chose Hampton. The entire family took the trip—in a station wagon full of all my stuff—to get me there. When we finally arrived—it is a 24-hour drive—my parents dropped me off with all my stuff and headed back home. I knew I would not see them again until Christmas.

Nonetheless Tara was excited about this new part of her journey.

I was so excited about going off to school. I didn't get scared when they dropped me off. I thought, 'oh this is fun!' After my parents left, the new students took a tour of the college. That was fun! During the tour, I met Jackie from New Jersey and we have been friends ever since that day!

In fact, Jackie and Tara became roommates.

We were best friends with Susan and Debbie who lived across the hall from us. We called ourselves the "Farleys" and I really don't know why. As freshman we had curfew so we would play bid whist to the wee hours of the morning with not much else to do besides study.

My parents really couldn't afford to bring me home for Thanksgiving and Spring Break while I attended Hampton. So my college friends invited me to their homes during those holidays. I had the opportunity to spend school breaks with Susan in New York City, Jackie in New Jersey, and Debbie in Beaufort, South Carolina. I also visited my best friend from high school, Jordiene who attended Cornell University. Having the opportunity to see these parts of the country helped me to understand one of the reasons why my mother wanted her children to go out of state to college.

Tara enjoyed college. Even the process of finding the right major provided a positive adventure. Initially intending to be a mass media major—*my mother told me that was something she thought I would enjoy*—after performing a commercial as part of a course requirement Tara changed her mind.

I had an accent, which my professors and classmates called a southern or country accent. We were required to write and perform a commercial. I chose to do a Hungry Jack Biscuits commercial. (She laughs) My classmates were nice, but I could tell they were really laughing at the way I sounded. I decided mass media was not for me.

Undeterred, Tara eventually discovered her passion—something she liked and had actually discovered in high school.

I took a home economics class from Ms. Stank in high school. I LOVED my home economics class! I loved to cook and sew! Once I was in college, I met someone who was majoring in Human Ecology—another name for Home Economics. I discovered that the Human Ecology major had a component that would allow me to study the things I enjoyed. So I changed my major to human ecology. It was the right decision. In the end I had a home economics degree with a focus on food and nutrition, and the urban extension program disciplines. This was a more well-rounded major, incorporating things that I really enjoyed doing.

Tara's selection of the Human Ecology major was fortuitous as the requirements of the discipline she chose would serve her well in her future professional life.

One aspect of being a Home Economist major was giving cooking demonstrations—like, how to make bread or how an appliance works. During college, I would have my best friends, Jackie, Susan, and Debbie, come to my room, and listen to me as I practiced giving a demonstration. I would say 'Hi I'm Tara and today we're going to make homemade bread. The first step is to do this and that and this and that and this and that...' It's actually how I started my career at Oklahoma Natural Gas (ONG) Company. They were looking for a home economist!

But before that job or any job Tara had to finish college. And although she finished all of her coursework a semester early, there was a detour . . .

Legacy and Other Options

Following in her mother, grandmother, and great-grandmother's footsteps, Tara arrived on Hampton's campus intending to pledge and become a member of the Delta Sigma Theta sorority. Without knowing why, Tara was not accepted into the chapter on Hampton's campus. Perhaps it was because she was a 'legacy pledge'—all of the women on her mother's side of the family were members of the Delta Sigma Theta sorority. While having family members who were already part of the sorority would seem to be an advantage, it was sometimes just the opposite. Tara believes such was the case for her—particularly since she met all of the other requirements for admission. She was disappointed . . .

. . . but what happened taught me never to give up on a dream; and if it's truly important, to take the necessary steps to make it a reality.

So despite that disappointment, or perhaps because of it, with a free semester in her senior year, and a desire to focus on something more positive Tara set her sights on pursuing another academic interest: gerontology.

I always had a particular affinity for the elderly; so with a semester without much to do, and with the help of a Hampton professor, we set about looking for a scholarship in gerontology.

That plan never came to fruition. Instead, Tara spent her last semester in college taking graduate courses in Public Administration at the University of Oklahoma—giving her a head start on a different graduate degree. Also during this hiatus in Oklahoma Tara became a Delta, pledging the Oklahoma City University chapter.

While my mother would have been okay if I had stayed at Hampton that last semester, my family members who were Deltas really wanted me to become a member of a sorority that they loved because of the sisterhood and the public service it provided world-wide. That was really important to them, so that's what I did with no regrets.

Working Woman

Technically, Tara started her work life at the age of 16 as a cashier at a five and dime store (TG&Y) in Oklahoma City making $2.10 per hour. Tara's mother would take half of her paycheck saving it for her.

However, her adult work life began after she graduated from Hampton in 1979. Tara hoped to find post-college employment in someplace other than Oklahoma. She was disappointed when she did not.

I felt like I should have been able to find a job away from home. In my mind, I wasn't supposed to come back home. Of my three best girlfriends in college—nobody went back home but me.

Shaking off this frustration, with her graduate degree in Public

Administration from the University of Oklahoma in hand, Tara was offered and accepted her first 'adult' job at the Urban League of Greater Oklahoma City.

I was the Program Director for the Northeast Neighborhood Technical Assistance Program. I helped neighborhoods form neighborhood associations in the Northeast quadrant of Oklahoma City.

Tara's job at the Urban League was short-lived.

An Urban League Board member—Mr. Will Williams who worked at Oklahoma Natural Gas Company (ONG)—announced during our board meeting that ONG was searching for a home economist. Immediately after the meeting, Mr. Williams gave me more specifics about the position, including the fact that it included a company car, a good salary, and an expense account. I was excited about this new opportunity. I was making $8,000 at the Urban League and the salary for the position at ONG was $18,000. And it was what I wanted to do! I was going to be a home economist! I couldn't believe it! I was so excited!

Tara's mother did not share her enthusiasm.

My mother was apprehensive about me leaving the job at the Urban League. She said, "You're going to leave the Urban League? That's a good job!" And it was. It was an excellent work environment to begin my professional career. I learned a great deal during my time at the Urban League. I developed my presentation skills, an understanding of how a board works, how to be a community advocate, and most importantly how to work with a diverse group of people. Our Executive Director, Mr. Leonard Benton, Mrs. Janice Scott, Mrs. Jeannie Smith from Leo's Barbeque, and Mrs. Henrietta Hicks from Boley, Oklahoma were all mentors that guided and directed me during my time at the Urban League They were all respected Black people within the Oklahoma City community whom my mother knew and trusted with her daughter. However, she didn't know Mr. Williams; so she didn't trust that he would help me to land my dream job as a Home Economist.

This would be a time in her life when Tara went against her mother's wishes and applied for the job at ONG. It initially may have seemed that her mother was right.

I didn't get the first position; but I got the second one. And once I got there, I loved it!

Tara was excited about the new job—her responsibilities would be what her college degree had prepared her to do.

ONG

I loved my new job! ONG supplied gas ranges to all the home economics classrooms in the Oklahoma middle schools, high schools, and colleges. Each Home Economist had her own territory. I would go into the classrooms and say, 'Hi my name is Tara. I work for Oklahoma Natural Gas and today I'm going to talk to you about the benefits of using natural gas. We are going to do this with this gas range by making a cake (or something else) today.' I would make a brownie sheet cake and then we used the top burners on the stove. The students got a demonstration and information about the benefits of using gas, and something good to eat!

There were only two African Americans Home Economist for ONG. My good sister friend Mary was in Tulsa, and I was in Oklahoma City. However, the women who managed the ONG test kitchens in both places were Black. They were instrumental in the success of all of the ONG Home Economists. In fact, I would not have successfully completed the training all Home Economist had to complete before we went to our assigned schools if it had not been for the test kitchen staff in Oklahoma City, my sheroes, Irene Counter and Imogene Woody. These women tested the recipes that were published in the gas bill and assisted us tremendously with our roles and responsibilities as Home Economists.

Even after our mission changed and we worked with small appliance stores to show their customers how to cook food on the gas grill, my role as Home Economist was my favorite job!

Tara spent her career at ONG and its subsidiary companies. There were successes and challenges, setbacks, and satisfactions. She experienced growth and renewal, lessons learned and opportunities to impact her job and her community in positive ways.

I worked for ONG, ONEOK and ONE Gas for 37 years which was the majority of my life. I started when I was 25 years old and retired at the age of 61. I had some exceptionally good years throughout my career and some were a bit more challenging. Often, I felt that I wasn't appreciated. I applied for several jobs that I felt would have been a good fit but unfortunately, I was not the successful candidate. I wonder if it was because I never had a so-called sponsor or mentor or perhaps because on two major occasions during my career at ONG, I had to fight for what I believed was right. I started my career as a Home Economist and later took on the roles of Dealer Representative, Builder Representative, and the Speakers Bureau representative. I ended my career as a Community Investment Consultant.

Although my career encompassed ups and downs, I learned how to choose the battles that I thought were important to fight, and to fight the right way in order to win. I also developed good friendships that I will cherish forever. We were a family. These are people that I have lunch with on a monthly basis even today.

Love & Marriage . . . and children

Gerry

In her new position as an ONG Home Economist, Tara could not have been happier in her professional life. Her personal life had also become interesting. Several months before she started work at the Urban League her cousin, Dr. Carole Hall Hardeman, introduced her to a young man from her church—Gerry Ravnell. Gerry was from Texas; so for their first big date he took Tara to the Texas State Fair.

Over the next year, their families would meet—one Christmas Tara's entire family drove to Mexia, Texas to meet Gerry's family. And after a year of dating, Tara fell in love and she and Gerry married. They had a beautiful wedding at Corpus Christi Catholic Church, with her college and high school friends serving as bridesmaids. Five years later, their twins—Jennifer and Jillian—were born. Their premature birth was a life-changing moment for the couple.

Jennifer & Jillian

Jennifer and Jillian were preemie babies, born on January 6, 1986. They were in the hospital from January until May. I didn't know I was having twins until I had them. Sometimes I blame myself for their premature birth. I didn't recognize the signs that I was approaching the stage where my babies were about to be born; and maybe I should have selected a different doctor who believed in ultrasounds. But this was my first pregnancy so I had no clue about the signs that my delivery was coming quick. My water broke on New Year's Eve. I was frightened knowing that my baby was not due until April. And it turned out my baby was babies! My life changed dramatically the day they were born. Not knowing whether they would survive was an emotional roller coaster. That's when my faith in God helped me to make it from day to day.

It was both Tara's faith in God, and her mother, whom she had relied upon all of her young life, who got Tara through this challenging time.

One Saturday afternoon, I unexpectedly ran into my mother on the steps of our church. The doctor had just told me that Jennifer probably wouldn't make it through the night. The babies were only a few days old; Jennifer weighed less than two pounds and Jillian weighed less than three pounds. I had come to the church to ask our priest to come to the hospital to give Jennifer last rites when I saw my mother and began to cry. It was the trauma of Jennifer's prognosis and the first time I ever remember my mother hugging me. The priest gave Jennifer her last rites. That was hard. But Jennifer made it!

But even after that, Gerry and I would go home each night realizing that there was nothing we could do about the girls' condition—they were at the best doctor, and we had to just turn it over to God. I remember being so tired during that time—going to the hospital in the mornings and then going to work this whole time; going to get something to eat . . . it was just a very difficult time.

Jillian came home in May and Jennifer came home in June. They were both basically healthy by the time they came home. Jennifer stayed in the hospital longer because she had a brain bleed that affected her left side, and still does to an unnoticeable extent.

Despite their somewhat inauspicious introduction to the world both Jennifer and Jillian grew and developed and are now college educated women with their own parental responsibilities. Jennifer has a bachelor's degree in Elementary Education and following in her grandmother's footsteps, she received a Master of Library Science. Jillian majored in Communication Disorders and is a Special Education Teacher and a Speech Language Disorders Assistant.

While Tara and Gerry divorced in 1992, they have a life-long bond because of their children and grandchildren. The girls now each have a child—Jillian has 5-year-old Jordyn; and Jennifer has 3-year-old Jacob. Tara and Gerry are proud grandparents.

Professional Changes

At about the same time that her marriage was ending, Tara's favorite job was ending when the company phased out its home economist program. She says ONG made a money decision at that time—a decision it came to regret.

ONG decided that the home economist program was not producing revenue dollars. But they were being short sighted, and as a result the company has now missed a whole generation of kids—the millennials—who are now home buyers but have not been exposed to the benefits of natural gas. Electricity is cheaper; so builders are going to install everything electric. In contrast, as home economists we were spreading the word about natural gas. Now the company is trying to figure out how to get that millennial group—my children's age group—that they missed when they were in high school, middle school, and college!

New Job

After the phase out, ONG's home economists became Dealer Representatives.

As Dealer Representatives we no longer went into schools to provide demonstrations in home economics classes. Instead, we interacted and helped appliance dealers that sold natural gas appliances. We worked with the salespeople doing demonstrations and advising them on the benefits of using natural gas rather than electricity so that they could pass along that advantage to their customers.

On a scale of one to ten, Tara's job in the Home Economics Program was *a ten!* The Dealer rep job was *an eight because I really loved the first job.* Tara was a dealer rep for a few years until those positions were also phased out.

Then those of us in that program were assigned to the building department where we became Builder Representatives. When there was a new housing development, we worked with the builder to make sure that the gas was installed before the homes were occupied. These jobs were all part of the marketing department.

Tara disliked the job.

First, the job wasn't interesting to me. I also felt that the good old boy network determined how builders were treated. There was an obvious inequity in the treatment of majority vs. minority builders, with minority builders getting the short end of the stick. Therefore, I made sure that I followed the guidelines, regulations, and procedures ensuring fair treatment for every builder.

When Tara complained, her job again changed. She no longer met with builders. Instead, she went from professional attire to jeans and casual attire while driving a truck all over central Oklahoma to ensure proper placement of gas meters.

I didn't pout or quit. I performed my duties as a good employee. However, I knew that I could not spend the remainder of my career driving a truck. I didn't enjoy my job nor did I feel like I was growing or learning. Sometimes we do things because we have to. It would have been financially detrimental for me to leave the company after 25 years. So I got in the truck every morning, did my job without complaining while planning to do something different.

Ironically, her manager unwittingly provided Tara with the ammunition to find her next best job.

I scheduled a meeting to talk to my manager about my current job responsibilities to see if we could come up with a win-win job situation for me and the company. She told me she didn't know what to do with me or how she could help. As our conversation progressed, she began raising her voice—loud enough to be heard outside of her office by co-workers. I admonished her for screaming at me as if I were a child and removed myself from what was becoming a volatile situation.

Although Tara and her manager were at an impasse, Tara soon came to realize the benefit of contacts and participation in organizations. That realization was Tara's salvation.

The day after this confrontation with my manager I had an off-site Board Development meeting with a community agency. During the meeting, I received calls from co-workers indicating that they heard the conversation between my manager and me. That encounter gave me the courage to go beyond my manager to get my career back on track; it also taught me the power of Black women.

I contacted some smart, savvy professional Black women in the organizations of which I had become a part seeking advice on how to approach the problem in a professional manner while obtaining the desired results—continuing a worthy career at ONG.

The advice Tara received would prove significant. Taking the recommended, appropriate internal action within the company with respect to the mistreatment to which she had been subjected culminated in a new, better position for Tara—one she would come to enjoy. ONG was developing a Speakers' Bureau though its Foundation. Tara was tapped to facilitate the work of the Bureau. But for the unfortunate circumstance with her manager it is unlikely Tara would have found her way to the position; however, like her first job with ONG, it was unexpectedly tailored to her skills.

I loved this newly created position. I was responsible for writing company programs that would be delivered to communities throughout the state of Oklahoma by area managers. Eventually, I traveled throughout the state speaking to senior citizen groups regarding the different customer service programs that we offered. This program became very beneficial to the company because ONG had previously closed all of our local offices no longer giving us the opportunity to have face to face contact with our customers, particularly seniors. Now I would be the face of our company and helpful to our senior customers. This was a win-win job situation.

I learned that crucial conversations could bring about a positive change. Within a 4-month time span I went from being a frustrated, unhappy employee to reinventing a Speakers Bureau that allowed me to do much of what I did as a Home Economist—speak to schools and civic groups about our company.

Personal Changes

In 1997, before the turmoil that led to her job at the Speakers Bureau, Tara would marry a man she admired and respected. Larry was an Area Relations manager for the local telephone company, who was instrumental in making sure the company's contributions were felt in the African American community in Oklahoma City. As Tara was also continuing to work within the Black community as a representative of her company, she and Larry met at a work-related community event. They dated for two years and were married for nine. Tara is wistful when discussing their divorce:

The divorce was unfortunate because we cared deeply for each other but were not on the same page financially. We lost our home and I moved in with Marc. This was at the same time I was moving into a new position at work. Our marriage just could not survive our differences.

Tara is neither embarrassed nor hesitant to discuss this time in her life.

Larry and I built a home in Forest Park. We eventually lost our home due to unforeseen circumstances. I'm not ashamed to talk about this time in my life. Unfortunately, we hit on hard times. However, during the time we lived in our home, my daughters were in high school and Larry had three children and a granddaughter who visited us often. We opened our home to family and friends; so I have some very great memories of the time that we spent there. I had to come to grips with the fact that our friends and family knew that we were having a hard time financially. I can remember my attorney saying, "If people can talk about Jesus, surely they can talk about you."

Tara was in her position with the Speakers Bureau for nearly five years.

After company organizational changes—ONEOK became ONE GAS—Tara went to work at the ONE Gas Foundation. She was happy about the new appointment. While she enjoyed the Speakers Bureau, all the travel and driving had started to take its toll on her.

New Job
Working for the Foundation a positive change.

I was elated because although I loved the Speakers Bureau the new job with the Foundation would be new and different. They placed three women to work in the Foundation; all of us about the same age. This was in 2015.

Tara embraced the mission of the Foundation.

The mission of the ONE Gas Foundation was about giving back to the communities where we live and work. I managed our United Way campaigns, our Matching Grants, and our Employee Volunteer Programs. I was proud that I was one of the chosen three to develop the ONE Gas Foundation. To end my career working within a segment of the company that ensured that our employees and the company gave back to the communities where employees lived and worked was extremely gratifying. I loved working in an environment that helped others.

On a scale of one to ten Tara says her final pre-retirement position with the company was *probably a seven because of the administrative part of it.* While she loved contributing to various organizations within the community on behalf of the Foundation, the paperwork associated with the position was sometimes daunting. That said, Tara believes that the end result—*giving back*—was worth it.

Calling it A Career
In October 2018 Tara retired. While initially a bit apprehensive about her decision—*people were saying things like, "Well, what are you going to do? There's only so much vacuuming you can do."*—Tara was ultimately ecstatic about her decision, looking forward to retirement. Never one to do nothing, she continues to serve on boards and committees, utilizing the skills she developed during her 30-year career to 'help'. The difference is that she is answerable only to herself. Tara's choices are now based upon what she wants to do and how she can best serve her community, while

at the same time leading a happy and fulfilling life. She also continues her somewhat newfound love of running—jogging 5–10 miles at least three times a week and participating in *half* marathons to the extent that time and her desire to do so permit.

So why did you Tara decide to retire? Although she had turned 60, people are now working into their 70s.

When I woke up in the morning, I didn't feel as if the time I was spending at ONG was the time I wanted to spend in my 'sweet spot.' When I wake up sometimes, I may want to go out and run. With my job I had to work around my ONG obligations to run. Or if I wanted to spend an extra day in Dallas with my daughter and granddaughter, I had to work around that. But in retirement I knew that I wouldn't have to work around anything anymore.

Tara admits having some trepidation about her decision to retire; and spent time reflecting on her career—the good and the bad—before finally deciding to retire.

Some aspects of my career were very disheartening—positions that I did not get, that would have furthered my career goals and benefitted the company. However, ONG was good for my family. When I was a single mom, I had the flexibility to pick Jennifer and Jillian up from school, go on field trips with them, and attend their school programs. I was able to be an active parent—serving as Vice President of the PTA one year. And the insurance was also a blessing. When the girls were born, they were in the hospital at OU Health Sciences Center for 6 months. Our bill was a million dollars. If I didn't have insurance, we could not have paid that bill.

With respect to the issue of racism in her workplace, Tara says,

People don't always have to call you the "N" word or say, 'I'm not gonna let you progress because you are Black," in order to manifest racism. I faced a different kind of racism as I moved up the corporate ladder—the good old boy system and not having a mentor. I did not find my mentors—Diane Buchle and Rhonda Mayhan—until my career was almost over. By then, I wanted my career to entail what I was passionate about and making a difference for others.

A more sobering reason to retire was a realization of her mortality.

My parents died young—my dad was 59 and my mother was 67; so whatever I can do while I'm healthy and of sound mind, I'm gonna go do it now! I want to see my grandchildren be great and do great things.

Retirement has meant that Tara's commitment to volunteerism has expanded. She has more time for organizations with which she has always been involved, and time for new groups as well. Tara has been a dedicated volunteer since she was a teenager.

Volunteering

My mother became a member of Jack and Jill when I was thirteen. As a teen growing up in Jack and Jill, I enjoyed it.

Returning home from college, Tara's mother helped her turn her teen experiences with Jack and Jill and other organizations into a lifelong passion.

When I returned home from college, I complained that I didn't have any friends and didn't know anyone. My best friend didn't return to Oklahoma after we graduated from high school, and the friends that remained in Oklahoma City had developed lives of their own. My mother suggested that I could keep from being bored by getting involved in the community. That was the best advice that she could have given me. Once I got involved, I was not bored. I made friends and my job eventually was all about giving back. I loved channeling my talents, time, and treasures through the organizations that I belong to in order to help the communities where I lived and grew up. I gained tremendously from being an active participant in my organizations.

My first volunteer adventure was as a co-brownie troop leader at St. John Baptist Church. Felicia McElroy was the co-leader, and we have remained friends for more than forty years.

I met the most influential people in my life through the organizations that I belong to and the places where I volunteered. I met Larry at the Capitol Chamber of Commerce and Urban League; and later I met Gregg through the Chamber of Commerce.

Ultimately, I became president of the local Oklahoma City Jack & Jill chapter and then a Regional Director. When I completed my term as Regional Director and gave my going out speech, the members gave me a standing ovation. The speech was more about what the members had done in our region for the Jack and Jill children and all the children that we reach through our program efforts. As a leader I believe that it is so important to recognize the people that make a program, an activity, a chapter successful. The members from Central Region named a leadership award after me—the Tara Bradley Leadership Award, which is bestowed bi-annually to a member in our region who exemplifies extraordinary leadership in their communities. I was truly honored to have been recognized by the members of Jack and Jill in the Central Region. I followed the same path of participation and leadership within The Links, Incorporated, and other organizations, including my church whether I was a member, committee chair, or officer.

Tara recognizes the continuing support of friends and family in her volunteer endeavors.

My college friends helped me to feel comfortable giving demonstrations, and Gerry helped me with the presentations that I had to give at work. When I became president of my local Links and Jack and Jill chapters, Larry supported my endeavors in his position for Southwestern Bell. He was particularly good by providing sponsorships and support for projects that we implemented in the Northeast quadrant of Oklahoma City. Gregg helped me to understand to not let others define who I am. He also helped me with my transition from being an employee with Oklahoma Natural Gas to retirement.

Recognizing all of the good emanating from the work of various groups in the community with which she has been affiliated, Tara has passed along the importance of such participation to her daughters.

As Jack and Jill teens, my daughters had an opportunity to gain confidence in themselves and serve in leadership positions. They had leadership opportunities in church and community organizations that were not obtainable at school. And I want to do more of that now.

In retirement Tara has the time to devote to these and other organizations and *to get up and just enjoy my house and Tara—whatever, however that looks.* So far, it looks like this:

My favorite post retirement past-times before the global COVID-19 pandemic were playing cards with the Queen of Hearts, lunching with the Much-a-dos, and serving on Boards that help senior citizens. My favorite post-retirement past-times during the pandemic have been planting flowers, enjoying a couple of glasses of wine every day, making wreaths, Zooming with family and friends, and sitting on my porch.

Influences

Tara recognizes several influences in her life—influences that have changed over time.

As a child my greatest influence was my mother. In college, it was my best friend from college—Jackie—because Jackie just had so much confidence; she was like a quiet storm and extremely smart. She was a beautiful person both inside and out, standing up for what she believed in. She's still like that today!

And while the two were always close, circumstances have brought Tara and her brother together on several occasions; so his influence—while different than her mother or Jackie's—is undeniable.

Marc and I have lived together quite a bit. He maintains, "I always had to stay with Tara." When we had the twins, Gerry's job was in Tulsa and I was working for ONG in Oklahoma City. So my mother said, "okay Marc give up your apartment," which he did. My mother's plan was that Marc would stay with me Monday through Friday while Gerry was in Tulsa and then he stayed with my mother on the weekends. And that's what Marc did. It was the first time he had to save me. When Gerry and I returned to Oklahoma City we built a beautiful home in Forest Park within walking distance of my parents' home. When we divorced, I couldn't afford the payments alone, so my mother said to Marc, "Okay you have to give up your apartment and go stay with your sister to help her pay her mortgage."

When Tara's second marriage ended, she again moved in with Marc, who had just been through his own divorce.

I said, 'Marc I have to come home because I don't have any place to go!' But it happened at the best time in my life because my girls were in college.

As we move through life, our influences change—from parents to friends to siblings . . . and sometimes to our significant other. So, for the last several years there has been a new influence in Tara's life . . .

Gregg

Now, my greatest influence is Gregg. He helps me to feel comfortable about who I am. He's a great supporter and encourages me to live my best life! When I was anxious about retiring Gregg said, 'it'll be ok Tara." He lifts me up when I'm down and affirms who I am. He's such a selfless person.

Tara met Gregg about almost eight years ago at a Chamber of Commerce meeting.

My supervisor at the time invited me to attend the Chamber of Commerce Legislative Picnic. Reluctantly, I agreed to attend. It was raining the evening of the event. My clothes were wet and I thought that my hair looked a "hot mess". When I pulled into the parking lot of the museum where the event was being held all I could think about was getting drenched. However, a good-looking man came to my car, shared his umbrella, and walked me to the door. It was Gregg Bohler. I was so impressed.

When it was time for dinner he said, "Would you ladies mind (my boss was with me) if I join you?" And so he sat and talked to us for a while. We talked about our jobs, and we talked about our families. He told me about his daughter Ariah who lived in Atlanta and how he visited her at least once a month. I could tell from our conversation that he adored Ariah and that she was a daddy's girl. From the time that I spent with him I just felt that he was a caring, smart, and really nice person. After we had dinner, he took time to circulate amongst the crowd. When I was leaving the event, he broke away from the group, and walked me back to my car. I think we exchanged cards.

After the picnic, Gregg would email me occasionally. It was a connection for us both. I really, really liked him and was on the wish factor—wishing and hoping that he really liked me. Finally he invited me to lunch. He had just buried his daughter—Ariah. He told me that fact; but it was clearly too painful to talk more. I wish I could have spent time with Gregg and Ariah together. Whatever his personal traumas, Gregg is kind and selfless; he lifts me up. His work ethic is impeccable and he's well respected by all. He's a wonderful person to me and my family.

Also, the women of Gregg's family are members of Delta

*Sigma Theta Sorority, which is another reason why I'm proud to be a Delta!
It gave me an added advantage with the women of his family whom I have
come to admire.*

Finally, in addition to the influence of her daughters Jillian and Jennifer, Tara's cousin, Sandra Rose, who became the matriarch of the family
when Tara's mother died, has been a sustaining influence and a light for
Tara.

Faith

Raised in the Catholic Church and attending Catholic schools for much
of her life, although Tara has ventured into other religions for various reasons at certain points in her life, she has returned to the Catholic church
where she worships and gives of her time where needed.

*I was born and raised as a Catholic, and I am a product of a good Cath-
olic education. However, society taught us that a family should worship together. So when I married Gerry, I became a Baptist. Gerry was a Minister
of Music for a small Baptist church in Oklahoma City—New Bethel Baptist
Church, which I joined so that I could attend church with my husband.
When Gerry and I moved to Tulsa because of his career we both joined a
Methodist Church—Christ Temple CME (Christian Methodist Episcopal).
This was a great fit for both of us because to us it was a combination of Baptist and Catholic. After Gerry and I divorced I returned to Corpus Christi
Catholic Church. What I realized is that church services have many of the
same components: a message, communion, prayer, and song. It's just delivered in different ways. What I found to be different in a church is the love
and fellowship of the congregation. I think it's so important to belong to a
church where you feel love and a spiritual connection to the congregation.*

Recent Challenges: Learning from Success and Defeat

Tara has experienced and met innumerable challenges in her life. The
most recent are her focus on fitness and furthering her involvement in
one of her favorite organizations—the Oklahoma City Chapter of The
Links, Incorporated. She learned from both.

*My most recent challenges have been taking two years out of my life to
train for a marathon, and then seeking the position of Vice-Area Director*

of the Links. I completed the marathon; however I was not the successful candidate for the Links' position. Although I was not the successful candidate with the Links organization, seeking the position helped me to understand how important it was that my physical, mental, and spiritual strength was intact in order to endure the campaign. Preparing for the marathon at which I was successful made that possible.

Evolution

For African American women our experiences, family love, influences, and maturity help us to evolve. Tara is evolving. She sees herself this way:

Today, Tara Bradley is becoming more and more comfortable with who she is and not dependent on what other people think or say—not needing or seeking the approval of other people. I don't feel like I have to please other people. I think I'm becoming more and more like that. Experiences, aging, reading, becoming more spiritual, and listening to my inner spirit has made a difference.

I am also pickier about who I choose to include in my circle of friends and I respect the small circle that I have now. This is especially important and necessary due to Covid-19. I must respect my fellow human beings, but it is not necessary to please everyone. And while I'm still very sensitive about some things, like my hair, Gregg has helped me to understand that what's most important is to always do your very best in all that you do and everything will work itself out. Sometimes I wonder what he thinks about my hair, but I've come to realize that my hair is not his issue; it is my issue. So I relax and enjoy us.

And, perhaps more importantly Tara says . . .

I'm happy. I feel good about who I am . . . I really do.

ANDREA CHARLTON
The Art of Resiliency

The experiences of life can cause us extreme pain. African American women experience that pain like anyone else. And like everyone else, our challenge is to determine how to move forward—past the pain. Speaking about our struggles through pain humanizes African American women to those who have never considered the human side of who we are—only the stereotypes. And for Black women, it may help us understand ourselves a bit better—how good, how great we are. That is part of the message of Andrea Charlton's story.

Once we hear/read her story, think about it, and know where she is today, we realize that there are and have been triumphs although there remains some pain. But her victory is that the pain that remains—that may always remain—has not kept her from moving forward, continuing to get up, *living her environment* as she says, and doing what needs to be done. Throughout some exceedingly difficult times, Andrea continued to get up; continued to say, '*okay, whatever I am facing and however hurt I am, I still must live my life.* Andrea has done that, and she continues to do so!

So . . .

How does a quiet, shy, studious youngster born in Jamaica find her voice and become a bold, unabashed champion of the underdog—whoever she sees in need? Such a transformation may happen for a variety of reasons. For Andrea (pronounced Aun—dray-a) Charlton it happened after she was thrown into a fight-or-perish situation. Rather than perish—or at least continue to be abused, ignored, and neglected—Andrea chose to fight. And in doing so she became a leader, albeit reluctant, and turned a journey of despair into one of triumph and peace.

The turning point in Andrea's life occurred with her naïve decision to enter Job Corps—naïve because wanting to leave home and find a better experience, she believed everything the Job Corps recruiters told her.

After graduating from high school I was looking for a job. I knew I had to get out of there [the home of her mother and stepfather]. When I went to the Labor Department to look for a job, the lady was telling me about Job Corps. She made it sound like I was going to go to a camp or something. They were advertising and saying I could learn a trade. This was my out. I could go to Job Corps, I would get paid to be there, they were going to teach me a trade, I thought it would be far better than my experience to that point. And then I got there and discovered that it wasn't a camp, it was more like a prison.

Andrea Charlton was born in 1961, in Mandeville, Manchester, Jamaica, to an unwed mother and a married politician father who had no desire to acknowledge her. When she was around two years old, her mother moved to Kingston, Jamaica. Andrea is not sure whether they left Mandeville because her mother wanted to leave or some other unknown reason.

I don't remember anything. I don't know anything about Mandeville. My memory for that is limited. I grew up in Kingston. My mother, I guess . . . this is my knowledge of what I know . . . she moved to Kingston, I guess she was on the run or whatever from her problem. She left me with a lady. I say she was on the run; maybe she was just leaving. Her mom was in London. She was supposed to be in school in Mandeville. And of course, she came up with a baby. And my father was a married man. So I think her leaving that area was because she had a child. She had already had me when she left. Because we don't have a close relationship, I don't know any more of the specifics of her leaving—whether she was forced out or left voluntarily. All I know is piecemeal—what I've been told by others.

Despite her efforts, Andrea's relationship with her mother is not and has not been close, precluding any detailed discussion about the first few years of Andrea's life.

It's like that part of her life, including me, she doesn't acknowledge—like I don't even exist as I'm talking to you right now. I don't have a relationship with her. We tried [to have a relationship], but we can't because in her mind others may find out the truth.

Perhaps compounding Andrea's sense of distance from her mother is the fact that when they reached Kingston her mother left her with someone else—not a relative, *just somebody who took people in.* The story Andrea was told is that she was only supposed to be with this person for a very short time, with her mother intending to come back to get her and take her to the United States to live with she and her new husband, whom her mother met in Kingston.

That never happened.

The one blessing of her abandonment was that the woman with whom Andrea was left was good to her.

Her name was Blanche Gross. I had a good relationship with her. I called her Mama at first because she was the only mother figure in my life. That was a good thing. To be honest, she was probably the only good thing in my whole life, even to this point. But after I left Aunt Blanche, that was it. I don't think I ever even saw her again. I missed her—she was good to me and the foundation of my life. But there wasn't anything I could do to get back to her. Aunt Blanche was the most influential person in my life to that point—in part because she was the only person I knew that cared anything for me. She is no longer alive. I'm saying that like I'm confident. I'm not certain, but

once I left her in Kingston, once I moved away from her, there wasn't any more contact. That was more because of circumstance than anything else. We weren't in the modern-day with a phone and all that stuff. We wrote letters, but that eventually faded away.

While living in Jamaica with Blanche Gross, Andrea was aware of her biological mother. She knew her mother's name was Patsy—the name by which Andrea refers to her mother. Andrea knew Patsy's husband's name was Thomas and that they had a daughter—Pauline—because they sent pictures and they would visit during summer vacation. Andrea eventually came to know her biological father's identity and that he was a political figure. It would be many years later after she left Jamaica before she had any contact with him.

Knowing of her mother's existence caused only a change in the name by which she referred to her surrogate mother.

I eventually called her Aunt Blanche. I called her mama first and then I called her Aunt Blanche because I knew I had a mother. So I just made the transition to calling her Aunt Blanche, which was fine with her because clearly, she was just taking care of me. She was taking care of two other girls at the time I was there—Joy and Denise. Denise's mom was in Jamaica, but Joy's mom was in New York. And then Joy's mom sent for her. So she left and went to New York with her family. And then Denise was with her mom, so it was just me there.

While Andrea was relatively happy living with Aunt Blanche in Kingston, they were poor. That fact became important as Andrea was about to enter the 7th grade.

I went to a Catholic school where we had to wear uniforms. Our uniforms changed entering into the seventh grade. Aunt Blanche, who was an old lady by this time, told me, "Your mom didn't send any money to get you a new uniform." Well, I was not going to go to school without a uniform because I would stand out. Everybody wore a uniform. So I didn't attend school that year. Aunt Blanche knew I wasn't going to school, but I got up every day as if I was going to school. I didn't go; I just went to the seaside. After you missed so many days, you couldn't go back anyway. We didn't have a phone so the school couldn't call. I don't know if they tried to come by. I don't know what they did.

This may have been the beginning of a quiet anger and resentment developing in Andrea towards her mother . . .

I think Patsy knew Aunt Blanche needed money for my uniform. You know you have a child out there! How do you sleep at night? You don't even know if your child is eating. Yes, she knew. She knew. And she had been sending money previously before she stopped. So I'm assuming she knew Blanche didn't have much income. We were poor. We lived in a community environment. There was a yard surrounded by houses and we shared the bathroom and the yard. The bathroom was basic—not like what we are accustomed to now. But that's all I knew. I didn't think of us or know we were poor at the time. That was not a factor at all. You understood there were limitations to what you could have, and you didn't live in luxury, but you didn't focus on or talk about being poor. I was not around rich people or other people that were doing better than we were, so my living conditions were the norm.

Shortly after this year away from school, Andrea would leave Jamaica. One of Patsy's brothers, Patrick who was still living in Jamaica, found out about Andrea's school situation; and he apparently told his mom— Andrea's grandmother—who was living in London. Whether they previously knew of Andrea's existence is unclear, *I don't believe she had any knowledge of my existence.* In any event, Andrea's grandmother came to Jamaica from London to set some changes in motion.

So it was like, that's not the way for me to grow up. And I think she eventually made Patsy, her daughter, bring me to live with her.

She would first, however, go to live with Patrick and his wife—a schoolteacher—in a town near where Andrea lived with Aunt Blanche. It was not a good move.

So my grandma came to Jamaica. I was 12 or going on 12 and had missed the 7th grade. And whatever their agreement was, her son Patrick and his wife took me in. . . . And that's where my whole world turned upside down.

Andrea did not object to the move—she was still in the dark about most things. So, although she was content living with Aunt Blanche, she was not consulted and simply did as she was told.

I didn't question anything because I didn't know these people. These people were like strangers to me. But since I knew from the time that I was very small that my mother was supposed to come to get me, it wasn't a question of whether I wanted to stay or go. I knew I had to go. I just didn't know when I was going to go. And since I wasn't in school, I thought the move was going to be a good thing for me. And maybe they thought that too; but when I went to live with Patrick and his wife Janice and their new baby, I don't think his wife wanted me there. Maybe Patrick agreed to the arrangement because it was what his mother told him to do. But immediately when I went to live with them it was a disaster.

Between the whippings for reasons she didn't understand and other abuses, almost as soon as she arrived at her uncle's home, Andrea wanted to return to live with Aunt Blanche. She understood Janice's dislike of her but at the same time, she knew that she had no choice about where she lived.

That was his [Patrick's] marriage, and they had a newborn. And they got something they didn't ask for is how I looked at it. I was a mistake that didn't or wouldn't go away. I may not have felt that way at the time because I didn't know. But reflecting on it I know this was the case.

Andrea stayed with her uncle and aunt for about a year; and for the most part, each day was miserable—except for school.

I was an above-average student, and I liked going to school because it was my escape—a way out for me. Janice could have been a good influence on me because she was a schoolteacher. But she was not. She seemed to resent me. I didn't tell anybody I was unhappy—there was nobody to tell.

While she focused on school, Andrea waited for her mother to send for her. She had been expecting that all of her life; and while living with Patrick and Janice was miserable, she expected things to get better. Eventually, she got a glimpse of what was to come . . . and it wasn't at all what she expected.

Back then I just knew that my mother was in America and she was going to send for me—and that had been what I was waiting for. That's all I knew. So I stayed with Janice and Patrick for a year or so.

But then I remember one time when Pauline, Patsy's daughter, and my sister—we're five years apart—came to Jamaica with her friend Charlene on vacation—this was an eye-opening time for me. Nobody told me differently so naturally, I know that's my sister, so I referred to her as my sister in front of Charlene. But I found out that it was supposed to be a secret. They came to Jamaica every year for their vacation and Pauline knew who I was. But this specific year when she came with her classmate, I didn't know I wasn't supposed to say anything. Everybody was upset. Pauline was very upset. Her little friend went back to America early. So, of course, I got in trouble— when didn't I get in trouble? They told me I talked too much—it was just crazy! They called Patsy and so their whole vacation was cut short.

There was another ugly secret Andrea has kept until now, which gave her even more reason to want to leave Jamaica. Her uncle was molesting her.

I was glad to get away from Patrick—some stuff happened that should not have happened. He molested me—Patrick did—Patsy's brother. I never told anyone as a child. It went on the whole time I was there. He would come into the room at night. Janice knew. I will go to my grave believing that Janice knew. I always think they know. I think that's why she treated me the way that she did. I don't fool with any of them. They now live in Florida. I have not confronted either of them; I don't think I would. Not this late in the game. He knows; Janice knows; I believe Patsy also knows. If she didn't know about Patrick she knows about her husband. They know.

Had Andrea known what leaving Jamaica would mean, she would hardly have been excited about moving to America; and would have likely tried to do everything in her 14-year-old power to avoid the move—probably running away from everybody: Patrick, Janice, Patsy, Pauline and especially Thomas, Patsy's husband.

On November 16, 1976, Andrea flew to America to live with her mother and stepfather in Baton Rouge, Louisiana.

At the time I thought it was a good thing because I didn't know anything different. However, because of the rest of my story—or at least my story well into adulthood—I wish I knew then what was going to happen because I would still be in Jamaica; I would have been satisfied in Jamaica.

A big issue was that Patsy had told very few people outside of her family of Andrea's existence, and the story she told to anyone outside the family was a lie: that Andrea was an orphan whom she and Thomas had adopted. Inexplicably, Patsy also never bothered to tell Andrea the "story" she was telling.

I don't hold Pauline or Thomas responsible for this part of it because I think the responsibility lies with Patsy. She was the only person I knew in the whole situation. So I came to America and I flew into New Orleans—a 45-minute drive from Baton Rouge. Somewhere on the way to Baton Rouge, somebody should have told me something! I'm brand new in the country; I don't know anything. Somebody should have said, "nobody knows anything about you"—like that I was Patsy's child. On the ride to Baton Rouge with Patsy and Thomas, somebody should have said something about what was going on that I didn't know about.

But Andrea found out the "story" by happenstance a little more than a week after her arrival—not from her family, but while attending a neighbor's family dinner.

They had Thanksgiving in November, which was a new holiday for me. We didn't celebrate that day in Jamaica. Patsy's neighbor, Ms. Irma, had a family of very nice people. So Pauline and I went to Ms. Irma's sister's house one evening during the Thanksgiving holiday. Patsy and Thomas did not go. When we arrived, I was introduced as "this is the little girl Patsy adopted." Maybe if they told me that was the story that they were telling I would have gone along with it because I wouldn't have known better. But they did not. So I said, 'I'm not adopted.' My God! Pauline fell out. I didn't understand why she was acting that way. She was about 10 at the time I came to America, but clearly, she also knew the story they were telling. I'm the only one in the dark.

Patsy and her husband were upset when Andrea and Pauline returned home. Andrea was initially baffled, but beginning to understand and becoming angry.

They were fussing and I asked, 'What did I do?' They responded that I was out telling their business. Really? Even to this day, I think I don't know how I'm telling your business. You all were out there telling a lie and you forgot to include me in on the lie. And that's not even the only lie you told.

Despite not wanting others to know their 'business' Andrea was treated differently than Pauline, and her mistreatment was sometimes obvious. Pauline was going to a private school and Andrea was going to the public school down the street.

That part I did feel—because I walked to school and you knew that was not the best school. But I went there anyway . . . But that's fine. And my treatment in the house was horrible! It was like, "this is mine, this is yours." I was treated differently. I had to clean up the house. One day Thomas was whipping me, and his cigarette ash fell on the carpet. Pauline went to pick it up and he said, "No, no that's what she's here for. Let her clean it up." He beat me; I caught whippings from him.

Thomas subsequently also began to molest Andrea. The difference this time was that Andrea told Patsy.

I remember one day Patsy was in Jamaica and he came into the room one night and got into the bed with me. And I was scared that night. I got up and went out the front door and I was on the porch. Pauline came out there with me and I remember she said, "Did Daddy do something to you?" I just looked at her and I didn't say anything. And then he came to the door and asked, "What you all doing out there?"—Like he's innocent and we're stupid! He told us to come back inside saying, "It's too late for y'all to be out there."

So when Patsy came back that Monday I sat and I told her what happened and that it had been happening. And so that evening Thomas sat on the love seat and Patsy and I sat on the couch and she said, "Thomas I can't believe what my daughter is telling me." And so he said, "that ain't none of my fucking child!" And she was crying, and I was crying, and he got up and went back into the room to watch his TV and that was that.

After that conversation, Patsy told Andrea she would leave Thomas when Pauline graduated from high school. That answer gave Andrea little comfort.

I was just shocked that he would say something like that. And if I meant anything to you[Patsy], you would leave now. The molestation did not stop. I think she knew because I withdrew from everything. I would come in and go to the room and stay there. I was just to myself.

Graduation/Nobody Came
Eventually, mercifully, Andrea graduated from high school—4th in a class of 414. Only Patsy and her friend attended. It hurt Andrea that with

all she had accomplished—after missing a year of school and being held back a year once she got to Baton Rouge—so little was made of her high school graduation. It reinforced her desire to leave "home" as soon as she could—a sentiment shared by others in the household.

Nobody came to my graduation but Patsy and her friend Cathy. Pauline didn't come. Thomas did not come. No other relatives came. Patsy took me to eat and that was it. Afterward, I heard Thomas saying, "when is she gonna get out of here? How much longer is she going to be here?" Patsy didn't say anything to me, but I think she knew I heard him. He wanted me to hear him. I understand that she may have been between a rock and a hard place, but if I'm supposed to be your child, you know . . .

Job Corps—From the fire to the frying pan

Andrea wanted to get out of the house and on her own more than Thomas wanted her out. So her priority after graduation was looking for a job. Patsy's friend Cathy seemed to have some sense of what was going on and tried to help Andrea by directing her to Job Corps. To Andrea, Job Corps sounded like the panacea!

When I went to the Labor Department to look for a job the person with whom I spoke told me about Job Corps. She made it sound like I was going to go to a camp or something. Their advertising said I could get a trade. This was my out! I could go to Job Corps, I would get paid to be there, they were going to teach me a trade! The photos in the pamphlets they provided showed me green grass and I thought it was far better than my experience to that point.

And then I got there and discovered that it wasn't a camp, it was a prison.

The details are vivid in Andrea's memory—even the date she arrived.

On December 8th I got on the Greyhound bus. I think I remember some of these dates so clearly because these were some of the most hurtful times in my life. So I'm on the bus to Job Corps—and that was the longest ride from Baton Rouge to San Marcos, Texas. And it wasn't so much that I wanted to go to Job Corps—at that point, I didn't have any wants; I knew I just needed to get away. We arrived at night. A bus came to pick us up from the bus station. I went to Job Corps with my little suitcase. They gave you a green blanket and a pillow and then we were escorted to a place like a barracks that had bunk beds.

While staying with her mother Andrea was primarily a loner. She tried to simply do what she was told and stay out of the way. This meant she had few friends and was a shy, soft-spoken teenager who spent most of her time being afraid. By choice rather than necessity, Job Corps ended that. If not the panacea, it was transformative for Andrea.

Up to that time, I was timid and scary and nervous; but once I got to Job Corps it was either you sink or swim—survival of the fittest! These were people my age, but most had been to prison or had been in trouble with the law. So you just pick who you are going to join in with and do what you need to do to get by. It was very much like a prison with gangs and everything. You couldn't leave—for the first 90 days, you couldn't even come off-site. After ninety days you could get a pass to go to Austin or San Marcos—and they gave you $18 every two weeks. This was 1980—December 8, 1980! I stayed there for six months. I had to go through a total transformation in terms of my personality to survive. I now wish I had been like that when I was at Patrick's; I wish I was like that when I was at Patsy's. But who knows I might have been dead by now because now I will stand up for myself.

Although Andrea quickly understood the reality of Job Corps, there were frightening incidents that are indelibly etched in her memory.

I discovered at Job Corps that you do what you gotta do, right? I think the scariest thing for me at Job Corps was when a guy was in his bed asleep—there was a woman's dorm and two men's dorms—and somebody cut his throat, killing him. They did some crazy stuff—something would always go down. I was so afraid—scared to death—of being there; fearful something would go wrong with me!

Andrea's fear turned into resolve . . .

After that incident, I said 'they will have to kill me. Either I'm going to kill the person, or the person will kill me. I'm not going out like this.' I was scared, and I knew I was scared. So I ganged up with the girls and guys from New Orleans—just like the New Yorkers had their group; everybody had a click. It was nothing I thought about, even though when I hear anything about Job Corps now, I'm reminded of what a bitter time that was.

In fact, Andrea rarely tells anybody that she was in Job Corps or talks about her experiences there—except when somebody says their kid is considering entering Job Corps. Without holding a long conversation, she urges caution.

College

Some good can usually be derived from any negative, which was true for Andrea's experience in Job Corps—it moved her into her future.

The one good thing about Job Corps is that if you had a high school diploma, it offered an opportunity for college. That's how I got to college. I had the choice to go to Texas A & I [now Texas A & M] in Kingsville, Texas, or Huston-Tillotson College (HT) in Austin. We visited both of them, and I ended up going to HT because it was a Black school, it was private, and it was religious.

The Job Corps program was for 24 months. So for the first six months Andrea was in the "prison" environment of the Job Corps location in San Marcos, Texas, where she received the $18 bi-monthly stipend. The last 18 months of the program she was enrolled as a student at Huston-Tillotson College in Austin, Texas. And while her stipend increased by the modest amount of five dollars to $23 every two weeks, her room, board, and books were paid for through the program—all essential benefits for Andrea, who was on her own.

Job Corps was consistent about how it introduced its participants to new environments—whether it was the San Marcos "campus" or college life.

You have to live your environment. We went to Huston-Tillotson during summer school. When I tell you that you have to live your environment, that's what I did. We arrived at HT on another green bus—there were seven or eight of us—on June 8th. They didn't bring us at night this time. We got off the big old green bus with our little blankets. Job Corps was painted on the side of the bus, so the other students knew who we were. I was embarrassed with those people looking at us. Now when I watch movies with prisoners getting off the bus, I say to myself, 'I bet that's how we looked.' I was so embarrassed, but I just had to keep telling myself, 'I'm going to get what I came for; I'm going to school for two years.'

We were going to stay on campus—not necessarily initially the best thing—but everything is a stepping-stone. When we got off the bus those students were horrible! Because they thought we were criminals they treated us badly. So I quickly realized that everything I did at Job Corps I just had to continue at HT: I still had to be tough.

The $23 stipend came faithfully every two weeks. But that was ok because we didn't know any different—$23 worked then. The other students knew every time we were getting our money because Job Corps came on campus and brought us the money—so again we all stood out. Initially, my attitude was they think I'm a criminal, I'm going to have to act like a criminal. Interestingly, however, I turned out to be friends with some of those people. But it was only after they realized that they didn't know who I was—that I was not dumb or bad.

In fact, Andrea became friends with most of the students, faculty, and administration at Huston-Tillotson. She was recruited by all of the sororities, became involved in a myriad of student activities—including becoming student council president when she was a senior in college—and was mentored by several faculty and staff, including HT's president. There were, however, various trials and tribulations in getting there—beginning soon after her arrival.

My transition to becoming friends with those people happened in many ways. I remember one incident very clearly. We were in the lunch line and a basketball player—I can see her face clearly—jumped in front of us in line like we didn't even exist. We didn't have the clothes everybody else had so we stood out. But I had gone through all that bull crap at home. And I said to my friend Michelle, 'If she does this shit one more time, I'm making an example of her!' So the next day we're in line, and of course, the same thing happens . . . until I confronted her, which means I charged at her and let her know that what she had done wasn't acceptable. We didn't have a physical confrontation, but she understood by the way I approached her that I was willing to fight. By the next day, I think everybody at HT knew who I was, and there were far fewer attempts at mistreating me.

Protector

At some point between arriving at Job Corps and moving to Huston-Tillotson College in Austin, Texas—and perhaps because of her own experiences as a child—Andrea developed a protective nature for others, propelling her to intercede on behalf of those who seemed incapable of protecting and defending themselves. It also helped that she had become a pretty big young woman since arriving in the United States.

When I came to America, I was 90 lbs. By the time I left Patsy's house, I was fat—food was my comfort. I mean fat—big!

Andrea's willingness to fight caused some problems at HT, but it also led to lasting friendships.

By the time I arrived at HT I was no longer the quiet meek person from Jamaica or Baton Rouge. I got in a lot of trouble at HT, but it wasn't my trouble. That means that if somebody was picking on someone I knew, I would stand up for them. I remember the first fight I had at HT. It was not my fight, but I had to fight for someone unable to defend herself. And so the next day I came out of my dorm and everybody was like "Hey Andrea! Hi Andrea." They were trying to be friendly. I eventually became friends with everybody—the people who were like me who I came with, and I was friends with the other people. I was friends with everybody. I didn't discriminate.

Sometimes these conflicts caused the sensitive side of Andrea to be revealed . . . the side that showed emotion. But woe to whoever caused it . . .

People saw the other side of me because I cried really easily—but that wasn't necessarily good either; because if I cried, I had to do something, which means if you made me cry, I had to fight.

That 'fighting spirit' ultimately followed Andrea into adulthood—and sometimes into the workplace, which had both positive and negative results. Unlike those who chose to remain silent in the face of discrimination or being overlooked for promotion and advancement, Andrea made her displeasure known. There were times when standing up for herself paid benefits, and like in college, caused others to admire Andrea's courage. At other times, however, she was marked as a 'troublemaker' and still overlooked for advancement.

I had co-workers who were going to just be quiet and sit down, but I'm going to let you know where I'm coming from—because I did good work.

Her "good work" was in accounting—Andrea's major in college—a major she had not planned for, but chose once she got to HT. Continuing her academic success from high school, Andrea made good grades in college and was on the honor roll while at HT. Nonetheless, the road was sometimes bumpy.

One week my name was on the marquee for honors and the next week I had to go to the Dean for fighting. And she would ask, "Andrea, what can we do to help you?" I would just sit there dumbfounded because I didn't know. I would try to explain to the Dean that someone was bothering one of the students and I was just interceding. And the Dean's question was "why did you think it was your business to intercede?" And I would say, 'because she couldn't defend herself.' Looking back, I guess I took on that role—a champion of the underdog—because I remembered a time where I was vulnerable and there was nobody there who would or could help me. Nobody came to my defense.

Reflecting on that time, Andrea chooses not to place blame, believing that in large part, few outside of her family—in Jamaica and Baton Rouge—knew what was going on. Those who did know did what they could; and whether or not it was helpful, Andrea appreciated the effort to help.

I don't think anybody came to my defense because they didn't know. I was a child and there was nobody outside the family circle who knew about it . . . except maybe for two of Patsy's friends. One of her friends knew what was going on but she didn't do anything because she wanted to stay friends with Patsy. Her other friend Cathy knew what was going on and she tried to help me—that's how I got to Job Corps—she thought she was doing something good. People try to help you the best way they can. And though Job Corps was not the best experience, she didn't know that. And to be honest, Job Corps was part of my life, and it helped to make me who I am. It was the only way I got out of the situation I was in. It made me stronger; I had to deal with my environment!

At the end of Job Corps' commitment, Andrea had two more years of study before she could receive her degree. Although she was working, she needed money to pay for those final two years. Despite her troubles, there were many at Huston Tillotson College willing to help:

When the Job Corps program at HT ended for me, I was able to get scholarships. Unbelievably those professors really liked me, so they helped me to stay there. I was a good student, so I applied for and received a Pell Grant. With that help and going to school year-round I was able to finish at HT. I finished high school in three years—having made up the 2-year gap—by going to summer school. And again at HT I finished college in three years. I was motivated because I didn't know where my next meal was coming from. I didn't have the luxury of taking longer.

Andrea had to use her wits, garnered from surviving the hard knocks of her life to that point, and the kindness of others to make it through. She had no family on which to rely.

During school breaks at HT, if I had no other choice, I would go back to Patsy's. But if I didn't have to I wouldn't. At Thanksgiving when everybody was going home, I would either stay at HT or somebody would say, "come home with me." And so sometimes I would go home with friends. That's when I really got to see what a real family looks like [crying]. Because those people did not treat me any differently than their other family members; they actually included me. Even now, they invite me to their family reunions, and I go. It was just really different.

Those who opened their homes to Andrea during this time were her *angels.* They were not just the students; but also their parents—something drew them to Andrea, seeing that she needed help and offering it. It started soon after Andrea arrived at Huston-Tillotson . . .

Angels for Andrea

When families brought their children to HT, they would bring all kinds of things with them: clothes, food, refrigerators. We [Job Corps folk] had our green blankets. I remember Mrs. Burke—the mother of a student I had only recently met—told me right off the bat to come to the store with them. I initially declined her invitation. She said, 'no come go with us,' and they bought me all this stuff. After that, she would send stuff—even when Debra would go home, she would send me like a care package. She was very nice to me. I don't even know if she necessarily knew of my situation, she was just from day one very nice. When she was leaving that first time, she said to me, "Ok, take care of my daughter." I said, 'OK I'm not gonna let anybody do anything to her.' When we were seniors finishing school Mrs. Burke told me, "Girl you looked like you were bad! You looked like, 'don't fool with me,' when I first met you." I didn't think that's what I gave off; it was not my intention. I guess it was the look I had developed to protect myself. Mrs. Burke asked me if I remembered when she asked me to take care of her "baby." I told her I did and wondered where that came from. She said, 'You looked like you could do that'. Throughout my whole time in college, she was good to me.

And there were other angels . . .

Some HT students from Florida were also very good to me. Even now I go to visit them, to their family reunions, it's like I'm a part of their family. And when I'm there they make sure I'm included in whatever they do. When I go to my mother's house, I'm like in the corner. While with these families from HT, nobody is making up stories about why I'm there like Patsy did, telling people, "her parents couldn't take care of her, so we are."

Andrea met a lot of those nice, caring people during her life at Huston-Tillotson College. That included some of the professors. She has remembered their kindnesses as well.

I still visit them. A few are getting older and can't do for themselves. After one of my professors retired, I would go wash her hair and sit with her because she had nobody else. And I didn't mind doing that. I'm by myself and I'm thinking one day somebody is going to have to do that for me.

College Graduation . . .

So it was graduation time. I was in the Honor Society and I was in a lot of other activities. I was the Student Government president.

Student Government President?! Let's back up . . .

Becoming a Leader

Unbeknownst to Andrea or probably anybody who knew her before she went to Job Corps, all of her life experiences, including Job Corpss, were preparing her to become a leader at HT—the reality of which Andrea is still reluctant to accept. However, what happened is undeniable. It started shortly after Andrea's arrival at HT and lasted throughout her college career.

Freshman Greeter

Freshman year I was the freshman greeter for the new people coming in—I think that's how I met Debra and her parents. I'm not sure how I got selected to do that; they just selected me, and I said ok. Really when I said it just happened, that's how it was because I was thinking if I was them, I would not pick me—I didn't have the clothes or anything. I guess they just overlooked that, which is why I'm glad I was a part of the Huston-Tillotson College—now University—Family.

Freshman year I was a member of the freshman student council—I was treasurer. I didn't seek out these things, but I didn't shy away from any of them either.

Zeta Phi Beta

In addition to her student government activities, she was highly sought after by all of the sororities on the campus. This was unfamiliar territory for Andrea.

When I got to HT, I didn't know anything about Greek and being in a sorority; so it didn't mean anything to me. I never thought about being a part of a sorority and did not think any of them would even want me—but all of them invited me. So I was simply interested because they asked. And I accepted all of the invitations so I could see which one I liked best. I was friends with a lot of people from all the different sororities and I liked all of them. People ask me all the time why I pledged Zeta and I can't say, because I went to everybody's rush function—free food! I listened to what everybody had to say.

The Zetas was the smallest sorority in terms of numbers on campus. I was not about to do all that stuff like stepping and dancing in the public that most of the sororities required. So I was not going to go with the ones which would try to put me out front and make a spectacle of me. The Zetas did not do all of that; so I selected them, and now I've been a Zeta for over 35 years. I love it! I love my sorors, I love everything about being a part of Zeta Phi Beta Sorority, Incorporated!

Andrea believed that the Zetas was the sorority most aligned with her personality—they were service-oriented. However, after her initial acceptance of the Zetas invitation to join, she 'got offline' because of some of the hazing the group still wanted to do.

Whenever my soror Sandra she sees me, she talks about how mean I was. I deny that I was mean and tell her, 'I just wasn't going to take any of that crap !' I wasn't going to run. I wasn't going to eat that crap that they try to make us eat. I wasn't going to do anything that would be detrimental to my health. You are not going to blindfold me and put anything in my mouth. And I was fat so no, I wasn't running up any hill. [Laughter] They had a hard time with me. But I made it through.

Once the Zetas realized that Andrea was serious about not being subjected to any of what she called the *stupid stuff* and because they *needed my GPA,* she was invited back and this time she joined with the idea that she wanted to assist in any way that she could in the service activities in which the Zetas were involved. Andrea is quick to note that after she joined the Zetas, new pledges rarely experienced the past hazing behavior from their big sisters.

Miss UNCF

The HBCUs have an annual *Miss UNCF (United Negro College Fund)* competition. It is designed to raise funds for the UNCF. Each HBCU has a representative in the competition. In her junior year, some of her fellow students suggested that Andrea run for Miss UNCF.

Now I know in my mind I couldn't be Miss UNCF because I didn't have the money for the dress; I didn't have any of that stuff. But those students urging me to run assured me that if I won, they would help out. Also, since by this time I was in a sorority, I believed my sorority sisters and others would see me through.

Andrea agreed to run for Miss UNCF. She didn't win.

The girl who won was very pretty, a nice size, with no money issues, so she needed to be the one to represent the school. I didn't need to be Miss UNCF, but I needed some scholarship money that came along with running for Miss UNCF and participating in the parade. So I was going to do what I needed to do to get some additional funds to go towards my schooling. So in the end, it was all ok.

Student Government President

Andrea maintains that becoming the student government president during her last year in college *came out of the blue.* Other students began encouraging her to run for the office. Initially, she declined because she did not want to talk in front of people.

That's not my cup of tea. Once I start to talk in front of people my voice starts shaking and I'm nervous. Recently I had to do a video for school [Andrea returned to school to get her Master's Degree]; you would think I was just going back to Job Corps. I was so nervous about doing the video. I've done Toastmasters and everything to get me out of that, but I'm still the same way today.

However, her fear of speaking in front of others was trumped when a friend from another sorority who was also running for Student Council President *started talking mess*. That *mess* triggered Andrea's decision to run.

Next thing I know I'm Student Government president. This was going into my senior year. I think part of the reason they wanted me to be Student Government president is because even though I was a Zeta I was friends with everyone. They knew that I was not going to show favoritism. For me, the Greeks, the non-Greeks, and all students were included. I became a friend to everyone. That is part of what got me elected. They knew that I did not have an allegiance or preference to anyone. I stood alone.

And she likely also stood alone in her matter-of-fact approach to her new role as student body president.

The student body president is limited in what s/he can do because everything you do you have to go through the school administration, and they have to approve it anyway. So students would come and say what they wanted and then I would take it to the Dean who would often say no. And so I'd go back and tell students of the Dean's decision—NO. And sometimes students were asking for something crazy and I'd say, 'you all know that's not going to happen.' My opinion was that the students who kept demanding the ridiculous stuff needed to go to class, which was what their parents sent them to school for—and to graduate. Quit being a permanent student. And then they always wanted to party, and I was not the party person. I would say to the Vice President, 'Are you going to be at the party because at 9 pm I'm headed for bed.' I was an accounting major. I knew I couldn't be down at the party because I could not spend an extra year in school. I didn't know if I was going to have money to come back to school that next year. I was going year-to-year and I had to get out as quickly as I could. Though I didn't say that out loud, in the back of my mind that is what it was.

Her approach neither alienated the students who elected her nor did it spoil her experience.

I did enjoy being the student government president. It went well. I enjoyed my whole college experience. Even though there was some conflict— mostly fighting—I enjoyed being in college.

Considering all of her activities while in college—most in a leadership capacity—Andrea reluctantly acknowledges that she was and is a leader . . .

. . . because sometimes even when you really don't want to do some-thing—like become student government president—you just have to step up to the plate to do what you have to do with what people want you to do.

Finally Graduation

For Andrea, remembering graduation *comes back to my little sadness.* She was graduating with Honors—she was 9th in her class. There was a ceremony requiring each Honors graduate to wear white. She asked her mother to buy her a white dress; her mother said she didn't have money for it.

She always gave me that sad story, but I knew different. I said 'ok, what-ever,' and told Mrs. Marshall I wouldn't participate in the Honors Day Pro-gram. But a good friend found out and said, "Girl my momma can get you a white dress." I said, no she doesn't have to do that. She said, "No, you gonna get a white dress; you are going to participate!" So I said ok and her mother, Mrs. Freeman, took me to the store and bought me a white dress. The cer-emony was on a Friday and on Saturday my mother sent a white top and white skirt. She had not given me any indication that she was going to do anything and sent everything late. So Mrs. Freeman got me a nice dress—if it had been from Goodwill, I would have still worn it. But this was a nice dress!

For the first time since Andrea had been in Austin, Patsy visited—for graduation. Andrea was wearing the dress Mrs. Freeman bought her, which did not sit well with Patsy.

My mother had an attitude. My friends didn't know anything, so they were being nice to her—but she had a little attitude with me because I was not wearing the dress that she bought me. But I had to wear Mrs. Freeman's dress. She had other kids and one graduating and she had sacrificed and got me the dress. So when I took off my robe, I wanted her to know how much I appreciated her thinking of me.

Reflections on Huston-Tillotson College—An HBCU

Andrea has only positive memories of Huston-Tillotson College—not just because she was able to get her college degree there, but because of the friendships she made and how well she was treated by the other students, the faculty, and the administration. They helped her financial-ly, got her out of situations, held her to high standards, and showed her kindnesses and a side of the world that she had never seen or experienced before. Thus, Andrea's journey celebrates the nurturing nature of an environment like that of an HBCU—an environment where people around you, the community around you, irrespective of what your experiences have been, lift you up instead of tearing you down.

Being a student at HT changed my world! Dr. King, Ms. McCracken, Mrs. Marshall—she's now Dr. Marshall—were all so helpful to me throughout my college career. Even Mrs. Marshall's husband, Dr. Marshall, whom I used to not like, guided me. The first time I met him I was late for his class. His back was to the class, and he didn't turn around. He just said, "Well thanks for joining us, Ms. Charlton. I hope tomorrow you can make it on time." I was embarrassed and just squeezed my fat ass into the chair. He was very good. Each of those professors was very good. Dr. Hicks was very good. She was so prim and proper. She didn't call you out loud but would ask you to stay behind. She would say, "You're a young lady; you don't have to act like that. You don't have to have the last word. Do you understand what I'm saying, Andrea? You're a smart young lady." I'd say, "Ok, can I go now?" She would say, "No you need to stand here and listen to what I'm saying." I liked all of them.

Perhaps the only thing Andrea's friends, faculty, and the administration at HT did not do is offer her that after-college advice. But they simply did not know that there was no one else giving her the necessary guidance to make after-college plans.

My entire time at HT was focused on finishing ASAP. However, because I didn't know what the next step was going to be, I had to go back to Patsy's in Baton Rouge. That was a mistake, but I went back because I didn't know what else to do nor did I have anywhere else to go. My focus had been on finishing school and getting my degree because back then everybody was telling me to get my degree and it would lead to something else. What I needed was somebody to tell me something else like go get a job while you're in school so you will have something when you get out. But I didn't have a car and I didn't have any money and I didn't know. And partly because I was so private, even those who were helping me didn't realize I needed that kind of guidance.

Post-Graduation—Back to Baton Rouge

When Andrea returned to Baton Rouge, she realized nothing had changed. Patsy had persisted in her lie—virtually no one in Baton Rouge knew that Andrea was Patsy's daughter, and Patsy was apparently not ready for that to change.

At the end of the 24-month Job Corps program participants received a final lump sum payment. For Andrea that was $1,600. And although she stayed at HT for one additional year to complete her degree, Andrea saved that money.

Despite the absence of change in her family life, when Andrea returned to Baton Rouge, she found a job there. Although she did not have a driver's license, she planned to buy a car, hoping Patsy and Thomas would be willing to add to the money she already had so that she could get a good car. Although they bought Pauline—who was still in high school—a new car, they were not willing to assist Andrea. Therefore, Andrea got up at five am every morning so she could ride back-and-forth to the job with a friend willing to pick her up. Undeterred, Andrea eventually saved enough money to buy the car she wanted—a Chevy Cavalier.

Unfortunately, because I couldn't drive, I wrecked the car when I hit a fire hydrant. When it happened, I politely got out of the car, picked up the fender, put it into the trunk, and carried on.

The condition of her car was the least of her worries as her relationship with Patsy worsened. After one particular argument culminating with Patsy hitting Andrea in the head with a frying pan, Andrea finally moved out and got her own apartment.

I didn't have money to furnish it; so I laid me a pallet on the floor until I could.

The final straw was an interview with the department store where Patsy worked. When Patsy found out about the interview, she told Andrea if the interviewer asked if she knew Patsy to tell them she was her aunt. She also cautioned Andrea that her employer did not ordinarily hire relatives.

I can't tell you how far down my heart dropped.

When the interviewer asked Andrea if she knew Patsy, Andrea said no. Andrea did not get the job, although Pauline was later hired by the same department store.

Moving On

Andrea knew she could no longer live in Baton Rouge. A friend in Austin suggested she consider moving to Austin. On a Friday during a visit to Austin shortly thereafter Andrea had an interview. They asked if she could start that Sunday.

I went back to Baton Rouge on Saturday, put my stuff in storage, moved out of my apartment, asked a friend to ride with me, telling her I would fly her back. She agreed, and I went to work on Sunday. That was March of 1986 and I've been in Austin ever since.

Andrea's after-college time in Baton Rouge had been yet another horrible experience. What occurred explains Andrea's sense of rejection.

My mother's rejection of me at various points has had a big impact on my life—in relationships. I push everybody away because everybody who has ever said they loved me, that love has proven to be too painful. My mother, my family—everyone who was supposed to protect me, did not. This was a major reason why I didn't have children. If I had become pregnant, I would have had an abortion. I feared that if something happened to me my child would have been treated the way I was. I didn't want my child to live the life I had to live as a child. I would be a good mother, but I had no faith if I wasn't around that s/he would be treated right.

Her father's rejection and the hurt it caused is also palpable. Andrea did not know him—although she met him and had several visits with him. Despite those visits . . .

He never showed any interest in me. I thought, 'I don't mean anything to you? I'm one of the children you have out here!'. He's deceased now. He was an important man in his community. He took care of others but not me. I do not believe he was given an opportunity to. I did not hold him responsible. I did not attend his funeral.

Overcoming rejection

Andrea has had a successful 30-year career as an accountant. She has found a place in her community and among friends. She is a vital and vibrant member of her church community, teaching Sunday school and Bible study for several years now. She has allowed people who needed a place to stay to reside in her home and, although she seems incredulous when she hears this, she has become a role model and a positive influence on others.

I have a friend at Abbott [Labs]. I met her not knowing her story. I would help with her kids—she and her husband and kids are like my family. Two days ago she said, "Andrea you were the person who made me go to college." I was like, 'really.' She said she admired me and the struggle I went through to get what I wanted. She said, " . . . and you always come out on top!" I never see myself coming out on top, but you never know how others view you or who you might influence. She said, "You inspired me to read a book, and to go back to school. She obtained an Associate's degree, a Bachelor's, a Masters, and has begun talking about obtaining her Ph.D. Her husband got his masters. Her kids also got their degrees, which include advanced degrees. I am so proud of them. I have other friends who have said 'because of you I did this, I had the strength to meet my challenges.'

Although nearing retirement age, Andrea recently received a second degree, a master's in Healthcare Administration.

I was attending a conference where the speaker said it's never too late to do what you want to do. I turned to a coworker who was also in attendance and said, 'you know what, I'm going to go back to school!' It is something I have always imagined. After returning from the conference I told a sorority sister about what I wanted to do, and she told me about a graduate online program at the University of Texas in Tyler, Texas. I enrolled.

❧

How did Andrea Charlton overcome the rejection of her parents and become professionally and personally successful? Andrea says she's not sure she has overcome that rejection.

I'm doing good talking to you. I used to not be able to talk about this. It has stunted my growth as a person. I could be doing a lot better, but I think this whole thing, this pain, holds me back. I probably would be in a relationship, maybe married with kids. But I'm grateful for where I am. Yes, God tested me and brought me to where I am, looking out for me. But education-wise I could have done better if I had the guidance I needed. Some choices I made in life would have been simpler. I have a nonchalant attitude, but I would have been more focused. I'm not sure if it's a facade or if I really don't care what you think. When I'm dealing with people, if I sense they are telling a lie, I cut them off immediately. That lying stuff just kills me. My whole life is a lie. I don't have time for people who lie.

Thus, Andrea's hurt/pain has resulted in self-doubt.

I don't consider anything I do to be successful, to be honest. I'm not sure why.

She does not recognize her greatness. And the only way sometimes that we do is to see ourselves through the eyes of others. She has heard and felt so much bad about herself that it is important that she hears the good so that it plants another seed that will hopefully lead to her understanding of the impact that she has had on others—allowing her to see herself as others do.

There is one thing that Andrea identifies as the reason that she has been able to persevere . . . her faith.

Faith is everything! It started when I was little. But it became really important. It has played an important role. When I started understanding Jesus Christ in my life was when I went to live with Patrick. That's when my whole world changed. I moved from somewhere I knew and was familiar with and where I considered myself happy, to live in Patrick's house, where I knew what was going on was not right even though I didn't know that kind of lifestyle. I was forced to use what I was taught at a young age to pray and pray fervently. I came to America and it was the same thing. My faith got me through—I would pray, read my bible, listen to anything spiritual—anything—that I could hang onto. When I didn't have anything else, I had my faith in God. I couldn't depend on anyone but God, and he always sees me through.

Andrea's faith also tells her she still has work to do—not so much for others, but herself.

I guess I should be able to let the past go and trust Christ totally, but I'm not there yet. My faith has made me stronger. Because if I give up on God, I'm out there with nothing. I go to church, try to do church work, go to bible study, I attend Bible Study Fellowship (BSF) and now I serve as a group leader in BSF. This has also been a good decision in my life.

The end result is positive. It has taught Andrea to be more open—talk about her pain—hopeful that at some point doing so will allow her to release it and fully heal.

I must tell you I have learned to be open. I used to be ashamed—I wouldn't want anybody to know what my life was like. Now whoever wants to know I'm ok with it. I learned to be ashamed of my mother—she was ashamed of me. She has said that she made a mistake so many years ago. To this day she is so ashamed of my being—I'm standing in front of her and she is so ashamed and she hasn't realized that I am not going anywhere.

Now, however, I think, what you see is what you get. Whether you like me or not. I'm not ashamed. I am a group leader in a bible study. This year I have older people in my class. I am amazed I'm here—leading these older ladies while I am struggling to understand how I made it to this point in my life. I often listen to their stories and can't be anything but grateful knowing I am here, by faith. It's all about God and Him pulling me through.

During a BSF church training event some of the participants suggested that I ask God what he wants me to do. So, I asked God what he wanted me to do. I asked him to break up this stone heart. Those in the training said to ask my pastor what he wanted me to do at the church. So, I asked the pastor what he wanted you to do at church. He asked me to be the announcing clerk. I wanted to do something else. I don't speak well . . . He kept encouraging me. My heart comes out of my mouth every Sunday—though it's gotten better. That's how I have to trust in God in all things. He will see me through. I was asked to do things as a result of this role as the announcing clerk and being superintendent over Sunday School. God has surely moved me from where I was to where I am. Things I had no dream of doing.

The Future

There is a sort of melancholy that remains a part of Andrea when considering the future—where does she go from here? At 58 years young, her future looks bright. But . . .

At this age I think of me as in the last days of my life, to be honest. I don't know. My focus is the people who come behind me to make sure if there's any way I can clear the way for them, that's where my focus is directed. Anybody that I see coming ahead of me that just needs that little support, I want to try to provide it. Because there are a lot of people that helped me along the way I want to be in that position where I can help.

I remember when I bought this house around the time of the flood in Texas. And I let a family stay here. I was amazed at how many people thought I was crazy. But when I think back from where I came from, if those people who I let stay here [and there have been others who have stayed with Andrea on several different occasions] come in and kill me, then so be it. Because when I was staying with people who were supposed to protect me, they didn't protect me. They left me wide open for anyone to come in and kill me. So if a stranger kills me, physically that's ok; because my spirit was killed by the treatment I received as a child.

Despite her pain, Andrea remains hopeful—both about where her life will lead her and even about her relationship with her mother.

I just wish [Patsy and I] could be open, genuine, and honest with each other rather than how we are with each other. When my mom came to America, she left me at two years old. I don't know if all this was intentional or not. She didn't look back—she abandoned me, she turned it into a lie to the point that you didn't even know it was a lie—she believed the lie she created. Even after her husband died, she continues with the same behavior—which left a big impact on my life. And I don't think it/she will change. I think she had the opportunity to do the right thing and didn't. I don't know if she is afraid or what. I have to just learn to accept her behavior and move on. That's just the way it is going to be. And I will continue to do what I do—not necessarily holding out hope that things will change.

I am hopeful. One thing: I would love to meet that person that I could spend the rest of my life with—however long that is. That's not something I ever hoped for before, but now I'm ready to move in that realm. If it doesn't happen, I'll be ok. But at this point in my life, that's something I think I'm ready to do. I am ready to just let the past be the past and move on.

But . . . sometimes other things intervene to not let the past rest—my mom. People tell me, "Oh, you shouldn't hold on to that. You should forgive." Now, I think I've come to the conclusion where yeah, I can forgive. But it doesn't mean that I can forget what happened or forgive to the point where I walk right into the same situation.

And there is still her deep, steadfast faith . . .

I have persevered by the grace of God. God has put people in my life that regardless of where I've been or what I do those people stand by me and support me, encourage me.

Andrea today

I think I'm still the same person and I still have that I don't care attitude, which is not what I should have. But I think I'm the same person I was when I was 13 years old—this scared rejected person that no one knows. I don't think I'm past that yet. Still being rejected; just out there by myself—nobody cares. Goes back to my mother. Even with all the people who embrace me. I still feel alone. I've tried to have a relationship with Patsy but it's not a normal relationship—of course. I never called her mother. Even in this adult time in our lives when friends are dying, nothing has changed. One night I was at a seminar about final preparation and she (Patsy) called. She asked what I was doing. I told her I was listening to a speech on how to be prepared. She asked why I was doing that. I said, 'When I die, I don't have anybody down here, so I need to have a plan. Even though I've donated my body to science, when they finish I want to be cremated.' She said to tell them to send my body to her. I asked her why? She replied so she could bury me next to her mother in Jamaica. I was puzzled. You don't want me when I am alive, why would you want me when I am no more? She got mad and we haven't spoken since that day. It has been approximately eight months now. I called and she has not called me back.

A month ago I was talking to my sister Pauline and telling her I was in school and was about to graduate. She asked me the date of graduation and said she wanted to attend. This graduation was not a big deal to me, I don't know if I was going to even participate in the graduation ceremonies. When I shared these thoughts with Pauline, she said even if I didn't march she would come down and we could spend time together. I shared how I felt during my graduation from high school—graduating 4th in my class and nobody was there for graduation. I did tell her she was a child and it was not her fault. Pauline says, "You always give me a pass." Pauline has changed I think because she has kids and all of them are now gone off to school or work. And her husband is with the FBI and she's home at times by herself. I remember when she lived in Illinois and Patsy would drive to Illinois to see Pauline and her family but could not/would not drive seven hours to visit me.

Doing something Different . . . A New Job???

Andrea is also now ready to retire from her position with the state and do *something else*. That means both a different job in a different location and perhaps using her latest degree.

I don't want to continue to drive to downtown Austin anymore. I would like to work at a school or hospital—3 to 5 days a week. I don't know if I want to do accounting. I went back to school in healthcare management. So I might like to do something in that field. There are options—I just want it to be something else. If the need is for accounting, I will do that. But I wouldn't go looking for an accounting job. I'd like to do something to help and care for the children and/or the elderly.

Life-changing moments . . .

For Andrea, the most life-changing moments are simple:

I guess getting to this point in my life. When I look back, and see where I've been—the valleys—it just makes me grateful. To try and just go back and say, what was the turning point? I don't think I could just pick one thing because truly it's faith, it's by the grace of God, every step of the way, whether I wanted that person in my life or not, He put somebody there to tell me to turn this way or don't go that way. Whether it was vocal or just in general. Even Job Corps was a blessing from God because I learned how to stand on my own and maybe I would not have otherwise. And I think I needed to learn to stand on my own.

Coming from Jamaica—a third world country—was life changing. I came from a depressed area in a third world country. I was very happy in that depressed area because I didn't know anything else. But when I came to a place which was supposed to make me better, it made me bitter. I have now overcome that, but at the time, I didn't have a voice. I couldn't say anything. I couldn't do anything be-cause I would have been out on the street. So when I think back, I real-ize things could have been worse—I could have had a baby at 12 or 11 or whatever age, or not gone to school—everything that society deemed to be where I should have ended up. So I'm grateful that those things didn't happen.

Paying it forward

Andrea struggles with what she had to endure in her young life before she was able to gain some control; and because the pain is still there and real, she sometimes wonders if death is not the peaceful answer,

People now say, "What is wrong with the life you lived? You live a good life." But I keep going back to that 13-year-old. I can't block that 13-year-old out. That's the core of me.

Then in realizing her many blessings, her concern is how to help others. Her accounting degree has helped Andrea personally and has allowed her to help others.

There are things that I have been able to accomplish that I couldn't even imagine at one time—sitting in this room in this house, to be able to go back to school would not be in my imagination 30 years ago. I will owe a lot of debt from school so that's why I want to sell my house so I won't be in debt. But that still wouldn't leave me with any money. I started paying on the loan; I got a letter saying you don't have to start paying until after graduation. But I was thinking that's why we are where we are in this country. Now I have paid one loan in full and then got a letter saying you don't have to pay now. I try to help others in financial debt because I hate being in that type of bondage. So I do what I can to educate those who are open and willing to listen to me.

When I read the scripture, it tells us you can make all the money in the world, but it will slip away like you have a hole in your pocket if you don't give any of it away to those in need. I tell the people at church to give God what is His. One lady said, 'I can't afford it.' But I say as long as you continue to say you can't afford it you won't be able to afford it. So I went to her house, helped her with a budget, took the tithe out. She said, "See that's what I've been telling you all along; I can't afford to tithe." I said, 'There are your tithes right there. I deducted it first before doing anything else. She said, "Oh you already took the tithe out?"

One Sunday she said she wanted to talk to me. She said she almost didn't give her tithe because her daughter needed a car and she wanted to help her with the car. I said, 'why can't you help her with your ninety percent? Why do you want to help her with God's ten percent?' So she said she gave the tithe anyway and did so happily as she remembered what I said. I said, Ok, let God do God's work.' After church, we were outside talking to a guy who had bought his wife a new car. We were happy for him. And I asked him what he was going to do with his wife's old car. He said, "I think I'm going to fix it up and sell it." I told him my friend's daughter was looking for a car.

He said, "She can have it." He told us the car needed tires and an alignment. She said she wanted to holler. I said, 'Yeah, this morning you wanted to rob God; now He's blessing you for being obedient.' She took the car and got an alignment, put two tires on the car, and her daughter drove that car for some years. She just told me a month ago the daughter went and bought a car, she didn't need a cosigner, she didn't buy a used car, she was able to buy a new car. God is so good to us. He sees our hearts. He is concerned with our hearts, while we are concerned about the things happening around us.

Advice/Takeaways

Through the myriad of experiences in her life—the good and the bad– it is not hard to imagine that Andrea has both reflections and advice. First, from Jamaica to Baton Rouge to Job Corps to HT/Austin and her life today Andrea says . . .

You have to live your environment. Embrace what you have been given and work it to the best of your abilities.

The Meaning of Love

During her journey, or perhaps because of it, Andrea has learned the meaning of love—a word that was for at least the first half of her life foreign to her.

For the longest. I didn't use the word love. I wouldn't tell anyone I loved them. I didn't know what love was. If somebody said they loved me I would flinch. I wanted to say, 'oh no don't. Don't love me.' When I heard the word love, all I could feel was pain, pain, pain. (Just thinking of all the pain that came with the people who were supposed to love me). But as I grew in my faith spiritually—I remember one day reading something that talked about how much God loves us. And flash! I thought, "you love me that much?" But I still couldn't even say the word. I might have been in my forties when I let the word 'love' come out of my mouth. I wouldn't even let people hug me. I didn't want anybody to be close to me. Now I will tell others, 'I love you' or even hug others.

I remember when I would go to church—I used to cringe when the people at church would hug me because I didn't want them to get any makeup on my clothes. I'd think, 'Ooh, I got to wash this.' Now I don't care; I don't think about that. It doesn't matter if they hug me. So I'm growing up a little. It's still not perfect. But for the past eight, nine years in this leadership role the people would say I love you. And I like it when I tell them I love them. I mean it; it feels good learning to love from the heart and not just repeating the phrase. I don't have that feeling of please don't love me or I don't need your love.

This year I had the older ladies in my BSF group. I was nervous about them. Most of these ladies had been in the program for over 30 years, but I think this has truly been one of my best groups. Since class ended, they sent me cards with little sweet notes like, 'you don't know how much you impacted my life,' 'You don't know how much you have made a difference in my life'. I was amazed! Last week I got a card from one of the ladies. In it, she wrote, "Andrea, I have been praying for you and your school. You were such a good leader! Continue to work in the vineyard for the Lord" It was affirming. It makes me want to continue to give because I always go back to the fact that somebody sacrificed for me. And it was someone who didn't even know me, was willing to take a chance on me. God has changed my view from my heart to allow and accept the love of others in my life.

While my focus seems to be helping younger people, I don't have a pref-erence. It's just whoever comes my way—some people will ask for help and others I just know that they need help. And I believe that to the extent you can help you should do so. I've learned that it doesn't even matter where I am or how I feel; there's always somebody in a worse situation than me. So instead of me focusing on my issues, I look for ways to help others to give back with what God has so richly blessed me with.

As a result of all of these experiences I have learned what love is; I learned also, not to use that word casually.

Regrets

Andrea has no regrets—about the bad or the good.

Even though all this stuff happened, I think it happened for a reason. And it made me into a better person. At one point, I thought it made me a bitter person. But I think it made me a better person as I move on. I re-member finally saying to myself, 'You gotta shake this off. You know, there's always worse.' And so I would go to the nursing home and sit and talk with people or go do something different.

In addition, I know that any kind of regret is just the opportunity to work on making that regret, not a regret—to turn it around. When I think of it and look at where I am now and think of where I could have been there is no need to be regretful because I know that by the grace of God I was led in the straight and narrow—a better path.

And so, of her journey thus far Andrea says . . .

It was not a sweet walk. It was a struggle. But in going through the struggle I was able to get to the other side. They say the diamond wasn't that shiny diamond all along; you have to pick it up, clean it up before you can see the value of it. I think that has been my journey, It wasn't a shiny diamond all along . . . I had to work at it . . . and so I continue to persevere.

BEVERLY PEGUES

SKIPPING WITH THE LORD

How many of us remember the first time we knew we had a relationship with a higher power? Can you readily share and describe what happened and how you felt? Beverly Jean Pegues-Tucker can. For her, the memory is vivid and easy to describe—

In the first grade I remember that I would hold God's hand and skip home from school with Him.

This experience left young Beverly feeling close to God and very much protected. Interestingly, Beverly did not think her experience was unique.

I thought God skipped with all the kids. I didn't find out that He didn't skip home with all the kids until I was in my 30s—I'm serious! I always felt very protected.

Both the sense of protection and being close to God through the physical act of skipping were not the result of Beverly being inundated with religious doctrine—

When I was a child, we didn't say prayers at night or anything like that. On Sundays, my mother would send us to church with my cousins—we grew up Methodist—but I never really got anything out of that church experience that enhanced my relationship with the Lord. We just knew that on Sunday we would get up and get dressed and go to church.

Beverly's close relationship with her grandmother, who was a Jehovah's Witness, gave her a different church experience as a child.

I went to church with my grandmother because I wanted to be with her.

Born in Columbus, Ohio, the oldest child of unmarried parents, Beverly was raised by her mom and her grandmother. In addition to the time they spent at home, Beverly's relationship with her grandmother was nurtured when the two went to Kingdom Hall, the church of the Jehovah's Witnesses.

My grandmother was a very mild, meek person; she had a lot of inner strength. She was very protective of me, which made me feel very confident. Even when I was young, there wasn't anything that I felt I couldn't do. She was Jehovah's Witness, and I used to love going with her to church. I didn't know what they were necessarily talking about or teaching, but I would leave school and run to get home in time to get on the bus with her when she was on her way to church. That was kind of special.

Beverly's grandmother died when Beverly was five years old, leaving a void in the life of her oldest grandchild.

Growing up During the Civil Rights Movement

As a child, Beverly felt very protected by God. Moreover, her experience as a young Black child growing up in Columbus, Ohio did not include overt instances of racism or living in an environment of second-class citizenship as was the case for Black people in the south and elsewhere. Nonetheless, Beverly was very much aware of and vocal about the civil rights movement and the mistreatment of Black people.

I always attended integrated schools. I never experienced segregation personally, although I was aware of it because of the political climate and things that were happening during that era. I graduated from high school in 1968. So I grew up during a very active time for the Civil Rights Movement that involved Martin Luther King, Malcolm X, and the Black Panther movement. It was a time of self-awareness—a time during which we were becoming more proactive, more politically aware and involved, wanting our voices to be heard.

Although not subjected to segregation and overt racism Beverly and her African American classmates were not satisfied to sit on the sidelines. They wanted to be involved in the movement in their own way—both by participating in protests and by taking an active role in their high school's student government. In 1966, while attending Linden McKinley, a predominately White high school, Beverly's cousin Paul was elected class president, Two years later Beverly was elected her class secretary. Both were the first Black students elected to those positions.

When the diversity in their student government did not seem to continue, the Black students organized their own group—the Artisans—which hosted events and addressed issues most specifically related to the African American student community.

Although her family was concerned about her involvement in protest activities, and afraid for her, they did not prohibit Beverly's involvement.

My parents never asked me not to participate, but they were concerned. They were afraid for their very strong-willed child and knew that if they were not watching me every minute that I probably would be involved in some way in the Civil Rights Movement.

Beverly's participation in the Movement changed because of her pregnancy.

Shortly after I graduated from high school I got married. I was 18 and two months pregnant, which prevented me from participating in marches or other protest activities. When I look back at it, I also know it was God protecting me at that time.

God was protecting Beverly because although she embraced Martin Luther King, Jr., and the spirit of non-violence she also could not fathom being beaten, bitten by dogs, and hosed by the police as was happening to protesters—particularly in the south—without fighting back. Beverly saw both Dr. Martin Luther King and Malcolm X as revolutionaries in their own right. She saw a place for non-violence, but also believed in her constitutional right and the necessity of self-defense.

I was probably a little more pro-Black Panther Movement than I was Dr. Martin Luther King's non-violence movement when I started seeing people get beat up on TV. I did not believe I could be beaten—it would be game on! They might kill me, but I would not go down without a fight. I would have fought them. I would have fought them! No doubt about it!

But I didn't feel like violence was the answer either. It was therefore sort of a conundrum for me.

Today, some fifty years later, Beverly sees herself in her Christian ministry as a revolutionary.

There are a lot of Christians I would put in that category—Christian leaders over the years, who are solid Christ-followers and revolutionary in their thoughts. They see the status quo and say, "it is time for a change."

High School Sweetheart

The person who helped to keep Beverly from becoming fully enmeshed in the Civil Rights struggle was her high school sweetheart, Terry. She and Terry started dating when he was a senior and she was a sophomore in high school.

He kept bugging me; kind of wore me down.

Terry graduated from high school two years before Beverly, going on to attend Central State University, an

HBCU in Wilberforce, Ohio. He and Beverly continued dating. Beverly was interested in the law and was looking to attend Kent State University when she graduated from high school.

Unsure about whether she wanted the responsibility of being a lawyer, but maintaining her interest in the legal profession, as a junior in high school Beverly decided to focus her attention on becoming a legal secretary. There were a series of business classes—a secretarial intensive program—that upon completion would provide the equivalent of a two-year associate's degree. Realizing the program was closely aligned with her future goals, Beverly enrolled in the program. The work was rigorous and because she entered the program late Beverly had to work hard to catch up and complete the program by the time she graduated. Her guidance counselor was skeptical about whether Beverly would be successful. She need not have been.

I was determined. I knew I was smart enough to do the work; the only question was whether I could finish in the time allotted. I told myself, 'I'm gonna do this!' So once enrolled in the program I worked like everything! I never caught up with the number one student, but I graduated second in that class. The guidance counselor said, "I don't know how you did that!"

The young couple's plans changed when Beverly got pregnant. Terry left college, they got married, he joined the military, and the family—now with the addition of their daughter LaTonya—moved to Colorado.

I felt like we should be together as a family. So when Terry enlisted in the military and was stationed in Colorado Springs, we moved with him. It was January of 1970. LaTonya was nine months old.

Although she believed it was important to move with Terry, leaving her close-knit family in Ohio was difficult for Beverly.

I cried the entire way to Colorado! And my precious little girl, LaTonya sat on my lap—you didn't have to have seat belts back then—almost the whole drive, wiping the tears out of my eyes saying, "Don't cry, Mommy. Don't cry." It was quite traumatic. To leave my mom? Oh my God, my mom. Oh, my goodness, it was horrible! But it was something I felt like I had to do because we were a family. And Terry wanted and expected us to come with him.

LaTonya

Although there would be other moments of change in Beverly's life, having her daughter LaTonya was perhaps her most life-changing moment.

Of course, the birth of my daughter was huge because becoming a parent changes your whole perspective. It challenges who you are, who you want to be, and who you want this person that you're raising to be. As a parent, I always wanted to make sure that I was imparting strong values, an excellent work ethic, solid morals, and concern for others into my daughter. It became my primary responsibility to let my daughter know that in addition to forging her own path she could also be a blessing to others, especially those who followed her. We all in some way leave something for this world, and I believe adhering to these principles would help determine LaTonya's mark on history.

Parenting is a full-time, life-long responsibility. Sometimes it will mean working long hours to provide for your family. It can also mean being very focused on the activities—school and extracurricular—in which your child is involved. For Beverly, her childhood experiences made the latter most important in raising LaTonya.

As a student, I did well academically. I was in the Honor Society and participated in several school activities, some of which my mother could not attend—like my induction into the Honor Society—because she was working. I didn't always understand why she could not attend. That was one of the reasons I wanted to be both very aware of and active in LaTonya's life. It is why we were very strategic about the school she went to, the classes she took, and her extracurricular activities. She was an avid reader, even in the summers, and we provided her with the opportunity to take piano, voice, swimming, and tennis lessons at various times. I simply wanted her to be a well-rounded person.

Divorce

Not long after they arrived in Colorado, Terry was deployed to Vietnam. But even before Terry's deployment Beverly's hope for the three of them as the perfect family began to show signs of stress: the couple was even discussing divorce. However, not wanting Terry to leave in the midst of a divorce Beverly decided to put any thoughts of divorce on hold, hoping that things would work out upon his return.

I didn't want Terry to have divorce on his mind in a war zone. We often corresponded while he was gone.

Unfortunately, upon his return, things did not work out.

When Terry got back, it was immediately apparent that he was affected by the war; and it became increasingly obvious that our relationship would not survive.

Four years after their family's arrival in Colorado, Beverly and Terry divorced.

Beverly chose not to return home to Ohio. Initially, it was because she was very satisfied in her work life—she was an administrative assistant/paralegal in a law firm in Colorado.

A bit later, she stayed because she had fallen in love . . . with Leonard Pegues.

Dream Job

After arriving and getting settled in Colorado Springs, and enrolling La-Tonya in daycare, Beverly began working. Initially, she took on several secretarial and administrative positions with local agencies and employers. She also renewed her involvement in political activism and volunteer work. Eventually, as a result of these latter two activities, she found her dream job—working as a paralegal in a law firm. It was the job she wanted and had planned for in high school, although she came to it unexpectedly.

A friend was running for state representative and a well-known attorney in Colorado Springs, Greg Walta, was his campaign manager. I handled a lot of administrative matters for the campaign, which required Greg and I to work together quite a bit. When there was an opening in Greg's law firm for a part-time legal secretary and paralegal, he asked me if I was interested. I said yes and was hired. No interview was required. I supported five attorneys in the firm. As the time passed, I took on additional responsibilities at the firm, ultimately becoming the firm's lead paralegal.

Leonard

Beverly met Leonard Pegues while both were volunteering in the Colorado Springs community working with wayward teens. Leonard, who was from Chicago, had come to Colorado Springs in the military and had completed his three years of service. He was 17 years older than Beverly.

Leonard was a handsome, much-pursued man in Colorado Springs. I think Leonard was attracted to me because I did not seem impressed with him. I saw him at the community events and Pikes Peak Community College, where we both took classes. Leonard was quite an interesting and re-markable guy.

Interesting and remarkable enough that Leonard and Beverly were married in May of 1975.

Leonard was well-traveled. He had a lot of incredible qualities. He had so many different life expe-riences, he was like reading a good book. He was an ex-tremely wise and brilliant man.

Although her mother thought Leonard was too old for her (Beverly was 25 and Leonard was 42), Bev-erly embraced the age dif-ference for what Leonard's years of life experiences added to her life.

I never thought about Leonard's age. I always felt like I had knowledge far beyond my own years and experience because I was able to live part of my life through the life that Leonard had already lived. When we got married, Leonard was intentional about investing in my life and in LaTonya's life.

After Leonard and Beverly married, this family of three were blessed with more than twenty-seven years together, until Leonard's death in 2001. Leonard devoted much of the last years of his life to Windows International (WIN), the ministry he and Beverly co-founded, traveling with her throughout the world, and offering his wisdom and insight along the way.

Higher Power . . . Conversion

While Beverly always thought of herself as a Christian—skipping with the Lord—reading and curiosity led her to explore other religions, New Age, and Transcendental Meditation.

I used to read books about different philosophers, of which Jesus was one. I knew in my heart that Jesus outranked everybody, but it wasn't until I actually had an encounter with the Lord and gave my life to the Lord that I realized the other religions amounted to idolatry. Although others may think of Christianity as idolatry, to me idolatry means putting something else above God, the Father. I am overwhelmed that God's love for humanity is so great that he would give His only begotten Son to pay the sin debt for all of humanity. My transforming conversion occurred in the late 80s.

At the time of her conversion, Beverly and a friend had started attending a Baptist Church in Colorado Springs—New Jerusalem—whose pastor was a community activist. Beverly views her path to conversion as simply seeking God.

I tell Christians concerned about their kids' salvation that the Bible is clear: if you seek you will find. Because anyone genuinely seeking the truth about God will find the Lord. Don't worry. During my journey, whether I was involved with Transcendental Meditation, or New Age, I was always seeking to connect with God. Being in search of God was innate to me. And I know why now: the Bible tells us in Ecclesiastes 3:6-9 that God puts a longing for eternity in the hearts of every person.

What assisted Beverly in her search after she joined New Jerusalem was taking part in a weekly Bible study group. But there was something much more personal—but publicly controversial—that Beverly describes as her turning point—both in terms of her faith and ultimately what led to her ministry.

Turning Point

It was the late 80s and Beverly discovered she was pregnant. She and Leonard decided Beverly would have an abortion. At the time, it was not a difficult decision.

I didn't think there was anything wrong with having an abortion. In my mind, I believed that a fetus was not a living person. We decided I would have an abortion. This is something I don't mind talking about as part of my journey as I think it will help others.

The abortion issue was hot in Colorado Springs at the time, and the words of an anti-abortion advocate sent Beverly into a tailspin.

My whole world fell apart. I went into such a state . . . I don't even know what to call it. I came home early from work. Leonard was in the kitchen cooking and the television was on and turned to the evening news. I said, 'Leonard did you hear what this man said? Oh my God, we killed our baby!' Leonard looked at me like I lost it. Then, almost immediately it felt like I was having a nervous breakdown or panic attack. I never had anything like that happen before or since. And I could not get settled with this whole thing.

Believing that she was literally losing her mind, Beverly called her doctor, hoping he could help. His words—which she describes as *the pro-choice line*—did not help.

She was so distraught that she considered suicide. Then she experienced something that would change her life.

I thought, 'I really don't deserve to live. I should commit suicide. I think I'll jump out of my bedroom window.' But then I thought, 'that isn't a good idea because I will only break my legs.' So I started praying the 23rd Psalm, "the Lord is my shepherd, I shall not want." I just kept praying that prayer. I would lay in the bed and I would pray the prayer. I'd walk around the bedroom, and I would pray the prayer, and then I'd lay back in the bed. At one point I thought about calling some of my New Age friends. But I knew the only One that could help me was God—this sin was between God and me. And then at one point as I was continuing to recite the 23rd Psalm, I noticed that there was this little light that popped up in the room. It was a small but very intense, bright light. I thought, 'how can that be? The sun is already moved from this side of the house. But I noticed that every time I would say the 23rd Psalm that light would get bigger. And I thought, 'I am really going crazy; there is no way that there could be light on this side of the house at this time of day.' Nonetheless, every time I said the 23rd Psalm the light got larger and brighter and higher. I recited the 23rd Psalm for a few hours. And all of a sudden, this great big white ball—like the sun it was so big and intense—rolled over me. And when it rolled over me—this encounter that I had with God—I was finally totally emotionally mentally okay. God set me free from the bondage I felt.

The sense of protection from Beverly's childhood returned.

I have to compare it with skipping home with God. I had to compare it with God, way back then, giving me such a tangible way of connecting with Him that yes, He would come to my rescue again. It meant that the guilt was gone, I felt forgiven by God because I asked God to forgive me. The crying about it was gone. The thoughts of suicide were gone, knowing that my baby was safe in heaven. God was saying, "I've got you; I'm protecting you. I'm with you." Then I read the scriptures where God says, "I'll never leave you or forsake you." Well, that's me! That's what God did. It was a major mile marker in my life. I love the Lord, and I am so thankful for Him forgiving my sins.

The next time Leonard checked to see how I was doing I said, 'God helped me, God delivered me. God healed me from this guilt. God has forgiven us.'

Beverly immersed herself in the Bible—reading and studying whenever possible. She also went to hear a well-known pastor—Carlton Pearson—who was speaking at a large evangelical church in Colorado Springs. Moved by his sermon, she began to look for a church that she could regularly connect to in the same way. Because the church at which Reverend Pearson spoke was a predominantly White church, Beverly initially resisted considering that church.

I was shocked that God would call me to that church because I didn't think White people were saved.

Despite these misgivings, at the urging of a good friend, she went back to the same church a few Sundays later; and then a third Sunday.

I said, 'God, you know these White people don't even know you.' But I noticed that the people were dancing and they were raising their hands. They were also very friendly. When we arrived, they were very loving and warm, seeking me out to talk. I was surprised. And I said to God, 'Look at this sea of White people.' The Lord said, "Beverly, close your eyes and concentrate on me." As soon as he told me that, the praise and worship leaders start singing this song, "Let all Earthly Distractions Fade Away, Concentrate on Him in Worship." I don't even know what they preached on that Sunday. I was too through; I cried through the rest of the church service.

On one of her visits to the church, Beverly completed a visitor card. Ironically, the church pastor pulled her card and contacted her.

And so he called me while he was driving back from Denver. He said, "This is Ted Haggard; I see you came to visit us." He asked me what I thought about the service and if I had any questions. And I said, 'Yeah, actually, I do have a question: are White people saved?' I assumed he almost wrecked his car because he started laughing so hard. The man was belly laughing. He asked me why I wouldn't think that White people are saved as well. I went down the list: Ku Klux Klan, social injustice . . . He acknowledged my concerns but assured me that some White people are saved.

Although still somewhat skeptical, Beverly decided she would start attending the church regularly. And although she did not always agree with the message in the sermons—Beverly's social justice orientation was not always reflected in the Sunday message—her unceasing study of the Bible allowed her to come to an understanding that was not undermined by what she might disagree with during a Sunday sermon.

And that put me on a pursuit of really reading the Bible, studying the Bible, learning the Bible, and applying the Word of God in my life. It absolutely changed my life . . . It changed my life!

Perhaps more profoundly, it put her on a path toward her ministry. And unexpectedly, Leonard joined the church as well.

To my surprise Leonard asked me about the service; I told him he should see for himself. He attended church with me the next Sunday, and after that, he rarely missed a Sunday. One glorious Sunday, Leonard joined the church.

Leonard's Christian Conversion

Beverly describes Leonard's conversion.

When I became serious about my walk with the Lord, Leonard did not know what to think. He thought surely this was another one of the religious pilgrimages that I would soon get over. All of a sudden, I was a different person. I wasn't the party person I used to be. I did not want to go out dancing anymore. The funny thing was Leonard did not like to dance but would placate me and take me out to dance the night away. After my encounter with God, Leonard started trying to coax me to go out dancing, but I wasn't interested. I spent my extra time learning more about the Lord and His Word. Leonard was still going out clubbing. I would pray and pray for him. God taught me how to stop nagging Leonard about his walk with the Lord. One day, the Lord said, "Pray it on him, don't lay it on him." That is when I started digging in and praying for Leonard to give his life to the Lord.

One morning Leonard was out and about, and I was at home. I heard a knock on our front door and got up to answer the door. The Lord showed me Leonard had a root system of sin from Colorado Springs to Denver (about one hour away). But every time I prayed, the root system was being chopped off and demolished. When I answered the door that blessed day, the Lord showed me that Leonard's ungodly root system had been destroyed. Shortly after the vision, Leonard gave his life to the Lord! What I learned from this journey is to trust in the Lord to do more in-depth work in Leonard and that it would be accomplished in God's time, not mine. My job was to pray and leave the rest to the Lord. Leonard's story has helped many people.

Beverly offered this suggestion to those who are called to minister to others.

We must be willing to take time with people, casually talking with them, and having meals with them in preparation for in-depth conversations. We need to get to know the people and their families that God gives us the honor to minister and pray. This way, we are not developing 'perceived' ideas. God will show us things we would probably miss. Time spent is time well invested in the lives of those who are precious to God. It is essential to build a relationship, especially if you need to bring correction. Your correction is more palatable when a connection has been established.

Show generosity by being willing to bless financially those you are ministering to by sending cards of encouragement, flowers, bringing by balloons from the dollar store, delivering pizza to a family having a hard day. Be willing not only to sew time but also financially.

It is not that my prayers are more powerful than others, but this is one thing that I have learned; we must preserve in our request before the Throne of God until He provides the answer. It may take longer than you want, but God is faithful, and He will answer.

The 10/40 Window Ministry

Beverly's initial conversation with the church pastor about the salvation of White people left a lasting impression—he had never forgotten her. So even though the rules of the church required a three-year membership before a member could serve on any church committee and Beverly had been there less than two years, the pastor contacted her asking her to serve on a committee. Though hesitant, she agreed. That was 1987, and her participation in the church grew from there.

On a particular Friday in 1992—the year LaTonya graduated from Howard University—Beverly broke out in hives. Leonard got medicine from the pharmacy, but it did not help. Beverly was miserable. So miserable that she decided not to go to the two church prayer meetings scheduled for the next day.

On Saturday I was still miserable and I told Leonard that I was going to stay home. After he left, I was lying in bed and I start praying. And the Lord spoke to me clear as a bell. He said, "The devil is trying to keep you from that prayer meeting!" I hurried up and got out of that bed! I was going to be healed at the prayer meeting.

Beverly made it to church and remained miserable throughout the first meeting.

I said, 'Lord, I thought when I got up you were going to heal me.'

Beverly decided to tell the leader of the second prayer group she could not stay. During that conversation, she discovered that there were Christian leaders from all over the world praying in the next room who were asking for interceptors—those praying to God on their behalf—to pray with them. Despite her misery, Beverly decided to participate. She did not know that her church pastor was one of the leaders, but as she began to pray, he interrupted her.

When ignoring him did not work, she followed him out of the room so as not to interrupt the other interceptors. The pastor began talking to Beverly about the "10/40 Window." Beverly had heard the term '10/40 Window'[6] once before in another prayer meeting but wasn't sure what her pastor was talking about. He told her that he was with the other leaders and had seen her coming in from the parking lot and told them, "There's the woman right there who should coordinate this effort for the 10/40 Window." Although flattered, Beverly pushed back because she had lots of other commitments with her job, community work, and her family

I told Pastor Ted that Leonard was trying to get me to stop doing as much; and that I needed to take some things off my plate, not add to it. So I said, no. He asked me to talk it over with Leonard and think about it. I agreed to do that, but when I left there, I was like, 'Whoa, God, what are you doing?'

Leonard initially agreed that adding the additional work would be too much—until Beverly told him about a chance encounter she had that day with a woman they met and prayed with in Washington, D.C., during the National Day of Prayer in May 1992. They were able to attend the National Prayer Day because it coincided with their daughter's college graduation from Howard University that same weekend. The woman with whom they prayed that day—Bobby Byerly—made quite an impression on them both. Thus, when Beverly told Leonard that she met Bobby Byerly again that day at the prayer meeting Leonard changed his mind.

You should have seen the look on his face. He said, "Are you trying to get me in trouble with God? You have to do this job!" It was obvious to Leonard and me that it was God. I mean, it was a setup from the Lord.

---

6. 10/40 Window"—an area in which approximately 2/3 of the world population resides, encompassing Saharan and Northern Africa, as well as most of Asia.

And that is how Beverly got involved with the 10/40 Window Ministry. She agreed to volunteer for one year and coordinate mobilization of the church globally. Her task was just to get the process up and started.

Our goal was to engage one million Christians across the globe to pray for four billion people or two-thirds of the world's population so they would be open to hearing the Gospel message.

Beverly and the committee met and surpassed their goal, mobilizing more than 20 million Christians to pray for the part of the world known as the 10/40 Window. And although Beverly initially only made a one-year commitment, she quit her dream law job—having a major falling out with her boss– and has been on the mission ever since. In addition to being an evangelical minister in the 10/40 Window with a focus on Northern Africa, Beverly ultimately is co-founder and President and the moving force behind Window International Network (WIN), a Christian organization developed to inform, equip and mobilize networks of prayer around the globe to empower effective evangelism, church growth and discipleship in the 10/40 Window.

Beverly describes the 10/40 Window Ministry this way . . .

The 10/40 Window is 10 degrees south and 40 degrees north of the

equator. Spanning the globe from North Africa, the Middle East, Asia, Southeast Asia, to Japan. representing 66% of the world's population.

It is the headquarters to Islam, Buddhism, Hinduism, atheism, tribalism, and agnostics. These countries are inhabited by nearly two billion people who have never heard of the redemption story and the love of Jesus Christ. They comprise 87% of the world's poorest people and the least educated. Corruption runs rampant in this region, the treatment of women is horrific, and wars and conflicts abound. It is illegal to take the Gospel into most countries. Forty-five of the top fifty nations that persecute Christians are in this region of the world. It has the highest martyred casualties.

The Lord tells us in Matthew 28:18-19, to go into all the world and to preach the Gospel. The leaders knew that God had given us His power and authority to spread the Gospel globally. But, because the 10/40 Window can be a dangerous place for Christians, we knew the project needed to be saturated in prayer. This meant we had to train the Church on how to engage in spiritual warfare to render Satan and his demons powerless (2 Corinthians 10:4-5). The Bible teaches us that our fight is not against flesh and blood. It is against principalities, powers of darkness, rulers of darkness in this age, and spiritual hosts of wickedness in heavenly places (Ephesians 6:12).

Can you believe that in the 21st Century, there are people who have never heard the Gospel message? Our ongoing prayer is that God grants us the opportunity to share the Gospel with those who have never heard about the love of Christ. Since the Church globally started praying for the 10/40 Window nations, hundreds of millions have come into the saving knowledge of Jesus Christ. Prayer changes things!

During Beverly's 28 years of ministry, she has visited nearly 50 countries. She has led dozens of prayer journeys, trained more than 18,000 leaders globally in 20 nations, and hosted and spoken at 36 prayer and leadership training summits. Some of the training took place in countries that are dangerous for Christians to live and minister. Beverly has authored and co-authored six books. She has hundreds of stories from her ventures with the Lord around the world. One in particular occurred in India.

One of the most memorable opening ceremonies was in Nagaland, India. We always start the training summits with the song, "We Speak to Nations." The Nagas were warriors and headhunters until the late 1940s when India gained its independence. With this backdrop, the Christians from the Naga tribe came out wearing the traditional Naga war clothing and carrying the 10/40 Window flags to "We Speak to Nations." It was electrifying! It attested to the transformative power that the Gospel of Jesus Christ brings to people, and God still calls us to be His spiritual warriors for the nations.

Biggest challenge for her ministry

Beverly's husband Leonard had become such an integral part of her ministry that when he died in 2001, she was not sure that she could continue without him, his support, love, and guidance.

When Leonard went home to be with the Lord in 2001, I didn't know how I could carry the spiritual and financial weight of the ministry without Len's support. When I prayed about it, God reminded me in His Word that He is married to the widow. Therefore, WIN and I were now God's responsibility. I can attest to the fact that He has faithfully been with me every step of the way. I learned to deal with Leonard's passing one day at a time. Thank God He was with me, and I never felt alone.

I try to be very careful that I'm hearing from God to do the things that I'm supposed to do, and not just because I think it's a good idea. I heard this one leader say, "God's will is his bill." So, if I'm doing what God tells me to do, it's His responsibility to make sure it's paid for; God's vision is His provision. That is how I have managed over the years, just trying to make sure that I'm hearing from God and doing things according to what He tells me to do.

Despite the trials of her ministry, punctuated by Leonard's death, Beverly feels that the ministry has been a success.

I believe that the ministry is fruitful because of the hundreds of millions of people who have come to the Lord. We started this whole prayer movement in 1993—and not just our ministry, but it has involved many other people who have become laborers in the harvest field to be able to take the Gospel to the Window. The Christian Church spends its resources among those who have heard the Gospel message repeatedly. But you can see the needle starting to move a little towards spending more funds in the least reached region of the world—the 10/40 Window.

Especially with the refugee crisis—more than 70 million displaced and refugees globally—most of those countries are in the 10/40 Window. These are people who are in these restricted access nations; therefore, workers preaching the Gospel in these nations risk being martyred. However, as refugees are moving into other countries without religious restrictions it is easier for Christians to be able to take the Gospel to them. Our responsibility is for people to hear; it is their responsibility whether they accept what they hear or not.

Academy of Black Arts

While Beverly's ministry has consumed most of her time, effort, and resources in the last twenty-eight years, there are other sources of pride—triumphs—along her journey. One, in particular, is the Academy of Black Arts (ABA)—a youth community performing arts group, which was based in the Colorado Springs African American community. The impetus of the group was to provide positive outlets and reinforcements for pre-teen and teenage boys and girls—like Beverly's daughter LaTonya and other young people in the community.

I would say overarching on a personal level, a major triumph would be the Academy of Black Arts (ABA), because we took kids whom people said would never graduate from high school, or go to college, or who wouldn't dadadadada, and helped to change their perspective in a positive way. We probably had about 100 or so kids who were involved with the Academy of Black Arts over the nine years that the organization existed. And with the exception of maybe two, all of them received their high school diplomas.

The group which Beverly and several other mothers and community-minded activists started, had their first performance—a play—at a local church. The church also had a prison ministry; so they took the play to prison—*an awesome experience for the kids and the prisoners alike.*

I think God used the ABA as a steppingstone to enrich the group and broaden their perspective on life allowing us to realize that people really do respond to and like the performing arts. It was also a way for Black kids to recognize their ability to do things they had not thought about. So we started doing little plays, holding dance classes, music classes, and the like. The community pitched in to help in whatever way it could when the ABA performed. Leonard was the set designer; Jackie Shepherd was in charge of tap dance. We had Sam Tabron, Claudia Brooks, Carl . . . there were a lot of people who would come in to do teaching and the training and everything.

There were also other culturally and educationally significant and enriching activities for children in the ABA.

I felt like we should also start partnering with the Black Student Union at Colorado College because I thought it was important to get the kids in a natural way used to being on a college campus so they could see it was no big deal—so that they could envision the possibilities for themselves. So we started performing plays at Colorado College at Armstrong Hall, having speakers from the college like Dr. Carruthers, or people who were in medicine. We used the campus library so that they would know it was no big deal going into a college library to do research. We spent the night at the Black Student Union. We brought our sleeping bags so they could really get immersed into a college environment. And I wanted to use that. Even though it wasn't really a Christian thing, I was being very directed by the Lord to do the things that would have a positive impact on the kids.

ABA's last big project was a performance of *The Wiz* in 1989. The ABA program ended around 1990. The students and the community were rightfully proud of this awe-inspiring performance.

Most of the kids in the program were graduating from high school. Younger kids wanted to join, but Beverly did not want the responsibility of taking another group of kids through that whole process. Some thirty years later, Beverly appreciates the efforts of the ABA participants and regularly hears from kids who graduated from the ABA expressing words of appreciation for her efforts. She would like to see similar efforts continue and become a mainstay in African American communities all over the country.

Many of the kids graduated from college; the last graduated six or seven years ago, even though it has been nearly 30 years since the program ended. She wrote me a letter saying, "Mrs. Pegues, the reason I finally finished college was because of you. Before ABA I never thought about going to college or anything like that." We have one woman who's a Ph.D. Several of them have received Masters' degrees. A lot of these kids would not have considered going to college before they came to the ABA.

Beverly believes that it is important to remind ourselves . . .

. . . that we still have a responsibility to build our community; we still have a responsibility to shape our community; we still have a responsibility to make sure our community knows our history. Listen, nobody needed to let my child know our history. That was my job! We have a culture and history. So I really feel that parents are going to have to re-educate themselves so that we can educate our children about Black History. But the church may still be one of the best places for something like this to happen—if it doesn't happen in the home. We all need to wake up, We have already lost a generation. White people cannot really teach our history.

Greatest Disappointment

Beverly expresses disappointment on two levels—as a political activist, and as an African American Christian.

My greatest disappointment is the way the United States of America mistreated our first African American president, Barack Obama. I was appalled to learn that the Republican leadership intended to do everything possible to make sure that Obama's presidency was not successful. That is when the uproar really should have started. There should have been so much pressure on Republican leadership for making such racist statements. But that did not happen. And the world was watching.

I was invited by Reverend William Okoye of All Christian Fellowship Missions Church in Abuja, Nigeria, to train their leaders and help prepare their church to send workers to the 10/40 Window. On the night of the 4th of November, I stayed up all night watching the election results from a foreign land. I really did hear from God that November day. What saddens me is that the Church in America did not lead the country into accepting and embracing our first African American President, Barack Obama. It would have been a game-changer globally because the world did not think democracy worked when it came to the United States electing an African

American to the highest office in the land. It was a God-given opportunity that was squandered.

Beverly's other disappointment revolves around the Christian response to the treatment of President Obama and the rise of overt racism in this country.

Beverly notes that although in previous years she had been on the President's Prayer Team—a group of Christian leaders who met to pray for political leadership and those in authority—the group disbanded after Barack Obama became president.

The Word in 1 Timothy 2:1-3 instructs Christian believers to pray for political leaders and those in authority. Doesn't this also include the African American President, Barack Obama? Surprisingly, Christian and political leaders repeatedly and graciously give second chances to Donald Trump with his documented lies, immoral behavior, and personal and political baggage. The way some high-profile Christian and political leaders treated President Obama is a disgrace and national embarrassment.

Beverly's other issue is how evangelical Christians have reacted or failed to react to the rise in overtly racist behavior against people of color in this country.

When the events of Charlottesville, Virginia were reported, with White supremacists carrying automatic rifles and espousing racist vitriol—"the Jews will not replace us", I feel that every pastor in America should have said, this is not acceptable. We are not neo-Nazis; this isn't who we are. They should have all come out against it rather than being silent. I have real problems with the silence of the Church.

I also ask myself, 'Why haven't African American Christian leaders been more vocal about this evil?' They should be roaring like lions as far as I'm concerned. I don't know why there isn't more outrage. The Bible says in Proverbs 31: 8-9, we are directed by the word of God to speak out for those who can't speak up for themselves—for the poor, the helpless, the needy to see that they get justice. So those who do not speak out are complicit in the harm.

After reading a book given to her about Dietrich Bonhoeffer—a German pastor, theologian, anti-Nazi dissident, and founding member of the Confession Church, which opposed efforts at Nazi control of the Protestant Church—Beverly is troubled about where we are today.

He [Bonhoeffer] said that Hitler was able to rise to power because of the financial struggles that people—and the Church—were having. As a result, the Church finally aligned itself with Hitler and became the Reich Church. They saw it as a financial issue. Jewish people were doing well. And although they ultimately knew that Hitler was doing bad things to the Jews, the Church chose not to object. Again, that's why silence in the face of evil is evil. It is a lesson for us today.

Beverly willingly shares her thoughts on such issues with others within and without the ministry, believing that in so doing change can occur.

Challenges for a Black Woman in the Ministry

Beverly has been in the ministry for nearly three decades, forging paths and doing the work she is God-directed to do. As an African American and as a woman, it has not been easy or necessarily fair. She recognizes this as a challenge, and while at times frustrated, she continues her mission.

It is a challenge being an African American woman in international ministry. I'm just really starting to recognize that if a White male was doing what I'm doing in the 10/40 Window, he would have no problem raising the funds needed to operate the ministry. Do you hear me? Because it's more

difficult as a woman and as a Black woman to raise the needed funds. Oh, there's no doubt!

She is not optimistic about change in the current patriarchy of Christianity.

I don't think it will change. But I know this is a calling of God on my life. So I have to keep pressing toward the mark of the high calling, and it's God's responsibility to make sure everything happens. And He has done that. It is a miracle that I was able to remain in our house and navigate all the financial obstacles that arose for so many years after Leonard passed. But like the old folks used to say, "God will make a way where there is no way." I can attest to this truth.

The church and the absence of women in leadership is a whole different subject. In fact, in general, the subject of men and women in leadership— within and without the church—is interesting. I think that has a lot to do with misogynistic attitudes that persist. It had a lot to do with Hillary Clinton not becoming the President of the United States. I think men just simply didn't want a woman in that position. Thus I pray that God will divinely position women in leadership to help solve crises in America and globally.

Takeaways

At 69, Beverly is now semi-retired from her ministry; having relinquished major responsibility for the daily operations of the 10/40 Window ministry in late 2019. She has had a wealth of life experiences– from young rebel to mother, wife, paralegal, and evangelical minister. She has seen much and done much. Her takeaway from all of this—and therefore her fundamental message—is faith.

I've seen a lot and experienced a lot. I remember being in one country where we almost had a head-on collision with somebody, and just crying out the name of Jesus saying, 'Jesus!' and the wheels that normally roll forward, start rolling sideways. So my takeaway is really Proverbs 3:5-6, "Trust in the Lord with all of your heart. Lean, not on your own understanding, but in all of your ways, acknowledge Him, and He will direct your path." That is the biggest takeaway that I have, the faithfulness of God. And knowing that God will respond not necessarily the way that I think, but he's going to respond in a way that is going to be the best for me, even though I can't see it at the time.

At one time after Leonard passed, it seemed that it would be best for me to have Leonard here, and we do ministry together. And I did not understand that, but I continued to trust in the Lord. There are a lot of decisions made and things that I see that I don't understand. But I do know that God is faithful. That is my biggest takeaway. And knowing that I can't trust in man, I can't trust in horses, chariots, or whatever. But I trust in the Lord, the maker of heaven and earth. That's my biggest takeaway. Because no matter what, I come back to God, the faithfulness of God. You know that song "Can't nobody do me like Jesus?" So in the midst of everything that we're going through, seek God, and include him in the formula of what's happening in your life.

The Future

Beverly was not without ideas about what is to come—both personally and professionally.

I feel like the rest of my journey is going to be training and encouraging emerging 10/40 Window leaders; I do a lot of that now. I'm always looking for emerging leaders So, my effort is to continue looking for those leaders, encouraging those leaders, being cheerleaders for those leaders, letting them know that you can make it, you can do it; it is helping them see something in themselves that they may not see, just like Pastor Ted saw in me. I wanted to make a lot of money. I never wanted to be a missionary, but Pastor Ted saw something in me that I didn't see. Sometimes others have the ability to see something in someone to spark something in them, to be who God has called them to be. As a community, we should encourage young men and women to fulfill the call of God that is on their lives. I pray this for my daughter, LaTonya, my son, Undray, the ABAers, the African American community, 10/40 Window leaders, and many others.

On the personal front, a few years ago Beverly was considering moving from the house she shared with Leonard. The house was a lot to handle for one person—especially because her ministry took her away from home so often. She was ambivalent about whether to stay in Colorado or move—perhaps closer to her family in Ohio. She expressed little interest in finding another life partner.

In three to five years I would have moved from the house, finding a smaller place to live. But me getting married again? If God said so I would. But it's not my preference. It would really have to be a God thing. I've thought about moving back to Ohio. I may end up getting a small condo or something in Ohio, maybe to go back and forth. But once I move from here, I don't know.

I don't know where I would go. But I haven't really thought about that part.
I think I'll do training. I probably will travel until I'm 80 or something.

Well . . . it was a God thing. In November 2018 after a whirlwind ro-
mance, Beverly married retired veteran, publisher, activist, and educator
Dr. James Tucker! They say when you are not looking that's when you find
your mate. Perhaps that was the case for Beverly. And she did move, as
she imagined she would—but not to a smaller place in Colorado Springs
or to Ohio. She moved to St. Louis, Missouri—a place that she had never
lived before, but the residence of her new husband, who has responsibility
for Undray, his non-verbal adult autistic son.

Although Beverly turned the day-to-day operation of her ministry
over to her successor, she will still travel and be involved in her ministry
in the 10/40 Window. She currently serves as a volunteer and President of
WIN's Board of Directors.

All of this did not take Beverly's predicted three to five years. It all
occurred in less than a year from our interview!

Not in our time . . . but in God's time!

FAEDRA CHATARD CARPENTER

Finding Her Place

Faedra Chatard Carpenter's biggest challenge growing up was *feeling out of place*. She and her two sisters and her parents were five of the very few Black people living in the then-small town of Bothell, Washington in the early 1970s. Her parents initially moved to Seattle, Washington after they married *because it was a place with schools where they felt like they could continue their studies*. Faedra's mother successfully pursued a Ph.D. in micro molecular biology, while her father, having completed medical school, was doing his residency in otolaryngology—ear, nose, and throat (ENT).

139

Once they started a family, Faedra's parents moved them to predominantly White *(I'm talking about maybe 1% Black)* Bothell (pronounced Baa-thell)—some twenty minutes from Seattle—where Faedra began her journey to find her space.

I am one of three daughters; I am the middle child. And despite many of the suggestions about the role of middle children, I was fine. I got along with my siblings and my parents. I did not feel dispossessed. My older sister was born in 1966. I was born in 1970, and my younger sister was born in 1975.

It was a happy childhood; just one where not many people she saw every day looked like her—so that she was often the only Black child—at school, among her friends, and at most gatherings.

Growing up in Bothell, my sisters and I were never in the same school. And when I was in elementary school, I was the only Black child. It's something that I remember that I knew; that I was aware of. First of all, because my mother was very, very conscious about making sure that we knew who we were and instilling pride in that—and making sure we had a sense of identity. So that was very important. She was always stressing that. And, of course, the other thing is that the other kids with whom I went to school would let us know.

And not always in very friendly ways . . .

My older sister was thrown into a big tin garbage can and bombarded with a bunch of racial epithets. On the playground growing up I would hear 'nigger' all the time . . . or things that they might consider innocuous like "Why is your hair like that?"

Despite these sometimes-harrowing childhood experiences, Faedra was—at least in elementary school—relatively undeterred by it all saying, *it was largely fine.*

Moreover, when her father decided he wanted to change paths from ENT to plastic surgery—which required the family to temporarily relocate to Gainesville, Florida—Faedra and her sisters had a sort of reprieve from being the "only."

My father was an otolaryngologist, and decided to move to Gainesville, Florida and go back to school to do a residency at the age of 40, with three kids, to become a board-certified plastic surgeon. [So when I was in the] 5th & 6th grades my parents put our house up for rent and we moved to

Florida. Moving to Florida was eye-opening. I went to a school called P.K. Yonge, which is a laboratory school connected to the University of Florida. It was eye-opening because of Black people! You saw them everywhere!

While Faedra's father began his residency program at the University of Florida, Faedra and her two sisters also developed ties with the University of Florida through their new school: P.K. Yonge, a K-12 developmental research school affiliated with the College of Education at the University of Florida. Entering P.K. Yonge was a formative experience for Faedra, not only because of the solid education she received while she was there, but also because her time there introduced her to new "life lessons":

P.K. Yonge School did a lot of pedagogical curricular testing [and] wanted a balanced demographic of all types of people. Supposedly, there was always a big, long waiting list of people who wanted to get into the school. But not for us. Me and my sisters were immediately accepted—because, apparently, the demographic of middle-class Black families was not exceptionally large. The socioeconomics of Gainesville at that time—or, at the very least, the socioeconomics of the families interested in P.K. Yonge, were really demarcated—the haves and the have nots. And so, we got accepted into the school immediately. And again, this was not about us being particularly worthy of acceptance, but rather exposes the reality of the racially-inscripted socio-economic divides. We were coming from a family, place, and experience that had given us a lot of resources as well as a different access to education. But our experience wasn't typical of other Black families in that area, at least not the ones on P.K. Yonge's waiting list. I don't think that waiting list boasted a lot of diversity.

Even amid this new "abundance" of Black folk in Gainesville, there were other dynamics at play at P.K. Yonge that still made it difficult for Faedra to feel like she really fit in. In addition to socioeconomics, part of this difficulty was related to the overall racially divisive nature of the school they attended (White students tended to socialize with other White kids and Black kids tended to socialize with other Black kids). But these were also compounded with the fact that Faedra and her sisters did not fit the mold of what some people think Black people "should look like" (that is, the erroneous expectation that all Black people necessarily exhibit a combination of dark skin, kinky hair, and broad features) and so, some feelings of displacement persisted.

Even when I went to Florida where there were far more brown people,

I was still always having to explain myself or assert my Blackness. I don't know if it has to do with Gainesville in particular and, perhaps, the highly segregated history of the city, but at that particular time, and at that particular school, problematic notions of what 'looked Black' persisted among Blacks and Whites, alike. Repeatedly, people didn't know how to 'place' me and my sisters. The idea of not being able to immediately identify me as Black was perplexing. I was like, 'What do you mean? I'm Black.' I didn't understand it. The very notion of color consciousness, which is something I write about a lot now in my scholarly work, was new to me. It wasn't until moving to Florida that I understood the way some people fixated on differences like "light skin" and "dark skin." In my early years growing up, I was always simply told by my parents that I was Black; the nuances were not emphasized.

And on occasion, Faedra felt she had to tell people—other children—that she was Black. This was especially important when she dealt with White children because she had to make sure they were comfortable with forming a friendship.

So I remember in the fifth grade a new person came to school. Her name was Shelby and I was having lunch with her and I remember saying, 'Shelby in case you didn't know I'm Black.' And I remember her chewing her lunch and eventually saying, "Oh that's okay. I had colored friends before." So it was always that kind of discomforting thing.

Two years after they arrived in Gainesville—with her father's residency complete—Faedra and her family moved back to Bothell and—at least for Faedra—an even more heightened sense of displacement. Because at this point issues of race, which still existed, were compounded by the fact that Faedra was also at an age where she was feeling physically awkward.

The bigger problem was in Junior High and the teen years. This was before Beyoncé, even before Vanessa Williams was Miss America, and before people were more open to valuing Black women and their beauty. I was getting no kind of attention, but I was getting a lot of ridicule and feeling displaced. I didn't think it was necessarily just racialized; I mean I was a little pudgy and a little nerdy, so regardless I didn't feel like I fit in. So it wasn't just because I was a Black child; those teenage years were awkward. Although, certainly, my feelings of physical awkwardness were compounded by the issue of feeling very isolated because I was Black. Just the day-to-day of being in Bothell, Washington was difficult.

The closest Faedra came to "fitting in" at that time was with her Mormon friends.

I had a small core of friends who, interestingly, were predominantly Mormon—members of the Church of Jesus Christ of Latter-day Saints (LDS). We were all in Honor classes together. These were my friends; they were nice to me. However, we sometimes had ideological clashes.

I remember in high school going to a friend's house and seeing a Dr. Seuss-like book—probably a grade school age picture book—that was created by someone from their church. And in the book were cartoon pictures that explained why different people in the world were living in different places—saying things like "God was really happy with these people who look like this and they lived over here, and God was not so happy with people who are naughty who look like this, and they were over here." I was trying to wrap my head around what I was seeing and reading; trying to understand the religious rationale behind what was clearly pointed racism. And trying to understand how my friends—good people—were interpreting this kind of material. It didn't make sense to me. And so [my friend] would try to explain it– and this was my very best friend—but it couldn't be explained away. I would just think, 'What are you being taught?' I think it wasn't until the 1970s that the Church of Jesus Christ of Latter-Day Saints opened up membership and positions of power to people who were Black. So I would say to her, 'So, before the 1970s, your church was basically saying that my grandmother didn't have a soul. Isn't that a problem?' These were the tensions and conflicts that I had to wrestle with—with people that were supposed to be my best friends! So this was the milieu in which I grew up.

It was still difficult for Faedra to find her place. Which is why her decision about the college she would attend was so important.

Spelman

A turning point for Faedra in her journey to *find her place* was Spelman College, an HBCU located in Atlanta, Georgia. Faedra's mother and several of her mother's family members and friends were Spelman graduates. Not surprisingly then, her mother wanted—expected—all of her daughters to go to Spelman. But—at least initially—all of her daughters did not agree.

My mother went to Spelman, my father went to Morehouse, and I think it was my mother's plan that every daughter of hers would go to Spelman. And we all did attend Spelman. None of us objected to going; but here's the thing: my mom was always talking about it, would always talk to you about it, ad nauseam, Spelman, Spelman, Spelman. And at first, I was like, 'I'm not going to Spelman! I'm going to Stanford, I'm going to Brown, I'm going to all these Ivy League schools!'

Mothers usually know their children—Faedra's mom was no exception. Realizing that her constant emphasis on Spelman was driving her daughter further away from her alma mater—and knowing how important it was that her daughter attend an HBCU (so why not Spelman?)—she finally got Faedra to agree to at least *visit* Spelman before she graduated from high school.

My Mom finally got smart with her tactics. I don't know who talked to her, but she shut it down; she stopped talking about Spelman. She said, "I'm not talking about it anymore, but you know all I want is for us to go for a campus visit. And we'll go for a visit to Spelman and I won't say anything else." And I said okay. My mom had dear friends there from her time at Spelman—in fact, one of the people teaching English was a friend of hers and I wanted to be an English major, so they arranged for me to visit that class. She also arranged for one of my older cousins, who was a sophomore at Spelman, to let me hang out with her for the weekend. We got to Atlanta on Thursday, I was hanging out on Friday, by Saturday I said, 'I'm not applying anywhere else. I'm going to Spelman!'

And Faedra did not submit a college application to any other school.

In hindsight, I should have thrown the net wider when it came to applying to schools, but by that point, Spelman was the only place I wanted to go. Growing up in the places I did definitely impacted how I got to Spelman . . . it [Spelman] gave me a sense of esteem I didn't have before. Look at the diversity . . . we don't all have to look this way or act that way; we don't all have to be Barbie dolls; there is no singular way of being or looking Black. Being at Spelman opened my world.

Her Place Among the Sisterhood

So, after her visit to Spelman, Faedra knew she wanted to be a part of the Spelman "Sisterhood." And her journey as a student at Spelman was broad and surprising and sweet and filled with nuances and twists and turns—from wearing long skirts, Oaxacan dresses, and Birkenstocks when she arrived on campus—to joining a sorority, becoming the coveted "Miss Maroon and White" [Miss Morehouse], and graduating with a degree in English. She absorbed it all and finally—at the end of her time at Spelman—began to find her place.

But first, she was dazzled by the diversity of Spelman's Sisterhood.

Talk about every shade and size of Black women from all over the world, from every faith, ideology, and political affiliation. The absolute diversity of all these Black women was so refreshing, so magical, and they were all bringing it! They were all brilliant and fabulous; and I felt, 'oh gosh, I'm so lucky to be among them.' That was affirming to me. I felt proud. I was rubbing elbows with all these women who I found so extraordinary; and I believed in The Sisterhood; and I found Sisterhood, and it was wonderful!

While the college experience is different for each person—and being a student at Spelman is no different—for eighteen-year-old Faedra Chatard her Spelman experience was really emboldening and affirming. It was everything she wanted it to be.

It was so wonderful that shortly after she arrived, she excitedly called her mother telling her about all of the new friends she made, boldly asking if she could extend her college career.

I was loving it so much mid-way through my freshman year that I called my mom and said, 'Mom can I stretch it out? Can I do this in five years instead of four?' I remember her laughing and me saying, 'But, I got, like, eight best friends!' which was so important to me, knowing my experience in grade school and junior high school and high school. And I remember my mother saying, "Okay, sure, you can stretch it out, but let's see how you feel towards the end." And she also said, ". . . and Faedra if you leave Spelman with one really good friend, you've done well." And today I have a lot of friends and amazing line sisters from Spelman, but I have one really dear, dear friend. And what a good friend she is. My mom was right; I did well.

Ultimately, Faedra graduated in four years. Those four years included being involved in student devised shows, serving as a member of Spelman's student government—and being elected Miss Maroon and White!

Miss Maroon and White: Miss Morehouse

Faedra came to Spelman as a freshman from Bothell, Washington, wearing *these big Mexican dresses, Birkenstocks*— looking very West Coast and "earthy." She soon discovered that *at many HBCUs, campus queens and their courts were a big thing.*

When you think of college queens at HBCUs, or at least at Spelman and Morehouse, it's something entirely different than what one may think of when one imagines "pageant culture." You also have to remember the history and significance of these pageants in contrast to, say, Miss America, or Miss USA or even small-town pageants. Vanessa Williams was crowned as Miss America in 1983—the very first Black winner since the pageant's inception in 1921. As Black people, young Black women, we have a history of being not included; not inscribed as being beautiful, intelligent, worthy of celebration. And this is the intervention that HBCU pageants have long enacted. Pageants at Black colleges and universities have been one way of celebrating the brilliance and beauty of Black womanhood; a way of celebrating Black women and placing them in a position of honor. They offer a platform for representation—on our own terms.

Faedra was intrigued by the Miss Maroon and White pageant and all that it represented. If there had been a bathing suit portion in the past, it was long gone; the emphasis now lay on talent, intelligence, a connection to the community, and legacy.

In terms of legacy, Faedra felt a direct connection as well since there was family history in relation to the multiple coronation courts that were part of the Maroon and White coronation network.

When my mother attended Spelman (she was class of '62), she was part of Morehouse's Coronation ceremony several times. She was Miss Torch (even the yearbook had its queen!), Miss Sphinx (representing Alpha Phi Alpha's pledge club), and, eventually, she was named Miss Alpha Phi Alpha. Her older sister, my Aunt Bean (class of '53), was First Attendant to Miss Maroon and White. And so I had long been privy to these folkloric accounts of these "royal" collegiate moments in my family.

As fun and nostalgic as the royal court experience appeared to Faedra, she had also heard the horror stories when it came to the Miss Maroon and White pageant: audience members booing or barking at contestants, rows and rows of people turning their backs on the contestants they didn't like—all kinds of dismissive antics, often proliferating with a domino effect.

You might as well have the Sandman with his cane pulling you off stage at the Apollo!

But still . . . she was intrigued. Faedra's intrigue eventually turned into something else for this self-described *relatively shy but blossoming* young woman from Bothell, Washington: she decided to run for Miss Maroon and White!

When I attended Spelman, I was growing into my own, learning to be comfortable in my own skin. I was trying to be comfortable dancing to the beat of my own drum. Again, I wore these big Mexican dresses, I wore Birkenstocks, I was real earthy. I was not, as they would say back in that day "fly"—I was not the one that people thought of as chic, or sophisticated, or "sexy"—or even particularly "cool." But that was okay. That was what was great about Spelman. I was accepted. I may not have been cosmopolitan, or chic, or whatever. But I was accepted as-is.

Now before her decision to run for Miss Maroon and White, a part of Faedra's blossoming had also been marked by pledging a sorority. During sophomore year, Faedra pledged and was initiated into Delta Sigma Theta Sorority, Incorporated. She was happy with her decision, enjoying the bonds she was developing with her sorors. Once she decided to run for Miss Maroon and White, however, those bonds would be tested.

It was sort of an unspoken but understood rule that if you're going to run for Miss Maroon and White—or anything, really, that would 'pit' you against someone else—well, Deltas don't go against each other. That breaks The Sisterhood. You have to be unified. You have to do it together. You don't do that. You do not do that! So, I told my best friend and line sister, Laura, that I was thinking about running for Miss Maroon and White. No one else had talked about running, and so I thought that I'd give it a try. She said, 'That's so exciting! Let's plan and we'll tell our sorors and line sisters!' And a few days later—we had not yet announced my intentions—Laura is at breakfast with a bunch of other line sisters and someone says, "Oh guess what? So and so (my other line sister) is going to run for Miss Maroon and White!" And this other line sister is a singer, she's very popular, beautiful, has the perfect little body—and is very cool—so, the whole package: smart and beautiful; magazine material. And I'm Faedra. And yes, I'm accepted, but I'm still "The Birkenstock girl." So my best friend has to say, "Well ladies, I think Faedra wants to run for Miss Maroon and White, too." And my line sisters, being very pragmatic, say, "Of course we love Faedra—but she can't be Miss Maroon and White! It can't be two Deltas—Delta's do not run against each other—and we already have the perfect candidate. Faedra 'beats to her own drum', and we love that, but she can't be Miss Maroon and White. She can't win." So Laura had to do the uncomfortable thing of coming back to me and having to share what our line sisters had said. Hearing all that was my only real painful experience at Spelman.

Faedra's feelings were hurt because she felt she was *just sort of being written off; it was like before; once again, I didn't fit in. I thought I had arrived at my Utopia, yet I still felt like I didn't fit in.*

Although the reaction of her sorority sisters hurt Faedra's feelings, it did not kill her spirit.

So, at first, I felt really dejected. And I began to doubt my ability to compete. I was never really trying to win per se; I just wanted to show that I was a contender—that I could compete among the best of them. I wanted to test my ability to navigate through that kind of pressure-filled experience. But then I started to doubt myself. And so I said, 'I understand; I'm not going to run.'

But her best friend, Laura, had her back. Although in supporting Faedra she, too, would be bucking tradition, she told Faedra, "You still have to run because I believe in you. If you want to do it, you have to know that you are just as capable and you are just as talented. If you want to run, I'll support you." Faedra appreciated the sacrifice her best friend was making. There was a serious risk of admonishment from other line sisters and "old head" sorors, but she didn't waver in her belief and support.

So with her own determination and Laura's support, Faedra decided to ignore the unspoken rule and run for Miss Maroon and White, anyway. At the very least, she felt like it would be a good experience in terms of stepping up to a challenge and she would be happy to simply not embarrass herself and, maybe, if she was lucky, she could even make it into the court of the eventual winner.

As expected, her sorors were not happy with her decision—it went against tradition. For Faedra . . .

It kind of propelled me further, creating more of a reason for me to run— it seemed like they were saying I wasn't good enough. Well, that is what they were saying. But I felt like I had something to offer, too. There's something about being discounted and dismissed. I'm very happy I decided to go ahead and put myself out there. It makes a good little story I can tell my daughter.

In the end, both Delta sorority sisters ran for Miss Maroon and White.

Faedra had to prepare for the evening gown competition, the talent competition, a question and answer segment, and a *little dance montages in-between the larger pageant segments.* It was work. A Morehouse man who was a "dancer in training" worked with Faedra several mornings a week starting at 5:30 a.m. *to teach me how to walk in heels.* Coached on the monologue by then-fellow Spelmanite, Cassie Davis (an actor who would later star in Tyler Perry's television sitcom *House of Payne* and its spinoff series *The Paynes),* Faedra had selected a unique dramatic monologue for her talent.

I did a piece from George C Wolfe's "The Colored Museum", a vignette called Git on Board.

The character Faedra portrayed in the piece is a flight attendant, Miss Pat, who takes the audience on a "Celebrity Slaveship" trip through African American history. She refers to the Middle Passage, the Civil Rights Movement, iconic figures such as Malcolm X, references pop-culture signifiers like Black music and the game of basketball—an assortment of tribulations and triumphs, a historical and cultural journey through tumultuous terrain. While the piece is funny, Faedra chose it because *it's also really, really deep; and it wasn't dancing, it wasn't singing I think it took people by surprise. It was material that they didn't expect in the Spring of 1991 during a collegiate pageant.*

Although not happy about the competition between sorors, the Sisterhood came through for both Faedra and her soror competitor.

A beautiful thing the night of the pageant was when some of my line sisters came backstage, they came to both of us, and fixed both of our hair, and looked at both of our gowns to make sure they were okay. I was happily surprised they were tending to me and fussing over me, too; and it was beautiful as it turned out.

Faedra *was* selected as Miss Maroon and White that night!

Her decision to run for Miss Maroon and White was a testament to Faedra of the depth of a genuine friendship, a symbol of her budding self-esteem, and a sign that she was finding her place in the world. And it left her without regret.

Of course, now the pageant it-self seems trivial—but not the lesson learned. Had I decided not to run I would have regretted it. I probably would have watched, and I would have said 'I could have done that.' It's a time I'm very proud to look back on knowing that I'm not haunted by the shoulda, coulda, woulda.

On hearing the decision that she was selected as Miss Maroon and White Faedra was happy—but also in shock. Her focus had not really been on winning, but having the courage—the gumption—to decide that she not only deserved to try but that her uniqueness could be celebrated. It was also about having the strength to assume the challenge of doing something that before she would not have considered because she felt so out of place.

Transitions

Spelman College allowed Faedra to find herself as an African American woman among the Sisterhood. Each experience at Spelman reaffirmed that. Now she had to find her professional place—what would be her life's work?

Faedra majored in English at Spelman, directing her energies towards becoming a teacher—a profession she believed she was destined for even as a child.

I was an English major at Spelman. When I left Spelman (after four, not five years as I had once envisioned!), one thing I knew is that I always wanted to teach. I didn't know what level; I just knew I wanted to teach. Even when I was little, my mom laughs about the fact that I would say 'I want to be a teacher.'

Faedra was also interested in theater, but not sure which path she should/would take. Writing and acting were both possibilities. While she knew that she was a good writer, despite her "blossoming" at Spelman, she did not believe that she could comfortably navigate the realities of an actor's life.

I loved theater but I was still relatively shy. And I knew that to be an actor your skin had to be much thicker than I knew mine could be because an actor's life is full of rejection; it's day-to-day rejection on the most basic level (you're "too this" or "not enough that"). So while I participated in student-developed celebrations and skits, I didn't formally pursue acting. Instead, I was an English major taking a lot of theater classes. Ultimately, however, I decided I would get a Master's (MA) in Theater after college, allowing me to teach in the field I loved.

Faedra chose a "reboot" theater program at Washington University in St. Louis (the year she applied the University was restarting a relatively small Master's program in theater) because *they were going to give me a full ride and a TA-ship. The fact that they were in the middle of rebuilding a previously defunct program was not significant to me. I was just impressed that it was going to be free!* Her choice of programs would ultimately lead her to something called "dramaturgy."

Dramaturgy

On her way to getting her Master's in Theater, with the help of two of her Washington University professors—and against the advice of her department chair—Faedra pursued an intern-styled fellowship as a professional "dramaturg." In doing so, Faedra was once again taking a risk to find her place professionally.

I had taken a lot of scholarly, academic classes to get my Master's degree. However, the professors I bonded with in that program were not the ones that prioritized research-oriented scholarship; they were the practitioners— my playwriting professor and a directing professor. These two would have me doing projects and production-related research for them. Near the end of my second year in the MA program, when I was about to graduate, both encouraged me to apply to a dramaturgy internship program in Washington DC at Arena Stage, this big regional theater. After all, they told me, "You have been working as a dramaturg." I had never heard that term before in my life! And they gave me this brochure, and each offered to provide a recommendation. The program was called the Allen Lee Hughes Fellow

Program, and they told me that the intent of the program was to bring diversity into the theater. They thought it would be a great opportunity for me.

But . . .

The chair of the theatre department strongly advised Faedra to skip the internship in DC and apply to graduate schools to get her Ph.D. instead. She considered his advice, did more research into dramaturgy, interviewed for the Arena Stage position, and when they offered her the position, Faedra grabbed it.

I was looking for 'real-life' experiences. I was like, 'but it's the real thing, it's life!' It was a prestigious opportunity. They had flown me in for a multi-day interview and activities, up against the other finalist, my competitor. I was there the whole weekend—and they picked me. I felt like I had to take the chance to see where this opportunity could lead.

Faedra was in DC for a year, *loving the work, loving working with artists, loving the experience of learning about play development, learning how to research and create packets of information and resources for the actors—*learning to be a dramaturg.

I answered significant questions, which can be especially helpful if a playwright is no longer living. I was doing all this research about the world of the plays for the ensemble and even though that is also within the director's purview, part of a dramaturg's job is to help bounce off ideas and gather information and be sort of an artistic respondent for the director and the actors. You also help with community engagement; you write the program articles, lead activities, help to promote discussions. You look at it from the perspective of the audience in addition to helping the director and actors. Every dramaturgical job is different depending on the play, what the demands are, what they need. A main central theme is that you're a bridge-builder for the audience. So you must determine what programming or assistance you can have in engaging them in the world of the play and the program. I loved it!

After the first year, Faedra was offered an opportunity to stay at Arena Stage, where she would be promoted to the role of literary associate. It was certainly worthy of consideration in light of how much she enjoyed her experience, and it paid benefits! But then again, Faedra's success in her initial stint as a dramaturg had caught the attention of others; thus, she was also offered a literary management/dramaturg position at Crossroads

Theater Company in New Brunswick, New Jersey. At the time, Crossroads was a full-blown regional theater and the most prestigious African American theater company in the nation. Both positions were compelling; and while the literary associate position with Arena Stage was familiar and felt more stable, the literary manager/dramaturg position felt like an important advancement. That being said, it was not offering any great benefits, it still wasn't that much money, and she would have to expect furloughs every summer. Nonetheless, the position at Crossroads had Faedra's heart.

I would be working under the amazing Sydné Mahone who was the director of play development there! I could be under her wing at this premier African American theater! And so I interviewed for that and I got it. And in terms of learning, it was all that I could have hoped for.

Faedra determined that at that time in her life her "place" was at Crossroads. She stayed for two years—with the benevolence of her parents.

It was a little safer because when I was on furlough, I had my parents help to support my dream and to live vicariously as an artist. They would help with my rent money; so thank you to my parents!

Then, after those two wonderful years at Crossroads, Faedra Chatard came to another turning point . . .

By this time I'm thinking, 'this is awesome, but I need some stability; I need some insurance; I need not to have to work at the Frog and Peach [as a restaurant hostess] in the summers to help pay the bills.' So that's when I decided to apply to Ph.D. programs with the goal of becoming a college professor. I wasn't really familiar with tenure at the time, but I knew it would be a more secure environment—and I could still work artistically with theaters as my schedule would allow. That was my goal.

So in her late 20s, Faedra applied to and was accepted into the Ph.D. program in Theater at Stanford University.

The focus of Faedra's Ph.D. was African American performance. When she articulated her intended focus to one of her professional mentors—her former boss at Arena Stage—he was less than enthusiastic upon hearing this news. He was thrilled about Faedra attending Stanford (he had written one of her recommendation letters), and as *an Emmy award-winning writer and scholar,* he had gone on to teach at New York

University (NYU)), but he was not impressed that Faedra's chosen course of study was African American performance. She remembers clearly how deeply it cut when he told her, "No, you're too good for that; you should do something like Shakespeare."

[It was as if he was saying] this is the model; this is the canon; this is what you should do because this is what's culturally acceptable. He thought that following what I wanted to do was going to limit me and be dismissed as not important. But I was like, 'Wait—this is important to me!' The truth of the matter is that now my chosen areas of study [Critical theories related to the study of Race, Gender, Class, and Sexuality within both staged performances and in the performance practices of everyday life] have been affirmed in many ways, and increasingly so. Contributing to these areas of knowledge has served me, my colleagues, my students—and all of academia—very well.

Nonetheless, Faedra acknowledges that the warning of her mentor was *impactful at the time:*

It made me question what I wanted to do, and, once again, I found myself acquiescing to the idea that someone else may know better. And again, the source of the wound was "friendly fire"; this time it was a mentor, a supporter, a Jewish scholar/artist who I thought would understand and who I trusted to have my best interest at heart. But I also knew what I wanted to do; so I decided to pursue what I wanted to do. I truly believe that if I had done what he suggested, I would not have the level of professional accomplishment and success that I have right now.

Faedra had found her professional place.

Professor Carpenter

As Faedra reached the point of ABD (All But Dissertation), having finished her classes with only her dissertation to complete, one of her professors suggested that she apply for an open adjunct professor position at the University of Maryland (UMD). It would allow her to finish her dissertation and have the inside track on a more permanent position there. Faedra took his advice, arriving at UMD to assume the role of adjunct professor as Faedra Chatard Carpenter—she had married her longtime friend, turned boyfriend, Donald Carpenter. They had met when she was still living in DC, before she had gone to California to pursue her doctoral studies, and before she had worked at Crossroads Theatre Company in New Jersey. When they met, however, they had quickly hit it off as friends; a friendship that lasted the test of time until, during Faedra's graduate studies at Stanford, they realized that they were destined to be *more* than friends. After dating for a year or so, long-distanced, Don proposed and so, after completing her coursework, Faedra returned to the DMV (the DC, Maryland, and Virginia area) and they married.

While successfully teaching as an adjunct professor at UMD, Faedra continued to work diligently on her dissertation and stay connected to the regional theatre scene within the DMV. When she began working as an adjunct, however, she couldn't help but notice that there were very few African American students in the graduate theatre program—as in *only one, and he was a Master's student. Still, at that time, he was probably only the second or third Black MA or Ph.D. student ever in that graduate program at Maryland.* However, much to Faedra's disappointment, he did not return for his second year; and it would be several more years before there was another African American student in the program.

After demonstrating her pedagogical aptitude—and the need for someone with her areas of specialty, the school subsequently invited Faedra to be a visiting professor. The visiting professorship was supposed to be for a year, but she was asked back for a second year. When another school inquired about her availability UMD responded by creating a tenure-track position for Faedra.

So that was lovely; it was wonderful to know that I was wanted. My journey as a teacher really started there. I used to feel a bit guilty about not having endured the pressures of a formal search and interview process; I was able to secure my tenure track position because I was already teaching in the program. But now I realize it's not that I didn't have an interview— but rather, unbeknownst to me, to all of us, I was actually experiencing an "interview process" of sorts: it's just that my process was almost a year-long, and entailed proving my value and contributions every day over a long period of time versus putting on my "best face" for 1-2 day interview process. So I came to realize that I was very fortunate with how things unfolded — definitely!— but that I also earned the opportunity to stay.

When Faedra began her tenure track position at UMD, there were no Black students in the MA/Ph.D. theatre program. It was not until her second year as a tenure track faculty member that Faedra had a chance to teach another African American Master's student; however, he was mentored by one of Faedra's colleague. Nevertheless, over time, the number of Black students in the program slowly increased, most asking to study under Faedra's tutelage.

I've taught at UMD for a little over 14 years now, and in the past 8 years, my department has witnessed tremendous growth. We've gone from having only one Black student matriculate—amongst all the active cohorts—to currently having five Black graduate students currently enrolled at the same time—and two Black Ph.D. students complete the program. Out of these, five are my advisees. I am thrilled and so proud! And two of my advisees are currently Ph.D. students, but they received their MA degrees under my guidance. Although they received coveted offers to pursue their doctoral degrees elsewhere, they opted to stay with me. What my advisees all have in common, however, is that they are tremendous scholars and tremendous people! They're all deeply invested in a sense of community and a sense of Sankofa—of looking and giving back. I am excited for them as well as inspired by them. Witnessing all that they are accomplishing does make me feel that my ability to mentor them, that being at UMD, has made a difference.

Not surprisingly, Faedra's favorite thing about being a professor *is my students.*

My students mean a lot to me; particularly my graduate students because I have formed a real connection with them. What I'm really excited about is that in the time I have been at UMD, an evolution of the African

American students in the graduate program has occurred. It took a while,
but gradually UMD became a place where African American students can
go and want to come to. I have wonderful colleagues and enjoy our interac-
tions, but I'm thrilled to be the advisor to my students—they feel like family.

Scholarly Writing

Having earned tenure and now holding the title of Associate Professor,
Faedra not only teaches, advises, and mentors her students, but her scholarly writing—addressing critical race theory and issues of identity in performance—has been significant and well-received. In articles, essays, and
interviews she has tackled difficult issues of race, gender, class, sexuality,
and identity *within both staged performances and in the performance prac-*
tices of everyday life.

Dr. Carpenter's book, *Coloring Whiteness: Acts of Critique in Black*
Performance (University of Michigan Press), received the Honorable
Mention for American Theater of Drama Society's John W. Frick Book
Award for the best book in American theater and drama in 2014 as well
as the Honorable Mention for American Society for Theater Research's
2015 Errol Hill Award for outstanding scholarship in African American
theater, drama, and/or performance studies.

Dr. Carpenter writes about art as a cultural expression, but also as
the performance of identity in everyday life. Her discussions of identity,
always interrogating the assumptions people make regarding others and
how this affects one's internal questioning about who they are, in many
ways, mirror her own struggle/journey to find her place.

An example of this is when Faedra wrote about a "nurse-in" that happened in a Starbucks coffee shop in Silver Spring, Maryland. Faedra wrote
a performance identity article about how breastfeeding is a contested performance of domesticity: on the one hand, *"It follows the social script that*
'I am a good mother' while at the same time others will judge you as this
'bad maternal body,' especially if you nurse in public because they perceive
that you are doing something that is deemed sexualized or inappropriate
within an American context.

I nursed both my kids, but nursing is a luxury. The notion is if you are
a good mom nursing your baby is best. But I had a private office at UMD;
I could pump; I had a fridge to keep my milk. But if I am working on my
feet at Walmart or in a factory, where am I going to do that? And when I
was nursing and not in my office, I—and other women—are often publicly

shamed with pointed looks, or even comments, when trying to nurse outside "acceptable parameters." I heard about a Starbucks on Cherry Hill Road [in Silver Spring, Maryland] where women were staging a nurse-in. A woman was nursing her baby—she was covered with a wrap—when the manager asked her to move to the bathroom to nurse. Nasty! So, thirty women came together, organized themselves, and descended on that Starbucks, and publicly breastfed in protest—domestic performance creating a show of resistance!

Dr. Carpenter also explores the problematic consequence of what she calls "presumed aural Whiteness," that is, the troubled concept that a Black person's use of Standard American English, or even the fact of their particular vocal quality may be equated to "sounding White." She provides a personal representative anecdote of this concept in *Coloring Whiteness*:

I write about theater, movies, and art as the performance of identity. In my book, Coloring Whiteness, I trace various symbols or motifs of Whiteness that Black artists use to interrogate ideas about what "Black" and "White" is—in doing so, many challenge all-too-common assumptions. One chapter opens up about aural perceptions and the "hearing of Whiteness." So, I describe how I was working as a dramaturg for a Black women's playwrighting group. I was pregnant with my son at the time and I was supposed to meet with this woman to help her develop her work. We couldn't meet on the initial date set, so I suggested we talk by phone. As a dramaturg, you ask a lot of questions. It's not my play so, hopefully, the questions will bring clarifying moments to you as the playwright. So, after reading this writer's work, the setting of her play seemed off to me. Her set descriptions painted the picture of the play being set in a hospital, but in other places, she insisted that it was a government office, so the descriptions didn't match. I first told the playwright all of the things I loved about the play, and then my need to understand her setting for the play. She was not having it. I persisted. She got really defensive and told me how a number of people who previously read the play did not raise the issue I had. Then she said, "But perhaps the problem is a cultural one—previously all the women who read the play have been Black women." I tried to be professional. The first thing I said, as calmly as possible, was, 'Just so you know, I am an African American woman, but I don't think my reading and interpretation is influenced by whether I'm Black or not.' She was quiet.

But let me just say the relationship got better; we met in person and when her play had its debut stage reading, she brought me flowers. It was lovely. The reason I included the anecdote in the book is to explore the question, so what was cueing her misinterpretation? What was the performance of identity she was reading, or not reading, that made her make assumptions about my Blackness or lack of Blackness? Because we do that. We all do that. There can be discussion about "He sounds Black," or "He sounds White," but you are going to always find someone who doesn't fit the mold. Bottom line, it's really about the training of your ear and how we literally learn how to speak, including the tenor and timbre and all those things that are gathered by our environment. It's not a racialized thing.

Coloring Whiteness is compelling, eye-opening, and thought-provoking on many fronts—not the least of which is the discussion of what Faedra refers to as "naturalized Whiteface"—pointing to Michael Jackson's physical appearance as evidence of her conjectures. For those who know baseball, similar observations and critiques have been directed towards former MLB player, Dominican American Sammy Sosa, and his changed physical appearance—marked skin lightening—in the last several years.

As much as I understand it and fall prey to the same impulse to pass judgment, we have to stop and realize that no one has the authority to be the arbiter of Blackness. When we ridicule people like Michael Jackson for changing their physicality, aren't we also then demarcating and limiting what Blackness could possibly be? Might that do more harm than good? So in my book, I talk about these perceptions of Whiteness, and the symbols that are used, and how Black artists use these ideas to demonstrate the complexity of identity. In my scholarly writing on performance, I am constantly asking, 'How do we perform identity?' As audiences and everyday life performers, what messages are we sending? What are we accepting? I often write about issues related to that. And I say in my book, upfront, this is not a book about White folks—it's a book about how Black folks use and acquire these ideas to explore things about ourselves; and, really, about how race and racism function.

Balancing
Having found her place professionally does not end Faedra's journey. Like most Black women, Faedra—the teacher, mentor, scholar, dramaturg, wife, and mother—has a lot for which she is responsible. Finding a way

to do it all well and have some time for herself—balancing—has been, is, and will continue to be a struggle.

Balancing is my biggest challenge—teaching, students, kids, husband, activities, and time for my own creativity—given all I want to do.

Finding Faedra's Creative Space . . . with the help of Gwendolyn Brooks

Is there more Faedra C. Carpenter wants to do?

Yes . . .

Although Faedra is an accomplished professor, dramaturg, wife, and mother, there is a creative spark burning within her yet to be satisfied— that of a creative writer.

Faedra was always a writer. She particularly liked to write poems—her fifth-grade teacher liked a poem she wrote about flags so much that she taped it to the door of her 5th grade classroom. Faedra's gift at writing poems was also something her mother appreciated and encouraged when she was a young girl.

When I was eleven—in the summer before the sixth grade—we were living in Gainesville Florida. One Saturday my mom called me from the library announcing, "Faedra, I need you to write a poem! Or do you have a poem?" I told her that I did not have a poem and asked her why she needed one. She told me there was a poetry contest and this very famous writer, Gwendolyn Brooks, was going to be the judge for the contest. My mom said, "and it's open to children, and you need to write a poem, and I'll come and get it!"

At the time Faedra did not really know who Gwendolyn Brooks was (*I was 11!*), but she enjoyed writing poetry; so she did as instructed and wrote a new poem. As promised, her mother picked it up and submitted it to the library. On the day the winners were announced, Faedra—in a *peach dress with ribbons in my hair*—and her mother went to the library for the announcement. Gwendolyn Brooks was present. After announcing the runner-up, Faedra Chatard was announced as the winner. And . . .

Gwendolyn Brooks gasps. We found out later that you were supposed to be sixteen, and I was only eleven and I won (laughs). There wasn't a big prize awaiting me; the prize was recognition from Gwendolyn Brooks. But what better prize could one ask for?!

Faedra continued her creative writing when the family moved back to Seattle. Every year from ninth through twelfth grade Faedra participated in the NAACP Afro-Academic, Cultural, Technological and Scientific Olympics (ACT-SO) Competition. The contest would start with the local competitions in Seattle. Every year Faedra went to Nationals in either poetry, oratory, or essay. In her junior year, she was awarded a national bronze medal in poetry, and she received the national gold in essay her senior year.

Faedra remembers her award-winning essay and recognizes now how it marks the birth of one of the themes in her academic writing: the exploration of African American identity.

It was about African American womanhood and beauty. I was greatly influenced by William Waring Cuney's poem "No Images."

Faedra knows the poem by heart:

She does not know her beauty, she thinks her brown body has no glory.
If she could dance naked under the palm trees and see her image in the river,

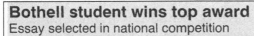

Bothell student wins top award
Essay selected in national competition

by Debby Smith
Citizen staff reporter

Faedra Noelle Chatard, a 1988 Bothell High School graduate, received two top prizes at the annual NAACP Afro-Academic, Cultural, Technological and Scientific Olympics in Washington, D.C.

The contest, for students in grades 9-12, consists of four divisions: humanities, performing arts, visual arts and science. These are further broken down into 21 categories.

Chatard took first place in the original essay category of the humanities division, winning $1,000 from the NAACP. She was also named the overall grand prize winner in the humanities division, winning a computer system from Digital Corp. and $3,000 from McDonald's Corp.

Chatard has entered the NAACP contest since ninth grade.

Every year she has proceeded from the regionals to the national competition.

"I'm lucky because I have done it every year that I was eligible," she said.

Last year she won the bronze medal in the poetry division and said she felt good about winning a gold medal in her last year of eligibility.

Her essay, "The Undeniable Beauty," she said, described the physical and internal beauty of black people and proposed that no group of people can be fit into a single mold, but rather each must be dealt with as an individual.

Chatard said she regularly enters writing contests.

"I'm a writer and that's just what I do. I love to write," she said.

"I've taken my writing very seriously and have spent years

working at it."

The subject of the essay, she said, was a reflection of the way she has been raised. She has always been taught to be proud of her heritage and to recognize the beautiful aspects of her race, she said.

Her writing coach for the essay contest, Geoff Gilmore, has helped her with her essays since she started in her ninth-grade year, when Gilmore was her English teacher.

"He has been a great coach," she said. "He wouldn't help me with ideas for my paper and never told me exactly what to do. He made me do it myself by asking me questions in answer to my questions to him. He made me think things through for myself."

On Aug. 31, Chatard will begin school at Spelman College, an all-girl university in Georgia, and

Monica Pihel photo

Faedra Noelle Chatard of Bothell with ribbon won in competition at Washington, D.C.

will major in English. For a career, Chatard said she hopes to be a psychiatrist or perhaps a broadcast journalist.

she would know. But there are no palm trees on the street, and dishwater gives back no images.

I literally did research about melanin or the broadness of our noses, what the physical features of many, not all, but many Black women are like, and explored the why in terms of anthropologic roots—it was a research paper, but very poetic—it addressed the "why" of physical differences while also celebrating Black beauty.

With that backdrop from high school, Faedra fully intended and believed that one day she would pursue her creative talents—writing creatively—in the same way that she eventually enmeshed herself in the academy. As yet that has not happened, which is disquieting to her.

It makes me sad, really. I feel like I had all this potential and I went safe and academic. I may have taken risks, but not enough. And so at this point, I'm pretty happy, but my greatest regret—the one regret that I'm not happy or proud about—is that I feel like I haven't fulfilled or appropriately pursued my creative talent. It's like being an actress. There is rejection in that, and I did not want to risk it. And the scholarly thing, especially once you get tenure and know people in your network, people may ask you to write a chapter in a book, it's no longer difficult to get that kind of recognition. So, certainly, I think getting tenure was great and the birth of my kids was absolutely the best life-changing experience of all, but when I think about my biggest regret at this point, it is that I lost or have not been exercising my creative talent. I have been good at cultivating other people, but I feel like I dropped—or, rather, threw that ball down—for myself. And although I can potentially pick the ball back up, I'm concerned that the creative muscle has atrophied.

It is more likely that Faedra's creative muscle has just been on hold while she tended to all the other life events that African American women tend to before they focus on themselves. Her novel is in outline form. The next step is giving herself permission to focus on something she wants to do and write the novel—and of course finding the time to do so.

Faedra's Advice:
What has Faedra gleaned from her journey that she wants to share? A few things:

Let's celebrate each other.

Faedra's daughter is the source of this piece of her advice:

I see this in my daughter—part of that self-confidence, and part of her celebrating other Black women, they go hand-in-hand. You can celebrate your friends' victories and someone's success as separate from your own. So you celebrate your community, you celebrate your friends, you lift each other up—as in "You Ain't Heavy, You're My Sister"—I believe in that.

*Which goes into her second piece of advice—don't worry about someone else—do **your** best.*

*But that means you can't be looking at your left and your right—comparing yourself to other people. You have to ask, what is **your** best, your fullest potential? One thing I like about having a daughter who is a competitive swimmer is that it is a sport that offers a great life lesson: don't be obsessed with "placing" one thru three, rather, what is **your** best time? Focus on that. And always improve on you. What is working to your full potential? And if you work to your full potential, then that is an automatic win. That is always winning. When you've done the best you can do, then try again and see how far can you go; how high you can go.*

So to put that in context for myself, I know right now I've done some things—I have tenure, I've written a book. All good. Now, what else can I do? I need to reach, and I need to continue to learn from those around me. Celebrate the victories that you have. Be triumphant in those and don't worry about Peter, Paul, June, and Jane—unless it's about holding their hand and bringing them up as well.

When Faedra became Miss Maroon and White back in college, she was shocked, but proud she had taken the risk. Today, she is finding her way back to that place where taking risks—within reason for a mother, wife, college professor, and dramaturg—is okay. And she seems to realize and acknowledge that her experiences while at Spelman may serve as a reminder of what she needs to do now.

Sometimes when I tell the story about becoming Miss Maroon and White, I think I need some of that back. Yeah, because right now I feel like I've checked some boxes, but I think I've gotten to a safe space—being a tenured associate professor at the University of Maryland*—and there are things that I want to do. I have a creative voice and a creative muscle that I need to begin exercising again. Even in my work as a dramaturg, I'm still in support of someone else's larger vision.

---

*Faedra has recently taken a position as an Associate Professor in the Department of Performing Arts at American University

My vision is of a young adult novel. I love young adult novels because similar to Family Theater, it's created for ages nine to ninety-nine. So it's not material targeted to just young people, but it is accessible for a young person. I have an idea that I've been mulling around for many years, inspired by my daughter, and I think about it all the time. But I have not yet made time or room because I'm too busy doing other things. But I know that's what I want to do. I have an outline and I've actually written the last line. I know how I want it to end, but I have that fear of not finishing, or failure, period. At Spelman, the fear of not placing did not exist for me. I was not fearful of not becoming Miss Maroon and White. I just wanted the experience. I wanted the process. It's so funny, I always talk to my students about "the process; process over product." But for the book I don't just want the process; I want to make sure that it's really good. So, there's the pressure of making it good. It's got to be good; it's got to do something at the end.

When I look back at the times when I just "did me" and I didn't worry about my decision—I wore Birkenstocks but thought I could still make the court of Miss Maroon and White; I decided to focus my Ph.D. on Afri-can American performance against the advice of one of my most influential mentors—because it was what I wanted to do—and I believe that approach has led to my successes and professional accomplishments.

Faedra Chatard Carpenter is far from completing her journey—and yearns to do more—maybe starting with the young adult novel. But she no longer feels out of place. Faedra is comfortable with who and where she is as she continues her journey.

I haven't achieved all that I could; I haven't arrived yet. I'm still on the journey.

ANGELA LAMBERT
LOVE IS AN ACTION WORD

The word 'love' is used freely and frequently today, among family, friends, and lovers. It is a word used in grief, happiness, in familial settings, and in moments of intense passion. Use of the word can have a deep-seated meaning as from a child to a parent, "I love you Momma" or can be thrown around to get more than you deserve, "But, baby, I looove you!" I often say Tina Turner had it right, *What's love got to do with it?* Does the fact that you love me justify beating and mistreating me, killing me, doing things you might not otherwise do, accepting behavior you might otherwise abhor and condemn, or simply failing to take care—of me, yourself, or others.

When used properly, *love is an action word.*

For Angela Jacqueline Lambert—abuse survivor, mother of two, political activist, teacher, and college graduate, returning to school in her 40s—the word 'love' is more than just a passive use of the word; instead . . .

Love is an action word. It's part of nurturing and it shows action. "I love you means" that you know that you are going to have a hot cooked meal, you have clean clothes, you have a place to live, you have shoes and the things that you need.

You care. And that is how Angela Lambert has lived her life. The youngest girl of eight siblings, with only a brother younger than she, Angela grew up *in a little town, little country town—El Reno, Oklahoma*, with her siblings and aunts and uncles and cousins, all living near to each other.

When Angela was six, she and her family moved to Oklahoma City after her mother discovered that Angela had been repeatedly molested by a teenage neighbor, a relative, who preyed on she and other girls in the neighborhood. Too afraid to tell her mother—having been threatened by her predator—her mother discovered her daughter's hidden horror inadvertently.

When my mother initially found out that I had been molested it was because she went to my sister's high school. She told us to wait in the car. I had gotten to the point where I couldn't hold my pee, my bowels, or anything. When my mom came back and saw what happened she said, "Ann, what are you doing? Why do you keep doing this?" I said, 'I don't even know,' and she took me to the emergency room. The doctors in the emergency room told her I had been ripped . . .

If that is hard to hear, imagine Angela's experience at 4 years old.

Once her two older siblings arrived at the hospital to be with Angela, her mother's mission was clear: she left to kill the rapist—her nephew; her sister's son.

Born in 1969, Angela lived in El Reno, Oklahoma with her mom, dad, two brothers, and two sisters. Her father worked with the railroad, in the oil field, and was a diesel truck driver—*wherever there was work*—and was therefore not home every day. Angela had four older siblings from her father's first marriage, her oldest brother being 20 years older than Angela.

Closer to her little brother in age than any of her other siblings, Angela was a self-described *little tomboy.*

I was with them shooting their bb guns and running the railroad tracks. The only thing I wouldn't do was catch crawdads. They caught them; I'd cook them.

Cooking came naturally to Angela—boasting that she was the best cook among her siblings—having been taught by her mother and grandmother when she was only four or five. So when not running the country roads of El Reno with her brother, Angie loved to cook. Her mother owned a café in El Reno where Angela worked clearing tables and taking orders even as a youngster.

It was like a little juke joint, serving soul food—fried chicken, hamburgers, pork chops, and some days she would have a blue plate special. I waited tables; I could take orders. I was a little girl, but children worked then, you knew what to do and how to do things. I didn't mind. I was a tomboy, but I preferred to be up under my mother and my grandmother. So whatever they were doing I was fine being with them.

Although her paternal grandmother lived 40 minutes away in Bridgeport, Oklahoma, Angela was close to and clearly spoiled by her.

Every weekend, my grandmother was coming to us or we were going to her. She and I had a special relationship. There was nothing that I couldn't ask for or anything she wouldn't find a way to let me do. If I didn't like what was being served for dinner—you know how back in the day they would eat wild food and I just wasn't a fan—I would call my grandmother and let her know 'they over her eating so and so'. She would tell me to put so and so on the phone and say, "go get my baby some chicken," or "go get my baby . . ." whatever I wanted. So she spoiled me. And then when everybody was away from home, she said, "Ain't nobody there baby; you gonna have to learn how to cook."

So whenever I saw her, I would be up under her in the kitchen watching and helping her—making dumplings or turning the ice cream churner for ice cream if that is what she wanted—it didn't matter whether it was cold or hot outside.

Angela seemed always to be with her mother and/or her grandmother, watching, helping, learning. She enjoyed being there—even if she didn't dare interject her own thoughts into adult conversation.

Even back then when kids were seen and not heard and Mama was in here talking amongst the ladies, I'd be sitting right around the corner with my back to the wall—ears wide open! I was listening to everything—from how to cook this to doing this and so and so happened and this and this. And the minute she needed something, I would jump up and run into the kitchen. If my mother said, "Oh I forgot to get so and so," I would have jumped to the kitchen and be coming out with it. Before she could get up, I was handing it to her. And she'd say, "Oh, thank you, baby." And I'd go right back and sit down. I just wanted to be around Mama.

Angela's neighborhood was friendly and familiar—many of her aunts and other family lived nearby.

On the way to my house I would go through the alley past Aunt Alice's house, and around the corner passing Aunt Salida's house. Family was all in the area. On our block, there were two aunts. And then through the alley, there was an aunt and then on the next street there was an aunt. The neighborhood school was maybe about five blocks up behind my Aunt Stella's house—she kept me and my brother, who was too young for school, during the day. Aunt Stella would be watching when I was going to school for half a day. I was in Head Start then and going in the afternoons.

One afternoon, while Angela was in kindergarten, Aunt Stella sent her to her Aunt Viola's house to get something—*I can't remember what it was.* She just had to walk through the alley a short way to get there, passing another aunt's house along the way. The rest of the story—even the short version is horrific.

I was walking over to my Aunt Viola's house to get whatever my Aunt Stella wanted. When I passed Aunt Allison's little disconnected-drive-garage by her house I thought I heard something. But I kept going. When I came back that way, I realized I did hear something, because he was there. He was in there. "He" was Eckard John, my Aunt Viola's son over whose house I went to pick up whatever Aunt Stella wanted. So when I was coming back, he was there and he said, "Get in here!" And he snatched me in there.

There were four other young girls in the garage—all of whom Angela knew. When Angie screamed, he threatened to kill her. He raped all of the little girls that day, including four-year-old Angela. While she was not sure what had happened—*I didn't know anything about sex at four years old*—she was scared and in pain and afraid he would kill her if she told anybody. But she did think about telling, until . . .

I was so afraid, but I still thought about telling somebody. Then his sister Cynthia after the fact (deep sigh)—I don't know if it was a day or two later—she said, "Angie, I promise it won't happen again." So I took her word, which is why I didn't say anything.

While Angela does not doubt that Cynthia's assurances were well-intentioned, she would soon realize that taking her word was a mistake. She was molested a second time by Cynthia's brother—within a few blocks of home, in her aunt's garage.

I was just a bloody mess. A bloody mess. So I went home, and Mama hadn't got there. Neither had any of my siblings, so, I cleaned myself up and did not tell anybody.

Happenstance, the physical consequences of the abuse, and her mother's wrath ultimately brought the assaults to an end.

So the next day Mom had gone to the school for my sister. Me and my older brother were waiting in the car. I said, 'I got to use the restroom.' And Jack said, "You already used the restroom." And that's when my bowels let loose. Mama came out there and said, What's going on with you? I think I need to take you to the emergency room." That's what she did and that's when the doctor came out and told her that I was just ripped up. So that's when I told her what happened. I had never seen my mother cry. When I told her what happened to me, she had this look about her that you knew . . . I knew something was going to happen—when she got that look . . .

No police were called. Angela's mother left the hospital.

Shortly thereafter, Angela and her family moved from El Reno to Oklahoma City. Her physical injuries healed, and for almost nine years Angela had no memory of what happened to her when she was four years old, or how her mother responded.

I suppressed all of this until I was like 13 years old. My childhood memories were for a time only of Oklahoma City. We left El Reno quick, fast, and in a hurry. Mama got over here and found a house to get us out of there. At 13 years old what happened to me started coming back in increments—like Sybil.

Even without necessarily knowing why, Angela was afraid in El Reno.

Until we moved here, I felt scared in El Reno. I didn't feel safe. So moving here, I felt safe. And I think that was a part of the suppression. It's like I was saying, 'So I can go on like this didn't happen.'

While she felt safe once they moved to Oklahoma City, Angela got a reputation for and believed herself to be *really mean*.

Once we got to Oklahoma City and I felt safe I was really mean, which meant I was in a lot of fights. I wasn't intentionally mean, but I just wasn't taking any stuff. If something went down and it wasn't right, I would make it right. Because I wasn't going to be violated anymore—physically, emotionally, or whatever. I wasn't going to be taken advantage of anymore. I was very defensive, very adamant: you are not going to knock this off my shoulder, you are not going to cross this line, none of that.

I have always been very vocal. If something was wrong, I would let it be known. It's something I feel I must do. If you allow someone to speak to you or treat you any kind of way that's how they will treat you—that's what they will do. If you give the person the opportunity, if you allow them the opportunity to speak to you or treat you any type of way, that's how they will treat you.

So at that time, you couldn't say nothing to me that was to the left without me bringing it right back to the center. I was very short-tempered; just wired. And my mother would say "Ann, don't let things that happened to you make you a bad person." She would talk to me as if trying to talk me through it: "Ann don't let what happened make you a bitter person or a bad person; Ann, don't always judge people because of what you have been through." She was just trying to talk me through it. It has helped in hindsight; but at the time, when I did not really know what she was talking about because I had suppressed it, no, it didn't help.

However, some of Angela's short-tempered meanness had a purpose—protection.

Since I was molested, I always was adamant about what a man/boy could/would do to me. Even as a young girl—8-12 years old, I would not allow any misbehavior by men and boys—this was even before the memory came back.

When Angela's memory began to return when she was 13 years old, her first memory was of being pulled into her aunt's garage. As she began to realize what might have happened, Angela was both deeply troubled and somewhat resentful of her mother because she thought nobody had done anything. When she asked her mother what happened, she would not tell her. However, still the quiet helpful child, able to listen to adult conversations, Angela ultimately realized that there were deep dark secrets in her molester's family—secrets the mother of her molester refused to acknowledge—that began to help her answer some of her questions.

My Aunt Viola was in denial. She said he hadn't done anything. Even when her daughter told her, 'he's doing this that and the other to me;' even when her son told her he was doing this, that, and the other, she wouldn't listen; even when her son would beat her unconscious and knock her out, she wouldn't acknowledge what had happened to him or that he was molesting his sister and his brother or do anything about it. And then hearing my mother and the others trying to convince my aunt to tell the truth about her children's upbringing made me think of what happened to me. That was the trigger.

Angela remembered more about what happened in her aunt's garage . . .

And I asked my mother, 'do you remember me telling you that Eckard John molested me?' She said, "yeah" but little else. My mother would never tell me what happened. She didn't go further with it. I later realized she was trying to protect me.

The "later" when her full memory of what happened returned was when Angela was 15.

The trigger for my memory was me getting pregnant at 15. I found out I was pregnant and as I began remembering that I had been molested and raped as a child, my mental state was such that do you know I was actually thinking that's who I was pregnant by—even though I had a boyfriend and it was 10 years before. It had me so confused and in such a mental state that it was incredibly crazy.

However, when Angela and her mother went to visit the mother of her baby's father, it all came flooding back.

I told my mother I wanted to keep and raise the baby; so we went to the baby's father's house to talk to his mother. After we returned home, for some reason I began to remember my mother going to my aunt's house and almost killing Eckard John (EJ). It was my mother going to the baby's father's house and supporting me at that time that triggered the memory. She was helping me, and I remembered what had happened. I said, 'Mama, when I was four and got raped and molested did you go to Aunt Viola's house and have EJ in the middle of street with a gun in his mouth? Viola was begging you, "Don't kill my son!"' She confirmed my memory of what she had done. I realized I saw what happened . . . by the time we got to my Aunt Viola's house from the hospital that's what was going on. Mama had snatched him out of his momma's house and had him in the middle of the street with a gun in his mouth, with his mother crying and pleading with my mother not to shoot him.

Angela's mother did not shoot her predator, but the memory restored her faith—especially in her mother.

Before that, I had been resentful. I loved my mother and always wanted to be up under her. But it was some resentment. I began to understand why she often told me, "Angie, you just alway been so strong; so resilient and strong—always taking care of everybody."

Pregnant @ 15

Angela had been 'taking care of everybody' to some extent, which made her pregnancy not as difficult as it might otherwise have been.

I got pregnant at 15 and had her at 16. I don't see it as having a great impact on me even at that age because I was already taking care of children, so it wasn't like it was something I didn't know how to do. It started with the two sets of children my mom had. I have nieces and nephews that I have raised. My siblings would bring their children home and leave them with Mom, and I would take care of them so my mom would not have to—me and my brother Jack.

Once Angela's daughter was born her brother and her mother were very supportive—financially and with their time.

Jackie has always known how to drive; he has always worked. He was always very supportive—he was my support system. Then my mother was very supportive, helping me take care of my daughter. I was still in high school—I did hair to help support me and my baby—so my mother would keep her while I was in school or working.

Because of her mother's support, even with all of her responsibilities, Angie was still able to enjoy being a teenager.

I was allowed to go out and do things. We used to go to Taco Bell and McDonald's and the roller rink. across the street from Cartwrights Barbershop right there on 23rd between Coltrane and Bryant. And we used to go down to the Tower Theater. So, I did get to do a few things.

Enjoying her teen years was fine although not Angela's primary concern. Angela was dedicated to her baby and finishing school—both promises she had made to her grandmother.

I really didn't want to do anything but stay home and raise my baby. My grandmother passed right after I had my baby. She told me, "Ann, whatever you do, raise your child." I took that to mean "raise your child; don't you leave your baby with nobody." She said, "You finish school and you raise your baby." So that's what I did. She was telling me not to let anyone else raise or be responsible for my baby.

Loss . . .

Angela's Grandmother

Angela's grandmother—the one who spoiled and doted on her and on whom Angela could call if she needed anything—moved to Oklahoma City so that she could have surgery. Angela was happy about the move because she was about to have her baby and her grandmother would be there. Unfortunately, the surgery was not a success. And although her grandmother was able to see Angela and her new baby, shortly after the baby's birth, she would die.

She was in her 70s and had come to Oklahoma City from Bridgeport, Oklahoma in March or April to have surgery, specifically to get a pacemaker. She left the hospital and went to rehab. After my baby was born in June, I would take her up to the rehab place to visit my grandmother. She was still talking and everything. But she didn't get better. Something went wrong—I think she got bad medical care. I do. One thing led to another and she died in August. Her death was a huge blow.

Angela describes her grandmother as the person who has had the greatest influence on her life so far.

My grandmother married my grandfather when she was 14. When he passed in the 70s, she never remarried. They had 140 acres and she worked that land; and we still have the land. We never lost the land. They raised potatoes and different things—even after her sons left home, she continued to work the land. I took from her being strong within yourself. To me, it wasn't like you just have to run off and get married. You can be your own woman and stand your own ground—regardless of what society says. She had her first child when she was 16, so she was not judging me when I got pregnant. "You haven't made a mistake; your baby is a blessing," she told me. Always, regardless of the situation, there was some good in it. She always spoke on the positive. She didn't down me about anything. I was always a full-figured girl, and she had no problem with that. When I was selling Girl Scout cookies, she made sure I was number one. She made sure I had the grandest dresses; the grandest whatever, I was going to be that girl. She was going to make sure. She always encouraged me. Always. She was just good to people, period. I try to emulate her.

Angela's Mother

The loss Angela experienced when her grandmother died was compounded by another loss several years later. Angela's mother—the person whom she always wanted to be near—died. Although Angela is frank in her assessment of the cause of her mother's illness and death, she was devastated.

My mother died when she was 63. She was really stubborn about addressing health issues. And her diet—she was still eating plantation plates— chitlins, pig feet, pigtails, and all of that—and she loved pop. She would drink Sprite and eat ice cream. She had diabetes, and wasn't taking care of herself, but did not die from it. She went to the hospital a couple of times regarding her diabetes. One of her stays ended up being like a month. She was always a full-figured woman, and then she started dropping weight. The last time we took her to the hospital for treatment of diabetes she had an aneurysm and died. That was 1997.

Angela's Daughters

After Angela's daughter ShaDellia was born, Angela finished high school and focused on supporting and raising her daughter. Angela met the man

I thought was my first true love in 1987 and they were married. Five years later, in 1992, Ambrosia was born. Angela and her husband separated in 1994 and were divorced in 1999. Angela had a pre-teen and a toddler to raise on her own. Her biggest concern was making sure her experience was not theirs.

When they were young, I worried all the time about my daughters being molested. All the time . . . all the time. I was always very open with my daughters about my experience as a child. I never ever hid that I was molested or any of that from them. Even in front of my brothers, I told them if a man or woman touches you that is unacceptable, and you have to let me know. They never got to spend the night away from home.

Her daughters seemed to understand.

Between my oldest daughter's birth and meeting and marrying my youngest daughter's father, ShaDellia today tells her friends, "I never saw men in our house or hanging around my momma." That was intentional. Because getting involved with somebody and knowing that he was going to be around my girls, I just couldn't do.

There were consequences for Angela personally. What she describes as the *wall* she put up never allowed anyone to get particularly close. There was one particular potential relationship that suffered because of the wall.

That's what happened with Tracy. I put up that wall. It kept me from dating . . . The wall was/is a defense or protection mechanism for me and my girls. I don't regret the wall as far as the way the journey has unfolded—although it kept me from a relationship with Tracy, but I can't say I regret it. I had to protect my babies. I'm grateful for my babies because they make me accountable.

Angela's protective nature had a positive residual affect for the community. Angela's house became known as the safe house—for family, friends, and those in need—hoping to help get people out of harm's way.

I was always the safe house. My oldest daughter had friends—a girl and boy who were sister and brother—who were getting beat by their father—the mother was as well. No sexual abuse, just physical abuse. Their mother would come to my house, and I would tell her she needed to get out. But she would say, "I don't have nowhere to go." One day the little girl went to school and her father had beaten her so bad ShaDellia called me and said,

"Momma I don't feel good; could you come and get me and Reesy?" I knew then that something had happened. So I called her mother and asked her to call the school and check Reesy out to me. She said ok. And so I went to get them. He had beat Reesy something terrible. So I told her we would go pick up her clothes and she would stay with us. She was afraid to go; afraid he would beat her mother and/or me. I told her, 'well he's not going to beat me up!' So we get to the house and her mother and father are both there and he's cussing and ranting. So I went in and told them to calm down so we could get Reesy's stuff and go or we could call the police. His mother's sister had come to get Reesy's brother. I told her, 'We got to take the children out of here.' So we did that. Reesy ended up staying with me until her mother split from her father and she went to stay at a woman's shelter—but it took her three months to do that.

In addition to the love of her grandmother and mother, and the birth of her children there have been several triumphs in Angela's life. First and foremost . . .

Being in my right mind. Because some people going through what I've been through would make them crazy. It's because standing my ground and knowing that I'm worthy of whatever it is I desire—being able to raise my children regardless of the fathers—regardless of my past; always being protective of them. Not putting me first, putting my children first—whether I missed out on a good husband, love, or whatever. They were first. That is my greatest triumph—knowing I'm in my right mind and that I always put my daughters first. That makes me triumphant.

After Angela raised her children, having done everything she needed and wanted to do in that regard, at 40+ years old she went back to school, getting a bachelor's degree in business *just to challenge myself and reinvent myself.* The process of getting her degree was enlightening.

Going to school and hearing things and reading things and seeing things, it makes you see the world in a whole new light. The education system is like any other system in America. It only works for us so much. For Us—as in people of color—it's going to only work so much. But for them [White folk] it works however they desire for it to work. It is said, "you can get a degree in basket weaving, as long as you get a degree." That works—that's true—for them. But for us, we better be the expert, the specialist, in whatever it is. The "American Way" does not work all the time; it does not work that way for everybody.

Recently, Angela has turned her attention to teaching—preschool and kindergarten. She sees problems. Among them, what she characterizes as a 'school to prison' mentality as manifested by the over-emphasis in many grade schools on children staying *on the yellow or blue or whatever colored line* when they are in the hall between classes.

Walking the yellow line: in prison, they have to walk a line. It is a school to prison mentality they are passing on to the children. They don't want them to learn. They are not setting our children up to be able to be successful at learning. Some of these kids lack guidance and structure at home and come to school out of control; others succumb to peer pressure—acting out like their classmates. You realize that there is a bell when you go to bed in prison, and a bell when it's time for lunch. The same thing is true in school: there is a bell in the morning, and afternoon, and evening. If we took the time to give them a hug, encourage, and lead them in a different way we would have a different outcome.

In our community, if you don't know how to build a relationship with our children, you don't need to be around these children—I don't want you to be around our children—whether you're a police officer or a teacher, whether you're Black or White. If you don't know how to develop positive relationships and how to do it with finesse and grace, I don't want you around my children.

Reflections

In the first 50 years of her life Angela has had the opportunity to observe much and has some thoughts and reflections:

Dumbing down

It's heart-wrenching to know they have watered us down and dumbed us down so much. I can see it even on television—and the subliminal messages we receive. From the 70s all the way to now, we—people of color—have been portrayed in a negative light; and it's time for it to stop.

Change

I have volunteered and I try to do things in the community to help. Each of us individually has a responsibility. I think even the ideology that we previously embraced—it takes a village—is broken. And that's where we have to get more people involved. There are certainly highly educated people who can do the job. But we also need people who just have that tact and candor that allows them to reach children. And we need more facilitators and educators who have those abilities, including the ability to nurture; that is what has been snatched away from our children. We need nurturers. Seven out of ten children in our grade school classrooms have not had that nurturing.

Parenting

When Angela says, *love is an action word*, it is not just a catchphrase to be adopted by others without more. She has specific guidelines for what we must do to make that phrase a reality.

Love is an action word. It's part of nurturing. It shows action. It means that you know that you are going to have a hot cooked meal, you have clean clothes, you have a place to live, you have shoes and the things that you need. That was my main focus for my girls—they never had to come home and worry about the lights, water, or gas being off. Because we were going to survive.

For Angela, the "action" part was a priority and she believes it must be a priority to both provide children with a sense of security but also as a way to model behavior.

That was my priority. To show them this is what you do. This is what you did. You don't have a man in and out of the house. This is what you do. You cook every day; when you have a child you cook. You are present. You show up at that school; you interact with their teachers, the committees, the PTA. You involve your children in sports and different things that they want to do—in the choir, in baseball and gymnastics, cheerleading. Whatever it is, you be involved.

It all boils down to being present.

Be present. That is what I would advise any young woman. Don't just put them in it—you must be present with them. I worked in the school system, so I could take my daughters to school and have dinner ready by the time they got out of school. I was home by the time they got out of school so they were not latchkey kids. There might have been a time or two when I was not right there when you got out of school, but I was right behind you.

It is about understanding your reality.

I had to have an income. And I did it. I was working in the beauty shop doing hair. So I said let me go drive a school bus. I can take them to school, get off the bus, go do hair, cook, go back and get them out of school, and we are all at home. I just figured out how to make it work so I was here. Especially when my baby Ambrozia got in school. My mother kept her until she went to school. I was working in the shop full time but knew I needed to be available to my kids. So I started doing hair at home, driving the bus, and making sure I was home for them with a hot meal. I did that until Ambrozia was in 5th grade and ShaDellia was a senior in high school.

I did hair to make it through high school. It was survival. When curls came out and I knew how to do a Jheri curl in 30 minutes—out of my house or I would go to your house if need be. I did what I needed so that we had what we needed, and my children never went without.

Regrets

Predator

One of Angela's regret involves her predator.

I wish I had tried to—before the forgiveness—I wish I would have been more of an advocate about molestation and tried to obtain information about the statute of limitations against that predator. Because I see where my mother not saying anything and his mother not saying anything allowed him to damage so many lives. That is a big regret for me—not putting it out there and getting him the rap sheet and all of this. The irreversible damage that I suffer and that others may have suffered and still suffer; I probably could have changed that reality. I regret not doing that.

She knows she is not culpable.

I know I am nowhere at fault. I will take some accountability, but I'm not a fault, because I didn't tell him to do it, I didn't encourage him. The accountability is for not speaking up. The silence. I'm accountable for that. And I think that is just silence. I was too caught up in my life; in maintaining for me and my children. I didn't want to expend my energies on that. I had to expend them where it was most important to me. But I thought about looking into the statute of limitations and trying to get him charged. I thought about it, just didn't do it. I regret my silence.

To give the person who molested Angela as a child much space in her story would do a disservice to Angela's resilience, forgiveness, love, caring for others, and her life of good works. Suffice it to say, she encountered him a few times in her life before he died. He taunted her until he saw she was not afraid. On one occasion . . .

. . . he comes up to me one day and says, "You the only one that didn't let it break you." I thought to myself, 'break me?' He said, "you the only one who didn't get strung out on drugs or ended up in a mental hospital; you the only one that raised your own children." And I'm thinking 'Wow! You would do that to someone to see if that would break them." Is that not a sick person?

Despite this encounter and with full memory of all that had happened to her as a child, four or five years after her daughter Ambrozia was born, Angela realized that the only way to fully move forward was to forgive her predator.

My youngest daughter was born in 1992. Probably about 1996—it was before Momma passed—I decided I had to forgive him. Before that I had not had anything to do with him, but to get myself straight and centered, I vowed I could forgive him and wish him well. I did that. It was for my peace of mind; I knew he was sick.

He was a pedophile who was never arrested. He died a violent death.

A Better Life for My Children
Good parents usually want their children to have more than they had, to have a good life. Angela is a good parent and has wanted that for her children. She expresses regret in not giving them more than she has.

Although I've always been able to provide for my children, I kind of regret not giving them a better life. They always say, "Momma you always gave us everything. You gave us more than some children with mommy and daddy at home. By the time we were sixteen, we both had cars!"

Angela Today
Angela Lambert has certainly been through the fire—since she was a small child. As a result, she recalls a time when she was *very very broken*. It was partly because of what she had been through, but also the

disadvantages—not based on her life choices—but how society discriminates against women, Black people, and *because I'm full-figured*. But she has ascended from the depths of despair stronger, more confident, healthier . . . and yes, still very protective.

I think I'm more confident with who I am. I'm okay with me, inside and out. Because I use to not be ok with me on the inside. I wouldn't say I was happy about being full-figured; but I didn't let it stop me. Whatever I wanted to do, I did: dance, dress, travel.

And I think that is just the struggle of it—the psychological damage—and overcoming that; being a whole person and being okay with me, and being ok with the past. That's who I am and I'm ok with the damage, that it left the scars. I'm ok with my scars; I didn't used to be ok with the scars. The rage only surfaces when it is provoked—it only comes to the surface if someone challenges me or attempts to hurt me or mine. That is why I try to stay even-toned and calm. I don't like the part of me that rages because I don't know where it might lead. It's still there; it's still a scar. And so it can come to the forefront, but I do what I do to the extent that I can to avoid that.

Advice
Angela has three major pieces of advice based on her journey so far:

Experience Life With Your Children

I would say to any young mother, remember to experience life with your children. If you want to get an education, get an education while they are getting an education. I think I should have tried to continue my education while they were getting their education. It may be difficult; but it's doable, it's been done. That shows your child that you are not asking them to do something that you're not doing. I was raised in a time when you do as I say, not as I do. That does not seem to work today. Rather, it seems now that to get a child to follow in your footsteps, or to take you at your word, you have to walk that walk in front of them. Also, if it's something you want to do, do it to better yourself at that time. There is no need or reason to wait.

And most importantly try to think of ways, to be present. You may have children at home and have been working on doing things for your child or children, but you're not present. So we must figure out ways to be present in our homes for our children at all times. With my girls, every day, Sunday through Thursday, they had a home-cooked meal with me. Friday,

Saturday, leftovers, take out, or whatever. But it is important to actually sit down at your table and have a meal together with your children.

Put us and ours first

As women, beginning with our ancestors—from the time we were taken and put on the ship and brought here to the present day—we have been taught to put other people first—our families, our children, and our husbands. All of them were stripped from us by the slave masters so we could nurse their children and clean their homes. We have had to put others first. We must get to a place where we put ourselves and ours first. That can only happen if we buckle down and stop trying to keep up with the Joneses. Create your reality. Speak your reality; be present in your reality—with your children, with your husband, with your family, with yourself!

I cannot always say why parents are absent. Sometimes it is because of a drug problem; or gambling, or something else. Sometimes its parents working so much they don't have the time it takes for their children. The reality is that if they are working for $7.50 an hour—as many parents must—they have to work all the time! Whatever the reason, we as individuals and as a community need to deal with it.

Modeling and Mentorship & Standing Up for our Children

Young people need to have peers who do the right thing. They can ignore us and what we do by saying, "it's just an old-fashioned way of looking at it." So having contemporaries who model positive behavior is important.

However, we also want to create some type of mentorship for young ladies and young men. It should be a mentorship program that is a part of their schooling as early as the kindergarten and first-grade—we have to engage our children earlier rather than later—that will help direct their attention to making sure our babies are reading and learning.

Finally, we need to stand up for our children. They are suspending these elementary children at an alarming rate—especially our kids. If little Johnny does it, little Johnny just needs a time out because little Johnny is going to be okay; little Johnny is going to do great things. But if it's little Jermaine, the rules are different. The police may be called. It seems that the answer to any problem with man woman or child who is Black—call the police.

We are a great people. Leave us alone and let us do, we will be an unstoppable empire.

For Angela, it is not just about saying, but about doing—it is about action.

Angela Lambert is Love in action!

GINGER CAMPBELL
FOLLOWING HER PASSION

Ginger Campbell's path was never intended to be traditional—and it has not been.

I already had my Grammy acceptance speech and my Oscar acceptance speech written and rehearsed before I was eighteen!

Raised with her sister Holly on a farm in the small village of Paw Paw, Michigan until she was ten by her Aunt Bea—who called her "Ginger" rather than her given name of Mary-Lynn—Ginger Campbell was naturally attracted to her surroundings.

I was very into anything kind of farmish . . . we had cows and horses, and my dog had puppies twice a year; so I was basically little Miss Farm Animal.

Her time on her aunt's farm infused Ginger with a life-long love of nature and the broad outdoors . . .

I loved it, yeah! Now I like being in nature. I like going hiking and stuff like that because I'm used to that outdoorsy kind of thing.

Of her name change, Ginger says Mary-Lynn *never resonated with me.*

My aunt named me Ginger when I was a few months old and it just stuck. So now only the bill collectors know my name is Mary-Lynn; I can differentiate them from other people.

So Mary-Lynn, aka Ginger, got an MBA and moved back to the country to commune with nature, right? Not at all. Ginger may have loved nature, but her passion was different—she always had different dreams for herself.

Always there was a part of me that wanted to work with celebrities. There were all of these people I could see on TV, and I'd say, 'I want to work with these people, I already know them!'

Ginger did not just want to know these people, she wanted to be one of them. She envisioned herself as both musician and actress—destined for success and acclaim.

By the time I was probably eighteen I had already written my Oscar speech and my Grammy speech. I wanted to be a singer. I was always attracted to music, and after taking guitar lessons I taught myself to play the piano.

Ginger's aunt supported her interest in music—as she did whenever Ginger expressed an interest in something, despite their limited resources—and bought her a toy piano.

I had one of those toy pianos . . . you remember those electric pianos or organs where you could press the chord—A, B, C, and all the chords—and then you got the music and then you just kind of hammered out the melody. And so from there, I would find an "F" chord on the piano. I would figure out this is a "C", this is an "A", and so then I didn't have to press the buttons. And because I knew basic chord structure from playing the guitar, I learned to play the piano. I remember playing 'Twinkle Twinkle Little Star' and my aunt just cried, "Oh look at her; she's a little virtuoso!" Really.

Ginger also wanted to be an actress, but *I sucked at it.*

Ginger was not destined to be either a musician or actress. Nonetheless, she has been enmeshed in the world of entertainment for the last 26 years—surrounded by the celebrities she dreamed of—working with Stevie Wonder, Whitney Houston, Eddie and Gerald Levert, Mo'Nique, and Dana Carvey among many others.

She followed her passion. However, the route was just a bit circuitous.

After the Farm . . .

Ginger's life on the farm came to a somewhat abrupt end when her mother—a legal secretary for a large law firm in Chicago—arrived one day to retrieve Ginger and her four-year-old sister.

They headed for her mother's home in Chicago. The transition for ten-year-old, light-skinned Ginger was a bit awkward.

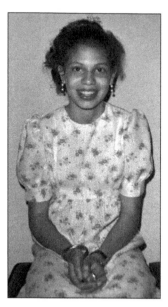

We lived on the north side of Chicago. When I lived with my aunt she passed for White; so I didn't really know I was Black. And then I moved to Chicago in the 70s, right in the middle of the Black Power Movement. Everybody is wearing dashikis; it's 'Right on be free!' It really took some acclimating.

Several years later, a much more race-aware high-school aged Ginger faced an even greater challenge when her family moved to Evanston.

By the time I got to high school, we had moved to Evanston where there were not a lot of people that looked like me. I remember the first day of high school walking into the bathroom and this girl said, "Iz you Black or iz you White; cuz I can't stand no half-breeds.'" I said, 'I'm Black.'

This encounter prompted Ginger to go *all the way the other way. I was splitting my verbs—it was making my mother crazy. I was just getting in trouble. Basically, I was just trying to fit in, and I didn't really feel like I fit in.*

Ginger says that it *just took a minute for it to all balance out.* However, Ginger's mother was not willing to wait . . . she moved Ginger to another school.

So my mom took me out of Evanston Township High School and put me in a private school in Lake Forest called Lake Forest Academy: Ferry Hall.

Once again, Ginger was in a different environment, trying to fit in—still a challenge as she was now going to school with children of the very rich—children who Ginger thought were seemingly abandoned at this boarding school by their parents.

[It] was like a dumping ground for the rich. All these kids came from very wealthy families; they did drugs, they did all this stuff and their parents didn't really seem to want them to come home—this was a boarding school.

She says going to school at Lake Forest Academy *kind of leveled me out.* Her rebellious nature waned and a greater focus on what she wanted to do began to develop.

Working since she was fourteen—for both Evanston Township and at various jobs at her mother's law firm in the summers (*I was good at it . . . plus I'm pretty likable. People just liked me)*—after finishing high school and then getting her Bachelor's degree from Lake Forest College, Ginger became more thoughtful about what she wanted to do—about finding her passion . . . with gentle nudging from her mother.

At some point, my mother asked, "Are you going to move out? When are you going to leave home?"

Recognizing the seriousness of her mother's questions, Ginger considered several possibilities: law school—a natural consideration in light of time spent at her mother's law firm (*I knew they made a lot of money)*— and getting an MBA.

Opting for business school because her GMAT scores would allow her to get into a top-rated school, she applied to Harvard, The Wharton School of the University of Pennsylvania, American University, and Northwestern's Kellogg School of Business. Wanting to go to a business school that allowed her to spend a year in another country, her first choice was Wharton, which had a joint MBA/MA program.

The school I really wanted to go to was Wharton because they had a joint MBA/MA program, which required you to go study someplace else. I really wanted to do an exchange program. When I was an undergraduate, I did a senior thesis—I was actually the first person at Lake Forest College to do a senior thesis on a computer—on adolescent pregnancy. I thought it was interesting that my mom had me young. A lot of my friends had gotten pregnant during high school. Mommy had always said to us she wasn't taking off work. She would take off at lunchtime with her Visa card to get us an abortion. She wasn't having teen pregnancy. That was always my fear. So I did the preliminary research my junior year when most students were going on exchange, and then I did the main research and wrote my thesis my senior year. Thus, I wasn't able to take advantage of the exchange program. So it was important to me that I go to a graduate school that had an exchange program.

Ginger believed that the business school that met her criteria was Wharton; however, she did not get into Wharton. She thinks that her mother's help, albeit well-intentioned, may have derailed her application.

Mommy was helping me with the Wharton application, but I should not have let her. The application required three personal items, three books, and three recordings. I had to say what they would be and why. Well, I had to have my Prince music and all this stuff. And Mommy read it and said "No!" She had me put John F. Kennedy, Martin Luther King . . . I know that's why I didn't get into Wharton. I know it, like I know it, like I know it! It wasn't me!

Despite her disappointment, Ginger was accepted by her other choices. Harvard became a non-option, however, because they did not offer adequate financial aid, and she was only lukewarm about the possibility of going to American University in Washington, D. C. On the other hand, Kellogg had an exchange program and offered her a full scholarship. The added bonus was that Ginger's Aunt Adrienne—a woman she idolized— had gone to Northwestern.

Ginger describes her Aunt Adrienne as one of the people who most influenced her life. Part of that influence included her decision to go to Northwestern.

One of the greatest influences on my life would be my Aunt Adrienne Bailey—I really emulated my life after her. She was my mom's friend—not really my aunt, but we called her aunt. I just saw Adrienne as so successful. She was big in the education realm—she used to work for the College Board and stuff like that. She always traveled a lot. She was very smart and someone who I think influenced me a great deal. Adrienne got all her frequent flyer miles on American, and that was the first airline where I had frequent flyer miles. Adrienne studied in France, so I studied in Spain; she got her Ph.D. from Northwestern, so I got my MBA from Northwestern.

Ginger's initial introduction to the Kellogg program and her classmates was a bit intimidating . . . *because it seemed everybody in our class knew business and I didn't.*

Charlie Baker, the current governor of Massachusetts, was her classmate. She recalls a case study being discussed on that first day of class. The class was tasked with trying to figure out the break-even point for a particular hospital. Ginger remembers that at the time . . .

I had no idea. I ain't got a clue. That's the whole reason I'm going to school! And Charlie broke that down so fast—I was impressed with his intellect.

Whatever her doubts, Ginger persevered. Along the way, she fulfilled her desire to participate in an exchange program. She went to Spain.

Initially, all these students were trying to go on Exchange. But as we got closer to the time for finding jobs many decided they didn't want to go on Exchange; they wanted to try to get jobs. But I still wanted to go someplace else. So, I went to Barcelona and studied there for a semester, which was so much fun! It was good; I wouldn't ever trade that experience . . . ever!

Barcelona also provided Ginger with a different perspective—a foreign perspective—about business school.

When I went to Spain, I took Finance in Spanish; and I was like, 'I don't understand it in English!' (Laughs). And it was Finance II. But in Spain, what we consider cheating they don't consider cheating. Because they believe that in business you have to collaborate with your team. So during finals, we would ask each other the answers to the questions so that we all could finish and pass the class. So I got through Finance II in Spanish! I thought, 'dodged that bullet.'

In addition to really enjoying the exchange experience, one of the long-term benefits of Ginger's time in Spain was that she learned Spanish—or at least what she refers to today as a *professional working proficiency* in Spanish. It has served her well over the years as a global marketing professional.

Despite her wonderful experience in Spain, when Ginger returned to the states, she was faced with a somewhat difficult reality:

I was probably one of three people who didn't get a job after Kellogg. Ah!

She had plenty of interviews—the prestige of an MBA from Northwestern's Kellogg School of Business was undeniable. However, Ginger's interview experiences were . . . different. She just didn't seem to fit the profile.

I guess I just didn't have what they were looking for. There was a woman that interviewed me, and she just looked monochrome. She was a pale White person with an air, a beige suit, and beige nail polish. I walked in with my red nail polish and I realized, 'there's not a vibe here.'

The absence of the right *vibe* persisted for Ginger throughout her myriad of interviews. During her interview at PepsiCo . . .

I saw a Hispanic or Mexican man sitting on a bench outside the building. He hadn't moved for fifteen minutes; I was worried and finally, I interrupted the interview to express my concern about the man who hadn't moved for fifteen minutes. The interviewer asked me if I needed contacts because the "man" was a statute.

Ginger's MBA from Kellogg was in International Business, Marketing, and Organizational Behavior. Yet, by the time she graduated she was still without a job. Above all else Ginger was practical. Thus, needing to generate income she did temporary work while testing a variety of possibilities—including an eight-day stint as a real estate agent. Finally, an old boyfriend directed her to the Mayor's Office of Special Events. The city's Special Events office at that time was responsible for the *Taste of Chicago, Blues Fest, Gospel Fest, and Jazz Fest.* These were *big, very complicated festivals and events: the Taste of Chicago hosted 2.5 million people, while the Blues Fest accommodated 500,000 people.* Ginger was assigned a variety of tasks from the beginning—from negotiating contracts (which she thought should be handled by the Legal Department) to raising money via sponsorships. While all of this was new to her, Ginger raised $1 million on her first sponsorship assignment!

Ginger was enjoying this job (*I knew I liked it and it was fun!*) that allowed her to utilize her academic training, introduced her to issues and concepts with which she was unfamiliar, and opened doors that permitted her to work with new and sometimes exciting people.

She was beginning to make a name for herself. In fact, Ginger was so successful in her first year with the City's Special Events Office that she got a promotion. But it was not without some drama.

At some point during all of this, there was this political drama playing out. Meanwhile, Harold Washington [the then first African American mayor of Chicago] had died, and there was this impromptu funeral; and just a lot of things going on. My supervisor made me Acting General Manager of Taste of Chicago. That meant everybody had to report to me—and they were NOT happy about it—I had the least amount of experience.

After Harold Washington's death and two years into Ginger's time working for the city of Chicago, the winds of political change made

Ginger's future tentative. First, Eugene Sawyer completed the balance of Washington's term; then Richard Daley, Jr. was making his bid to become mayor. And despite her success, the person who brought her in had been demoted and Ginger was a consultant to the city—not getting benefits. All of this made the timing of a call she received perfect.

A friend from Kellogg called me and said, "Ginger, Jim Harris [a guy who graduated from Kellogg the year before] has started an entertainment marketing company and he is looking for people to do this tour." I was like 'what's his number?'

It was a rock concert tour with Steve Winwood. They were looking for a tour sponsor—Michelob to be specific. At the time, Michelob's slogan was very popular, "The Night Belongs to Michelob." Ginger successfully recruited Michelob to sponsor the tour and then proceeded to travel with the band on the rock and roll tour. She says she *had a ball!*

It was a 33-city tour. It started in St. Louis—home of Michelob/Anheuser Busch—and it ended in Toronto. And I did that all summer—the summer of '88. It was the most fun a 28-year-old could ever have! It was sooo much fun! My job was to do radio promotions. So, I was working with the bands; and sometimes we would take the band bus and go to various places. We had these nice neon lights, and jackets and sweatshirts—part of the swag we would give to radio station winners. My other job was the pre and post hospitality part. Basically, my job was to drink beer that summer and host parties and drink all night with the band—so that's what I did. We played Radio City Music Hall; we played out here (LA) at the Universal Amphitheater. I got to see a lot of places I had never been to before.

This was all working towards event production—but I didn't know it yet.

The only problem when the tour ended: Ginger was unemployed—again.

So the tour is over and once again I'm unemployed. And I'm wondering why it is my life story to keep getting jobs and not to have jobs.

Despite this anxiety-inducing query, Ginger started looking for another job. Back in Chicago—and back living in her mother's home—a friend who was working for a company marketing corporate events told Ginger that they were in search of someone with experience marketing festivals. That was Ginger. She made the call and got the job. Perfect. It allowed Ginger to acquire a new skill—learning to market corporate events—in exchange for her expertise with festivals. She easily and quickly demonstrated she was up for the challenge.

Her first assignment was to promote a festival featuring the Temptations—without an advertising budget. The firm had received a large fee to promote the festivals and was under pressure to make sure there was a significant audience. Ginger called Chicago radio legend Herb Kent. He agreed that he would promote the festival if she could get him an interview with Otis Williams—at the time, one of only two remaining original members of the Temptations—the other being Melvin Franklin. Of course, Ginger got Herb the interview—with both of them!

They were performing that night; I just went in and asked Otis to do the interview. This was after I opened the door and they were all in there getting dressed—a sight I couldn't unsee.

That is how it went for the sometimes jobless Ginger. Whenever there was a new opportunity—often fraught with known and unknown challenges and obstacles—Ginger grabbed the opportunity and met the challenge, overcame the obstacle.

Ginger continued working with the company, honing skills that would serve her well, while also enhancing the firm's portfolio when she added a large corporate client—a move that would become even more relevant as she moved closer towards her ultimate goal.

I stayed on with Paulette; she taught me how to do corporate special events the right way. Some people think you get on the phone and call a caterer and you're a special events planner. But she really taught me the right way to do things. During that time I would go out on sales calls and I was able to get Hewlett Packard as a client.

At this point, professionally, Ginger was in a good space. She was doing the kinds of things she was coming to love—and being very successful in the process.

Sometimes our professional and personal lives mesh perfectly. Sometimes they do not. The latter was the case for Ginger as she was about to turn thirty.

A surprise visit from her recently married mother and her new husband started it all. Ginger was now living alone in the home she and her mother and sister shared in Evanston.

My house was now the place that used to be my Mom's house. But she moved to Albuquerque. In 1987 she announced, "either you are gonna move, or I'm gonna move. I give you one year." Then she left.

Ginger arrived home from work one day to find her mother and stepfather in her house. Her mother still had a key and had let herself in. Her mom's initial response to, *why are you guys here?* was to tell Ginger that they wanted to share their wedding photos with her. However . . .

Then my mom blurts out, 'Cameron has AIDS!'

Cameron was someone Ginger dated—long enough for her family to know him—but with whom she had recently ended a relationship. She knew he was sick—the last she heard they thought it was pneumonia, but further tests were pending.

I don't know what to do. But I'm wondering why his family called my mother—I'm 30, why didn't they call me? Somebody told my sister Holly, who was out on a date with her to-be husband. I'm thinking this is all bad; there's just drama going on.

The news was obviously disturbing, and Ginger needed something—someone—to help curb her rising panic.

So I pick up the phone and call my cousin Marina who lives in Los Angeles. I tell her what has happened. She's an unemotional person and she said, "Do you feel like you have AIDS?" And I said, 'No.' She said, "Then you don't.' I was like 'oh, ok.' That made me feel better.

Despite her cousin's reassurances, Ginger recalls this being *a time when AIDS was really a gay man's disease and it was something to be super ashamed of.*

When I went to get my AIDS test I couldn't go through my insurance because it was something that would follow me. I can remember going to the doctor and the doctor saying, "Well you know they have some really good treatments for it; and you could live ten more years; and I remember saying, 'But I'll only be 41 then. That doesn't really work for me.'

Thankfully, Ginger did not have AIDS, although she had to get tested every three months for a year to make sure. Moreover, everyone in her circle knew Cameron and knew he had AIDS; it impacted the way they began to interact with Ginger.

I can remember going to a party and I hugged someone and another person walked up behind me and said, "That's Ginger Campbell, her boy-friend Cameron has AIDS," basically warning them to be careful because at that time nobody knew how AIDS was transmitted. There was a lot of disinformation and misinformation about it.

It was more than Ginger was willing to handle on the advent of her 30th year. It was time for Ginger to journey out of Chicago.

I was like, I can't deal with this. I had been wanting to move to Los Angeles. Maybe this was the time to do it. I talked to my cousin Marina; then—I don't remember how it all happened now—somehow, I found out that Paulette's ex-partner knew a woman out in California. I talked to her, met with her, and ended up getting hired. So when I moved to LA in September of 1991, I had a job.

Ginger also arrived in LA with a client—Hewlett Packard (HP) decided they wanted to continue to work with Ginger notwithstanding her move to Los Angeles.

While the new job only lasted nine months—she and her new boss ultimately could not find common ground—Ginger was becoming comfortable with her new home in Los Angeles. Now it was time for her next—and best—move, her own company.

SNAP Productions—named so because Ginger's grandfather used to call her "Gingersnap"—was born in 1992. Ginger only had one client—HP—and one prospective client, a Japanese tour company that she wanted to become her client.

I had been going after this Japanese tour company because Japanese tour companies were a big business in Los Angeles. They were bringing a lot of people over here. I told the company representative that I was going to start my own business. I offered him the options of staying with the previous company, in which case I would try to get someone to work with him, or I would try to see if I could do the first couple of events as a contractor just to ease the transition; or—literally as an afterthought—you can go with me. And two days later he said, "I'll go with you."

I almost panicked realizing I had to do this—and I was on my own. But I did not. I started my own business with the Japanese company and HP.

It was never completely smooth sailing: when HP closed its Midwest Office—where all of her work for HP was coming from—Ginger lost HP as a client.

But then . . . she added Motown.

I ran into this guy who worked for Motown, and I always wanted to work for a record company—that was my dream. So I was calling and calling him, but he would never take my calls. However, it turns out that two Gingers were calling him—me and the other Ginger who was with Essence. So he told his assistant to call Ginger from Essence. When he came on the telephone, he started talking to me about a shoot and I said, 'What shoot? What are you talking about?' He must have realized the mistake when he said, "Is this Ginger Campbell?" The administrative assistant, Dani, didn't do this on purpose—I didn't know her; it was her first administrative assistant job.

And because of the mistake Ginger was hired as a consultant . . .

. . . not for a lot of money—I was a consultant again. I don't know if it is karma that I can't get a good corporate job!

Nonetheless, Ginger was hired as Motown Publicity Manager and started to live her dream.

I'm in the music industry! And I'm working with Boyz II Men, and I'm going to some of the awards shows! This is when Arsenio Hall had his show and we were going and hanging out at Arsenio's Greenroom and I loved this! I just loved this!

Things were going well. Uh oh . . .

Sometime around February 1993, Ginger was back in Chicago on business. She recalls feeling ill after dinner one evening but attributed it to the cleanse she had recently done. However, when she woke up the next morning her skin was green!

In January or February of 1993, I was getting really nauseous—I was not sure what was wrong with me. I had just done a cleanse, which I had never done before. I thought that was what was making me ill. Paulette and I had reconnected so I was back in Chicago. I remember eating a salad and afterward my back was hurting. I woke up the next morning—I'm peeing brown, the whites of my eyes are brown and my skin is green. I didn't know what was wrong with me.

Ginger had hepatitis—but non-A, non-B, non-C. It apparently related back to the issue of AIDS.

What we were able to piece together is that for those people who didn't come down with AIDS, hepatitis can sometimes be a reaction. And I never came down with HIV, but I was really sick for about 5 months.

While her physical condition made for a difficult several months—Ginger never stopped working.

I would do events and I would have to sleep. All the while I was fighting my boss in LA because she never gave me my final paycheck. I was doing events with HP and trying to stay on top of work, but I was sleeping and sleeping and sleeping because I was sick. I would fly places. I was taking this Chinese medicine—this tea—for five months because it seemed to be the only thing that would help what I had. But I swear it had Eye of Newt and bugs in it because they plumped when you boiled it. But I was like, 'You gotta drink this tea.'

Ginger's primary concern was not the disease—but getting her work done.

I wasn't afraid; I was concerned because I'm working for myself and I got to make money and I'm sick. I would hire friends to do events or to go with me but I didn't have anyone that I could shoot the work off to.

What perhaps should have caused her to miss a beat, was more inconvenience than roadblock. She says the possibility of having AIDS scared her until she knew she did not; but with the hepatitis diagnosis, it was not fear but the need to find time to recover.

When I got hepatitis, I wasn't so much scared as I needed to rest. My body was so fatigued, and to get better I needed a lot of rest, but I didn't have a mound of money I was sitting on. I had enough but needed to keep working to stay afloat. That was my dilemma. In the meantime, Cameron died. I had kept in contact with him. I had to go to site surveys while still trying to get myself together. I'll never forget one week I had to leave Los Angeles, go to Austin for a site survey, fly to Chicago; then leave Chicago and go straight to San Francisco for his [Cameron's] funeral.

Nothing was easy for Ginger, but everything was manageable—and sometimes she had a lot of fun—just living her dream—and always *hustling.* The PR job at Motown was going away because the person whose place she took was coming back. But Motown needed somebody in R&B Promotions—Ginger took that on. At the same time, she got a *BIG job with the Japanese tour company and made a bunch of money!* So once her

Motown gig went completely away, she was doing pretty well. She had taken on a job with the Black Entertainment and Sports Lawyers Association and was about to do an event with them in the Bahamas . . . *cuz I always did the fabulous meetings with them outside the country.*

And then Ginger got robbed . . .

I returned to my house one afternoon to find the door open and my cat outside looking at me, like "Why am I out here?" I walked in and realized that I had been robbed. The police said they thought they would come back because they didn't get everything. They just took the little things they could fence like speakers and little electronic stuff.

Alarmed by both the burglary and the police prediction that the burglars might return, Ginger's mom suggested that she get a male friend to stay with her for a few days, which she did.

. . . So, of course, I get pregnant that night; and now a whole new drama.

By this time, October 1995, Ginger is thirty-five years old. She had never been pregnant—had not been dating anyone for a while.

And I'm like this is not my paradigm of what I believe should be happening here. I didn't know what I was going to do but I had to produce another event in Aruba for the Black Entertainment and Sports Lawyers Association. So I did another Ginger thing: I went to Aruba and said 'I will deal with this when I get back. I'm just going to go do the event.'

When she returned from Aruba ten days later, Ginger had what she describes as *an epiphany.*

I said this is the first time you have had an opportunity to have a child; you may not have another opportunity. You should probably move forward with it.

When she told her daughter's father that she had decided to have the baby—believing that the two of them would be able to co-parent—he was anything but enthusiastic, attempting to dissuade her from her decision. He went so far as to predict that Ginger would be *an unfit mother because I was trying to do the Hollywood thing.*

Wounded by this prediction, and not quite sure what she was going to do, Ginger, remained steadfast in her decision to have the baby. There were, of course, challenges—from friends and her clients.

I decided I was going to go with it. But then I felt like I ran into a black period because my friends were all going out and doing stuff and they kinda stopped calling me. Money dried up. People stopped giving me work; it was like they were saying you need to just stay home and be pregnant. I was like I don't think I'm gonna have a home if I don't get work. This did not happen at an opportune time in my life.

But, true to her spirit, during her pregnancy, in addition to her work with the Japanese tour company Ginger found a temporary job producing events for the California African American Museum.

Then Myko Lyric was born.

Ginger's mom came to visit to help with the baby and with finances as Ginger was still not getting much work. She also received help from an unexpected source—Myko's other grandmother.

His mother, Marcie, kept trying to reach out to me and I wasn't trying to be mean because it was her grandchild. But I thought she was doing it more to assure Nick's place in the baby's life. But it turned out that she just wanted a relationship with her grandchild. That opened up a whole new world because Marcie was really good with the baby. She was in Chicago, but financially she helped me a great deal.

As a result of Marcie's reaching out, Ginger describes her as a major influence in her life—someone who could raise Ginger's spirits when things got difficult.

Myko's grandmother Marcie was a big influence because she always did her best to keep me lifted. You always need someone like that—my mom as well. But Marcie was not my blood, yet she was so invested in her grandchild; and was so grateful to me—she would cry

sometimes and say, "I know people who were not allowed access to their grandchildren. They would have to look at them through the gate at school or something like that." I could never be that way. Myko deserves to know who her family is. I mean that would just be plain wrong for me to do that. But she would say, "But it happens all the time." So the fact that she was always so grateful and gracious with me helped build up my gratitude. And sometimes when things were bad, she made them better.

Even with the assistance of both grandmothers, Ginger knew that the responsibility for Myko was hers. They were by themselves in California, which reinforced Ginger's decision to have her own business—allowing her the flexibility that a traditional 9 to 5 job—no matter how much it paid—would not permit.

So now I got this baby and I need a J-O-B but I'm not getting a J-O-B; so I just had to continue with the Museum and other projects I could pick up. I still dabbled in doing some work for the music business.

Then I felt like I needed to work for myself as Myko was growing up. On Mother's Day, Father's Day, Grandparents Day, whatever, I didn't want her to not be represented, and her not to feel like she was supported. So I was just taking care of Myko, getting her to every lesson—she excelled at dance and I wanted her to continue with dance lessons. She really liked acting, so I also wanted her to continue in that sort of thing. I really pretty much devoted my life to her while at the same time stressing and doing whatever I could to rally up some money. And I wanted to be available to her—that's really hard to do when you have a job.

Ginger landed a temporary position with City of Hope that kept her occupied for about a year. She was working with their LA Marathon producing first their senior walk and later their 5K.

I've always found a way to make it even though it looks kind of dire and not so good; you know, the sun shines somewhere. (Smile in her voice).

With this philosophy, even before Myko was born—when Ginger had hepatitis—she had to manage medical costs without insurance.

I paid cash; and luckily when I had hepatitis, I had just done some events for HP so I had some money.

Ginger did not and does not necessarily view these things that happened as obstacles; she just *always has to find the workaround.*

So, when she was pregnant with Myko Lyric, and had no insurance Ginger found a "*workaround*" with her doctor.

I didn't really have a choice. I got pregnant; I didn't have insurance. I went to a MediCal doctor because of my income. He gave me all the wrong prenatal vitamins; it was awful! So I called people. One of my friends who got me through that period was Gary Watson who is Myko's godfather. I called Gary's sister and asked if she could recommend an OB/GYN and told her, 'I don't have insurance.' She gave me the name of this guy, Dr. Arthur Johnson, and I told him, 'I don't have any insurance.' He said, ""OK, if I deliver your baby it's going to be $3000; if you have to have a Cesarean it's going to be $3500." I said, 'Ok, I'll pay you cash.' So as you get later in the pregnancy—he was a Black doctor—you gotta go to the doctor all the time. He'd say, "You see the squares on this floor? Every square costs me $12; multiply that." When I found out I had to have a C-section, I'm like, 'oh shit!' But I was at Cedars—so I wasn't too concerned about the hospital bill, but I had to be in the hospital for about 5 days because of the C-section! So, it took me a minute; but I would write him a check every month. I remember the last check was for $67 and I wrote a note that said, 'Dear Dr. Johnson, this represents my last payment to you. Please forward the title to the baby to me as she is now bought and paid for!' He wrote me back saying, "You gave me your word and you kept it." It was not necessarily in his time frame; but I was going to pay him.

When producing an event or doing a PR campaign, Ginger says something will inevitably go wrong. She had a workaround.

But if you planned it well enough you can usually find a workaround. Now in my life I'm not such a good planner—in my personal life. But I think you have to be resilient. You have to be able to . . . you can't just give up. I mean there have been times when things were difficult; but I have to keep moving forward, because if I don't and wallow in it . . .

At the time of our interview she was awaiting a long-overdue payment from a client.

I finished a job in Miami and the guy hasn't paid me. Do you know how badly I need that money?! Every day I have written him emails. He knows how badly I need that money, but I don't have it. So, you know what? I have

*to breeze through it. You just
have to breeze through it. Resilience and perseverance have
been two of the trademarks of
my life.*

SNAP, Productions provid-
ed significant PR work for a
client—five events in five days
in five different cities. A long-
term client in dire straits himself, Ginger continued to work
despite the fact that the client
cut her fee by $10,000.00, and
despite the fact that she came
down with the flu the day she
was leaving for the first city
because I had been working like a madwoman. Moreover, although her
contract required payment in full by a date certain, she was being paid
incrementally, and was still owed a substantial sum of money nearly five
months later.

Despite these glitches that are part of having her own business, today
Ginger looks for work that resonates with her. She enjoys projects where
the objective is to empower, inspire, educate, and uplift people.

*I like working with projects that do good in the world. I like working
with people who I feel are elevating or uplifting or helping the human condition. So I have tried—especially in the last four or five years—to pick things
and work with people who want to help—who want to give scholarships to
young kids or mentor them or do those kinds of things.*

She still enjoys working on entertainment events, but has learned
that some large companies are cheap—not wanting to *give up any money;* some talent—people whom you've held in such high regard—are *just
awful;* while *some people you work with are just really really nice.* She has
learned to work with all of them, while acknowledging that *some are more
challenging than others.* Ginger hints at the identities of some of the more
awful talent, but discreetly chooses not to name names. She does say,

*The press that some reps put out is not reality. And I've had to tell several
people not to believe their own press.*

Through all of the nuances of operating her own business in the last 20+ years, Ginger's one constant has been her daughter, Myko Lyric, whose birth she describes as the *most important life-changing event in my life—* professionally and personally.

I would say having my daughter has been the most important life-changing event for me because it completely changed everything that I did. It was all about me and then it became all about her.

Now 24, Myko graduated from New York University in May 2018, quickly thereafter heading to Europe for a month-long adventure. Of her relationship with Myko, Ginger's initial description lends itself to what can be characterized as a typical mother-daughter relationship with hilarious details:

I need her cousins to really tell you about our relationship, but Myko used to always say I was all up in her business; and when she was leaving for school she said, "Mom this talking every day has got to stop. I can't talk to you every day." I said, 'Ok.' So who calls me three times a day, right? "I got a pimple; I think it's a cyst! I'm having this . . ." After graduation, when she took a trip to Europe, she called me every single day.

I was at the gas station and you know you're not supposed to talk on your cell phone while you're putting gas in your car; but I see this call from Myko and it's a face-time audio; and I hit the phone to respond and say, 'Myko I'm at a gas station; I can't talk right now. I will call you when I get to Trader Joe's.' Then I realize I didn't hit the speaker button; so when I do, I hear, "Mom stop talking; Mom stop talking." And I say, 'I couldn't hear you. I'll call you back.' She says, "Mom I'm locked out of my Airbnb!" She was in Venice, Italy. I am standing on the corner of Olympic and La Brea at a gas station in Los Angeles. I'm thinking what can I do? So I ask, 'Did you try the key before you left?' I don't know if she is outside on the street or if she is inside the apartment. I have no idea. I'm thinking I could call the police; but I don't know the address. Then our call just disconnects. I actually think Myko just hung up on me. But I choose to believe that it just miraculously disconnected. Then I look down at the phone and I see, "MOM ANSWER YOUR PHONE; MOM, ANSWER YOUR PHONE!" All these admonitions in capital letters. Then the next thing I hear is, "I got in." So somebody heard her and let her in.

So, I think we have a really good relationship. She called me every day while she was in Europe and was with her boyfriend for the latter half of it. So I think it's good. I think we have that mother-daughter thing. Plus the dynamic that I never had when Myko got on my last nerve was 'go talk to your father'—that was not an option. I never had that. Her father has never been a big influence in her life. Her grandmother—his mom—and his sister have been. But not him. He's just generally not been there.

While Ginger has found a "workaround" for many of the challenges in her life—the expected and unexpected—most of the unexpected and some of the expected of running a business solo has been stress-producing, and there has not always been a workaround to address how to deal with the stress. Ginger knew she had to find an answer.

The Agape Spiritual Center in Los Angeles—which she started visiting seven years ago—has provided some of those answers. Ginger describes the Agape Spiritual Center *as a place to learn the truth about life. That Life is Good. That the Universe is always for you. That changing your thoughts can change your life.* She started going to the Center because . . .

I just seemed to be a person besieged by worry and doubt—all those kinds of things.

Some of that doubt creeps in when she looks at her Kellogg classmates.

When I look at myself compared to a lot of my Kellogg friends, I feel like they are doing sooo well; they are making a bunch of money. They don't have to worry about how they're going to pay their rent. They got houses and wives and that sort of thing; I feel kind of inconsequential. I don't feel as successful. I think it is in part because I have never been married—and not close to it. It would be nice to just have someone so that the onus is not always only on me to make everything happen.

Success, as well as happiness is not measured in money—facts about which Ginger is well aware; yet, for a while—as much as she enjoyed her independence as an entrepreneur—the doubts would creep in. That is when her experience at the Agape Center began to matter.

I started going to Agape Spiritual Center. Michael Beckwith runs it here in Los Angeles. I took a lot of classes there and I feel like it's helped. I'm not exalted or at a Zen level, but I feel like, given the fact that my lifestyle is stressful, and I still have an issue with trust, I have relaxed a little bit more into it. Like running numbers through my bank accounts at night—I don't do as much of that.

Ginger says that since she started going to the Agape Spiritual Center,

I'm calmer. I'm not sure about being less stressed. I am responsible for my daughter. I'm responsible for how I live. I have to hustle for every dollar I take in. But I'm calmer.

Agape has also helped Ginger appreciate what she has been able to provide for herself.

I was cracking up yesterday and then I said I don't know when I'm getting my next check but I got a brand-new BMW sitting in my driveway. I don't really know how it's getting paid for, but somehow, I will find a payment this month and it's all going to work out. So you gotta stop feeling that there's no prosperity around you because, just look at it! So I just have to get out of this, 'I don't have' thing. Marcie was good at helping me balance that. So that's why I appreciate Agape now; because you know whatever you put your attention on you get more of it. So I want more of the good things. I don't want more of the bad things.

Ginger is proud of the reputation she has developed as a Branding, Public Relations and Event Production Specialist. It was long hours, hard work, hustling, workarounds and whatever it took to get the job done. And she is successful, having been in her own business since 1992—and Ginger is handling her business. Everybody is not able to do that; in fact, a whole lot of people—perhaps some of her "successful" Kellogg classmates—are unable to do that.

And there is joy and humor in her life—something she came to realize was so important.

I learned that having a good sense of humor is important. At some point you just have to be able to laugh—even if you laugh to keep from crying. I think if I can laugh at me, I won't take myself or my situation so seriously.

Ginger describes herself as a *creative person*; and today at nearly 60 years old, and with lessons learned from her time with the Agape Center, she is looking to a future in which she continues to do the work she has come to love—but with a few changes.

I'm at a point where I want to enjoy life. I don't want to be in this constant stress. My sister is always asking, "Why don't you come back home?" And there's a part of me that wouldn't mind going back to Chicago, but all my business contacts are here. So that would be challenging. I'd like to just be able to exhale sometime—know that it's all good and I can do some of the things I want to do without worrying. I mean like I don't have to answer the telephone if I am out of town on vacation. And I want to take a vacation! I want to set my butt in the Caribbean sometime and enjoy it. I think that will happen; it's just getting through life's valleys.

What about the future?
First on Ginger's list for the future is continued success for Myko Lyric. You can see the smile on her face and hear the lilt in her voice when she talks about her daughter.

I mean she's an amazing dancer. She put music together, and has taken a six-week intensive with Alvin Ailey. So, I feel like that is a big thing in my life—being encouraging—just letting people be themselves. Obviously, there is some guidance that goes on; but you want to encourage people to do what they want.

What about when she looks to her future?

Well, number one, I'd like to see a lot more contracts so I can hire some people, allowing me to get out of the day-to-day. And I'd rather work on the business than in the business. I think I could be more effective in strategy and stuff. I'm bossy so I doubt I'd completely extricate myself; but at the same time, I would like to mentor and build up my successor so I have somebody to take this over. Number two, it would be great to have a boyfriend or be married; but if not, I just want to be around good friends—laugh, drink my wine, and do some traveling. Certainly, I want to enjoy life a little bit more and really work on pulling myself out of the stressors—by just shifting my consciousness to a certain extent because while I feel like I've made headway there's a lot more headway to make. Gandhi or the Dali Lama or somebody said, "If you change the way you look at things, the things you look at will change." Somebody said that—it's very profound! I like that.

When asked how her journey thus far has changed her, Ginger says:

Well, I think some of my idealism is gone, which I don't think is necessarily a good thing; but I think I'm wiser. I think I'm less intimidated by people.

I guess as you get older you just get a better sense of self—what works for you, what doesn't work for you—you are more inclined to speak your mind as opposed to just go along to get along. I have less to lose. And if you don't really resonate with me; I don't want to spend my time making you like me.

Words of wisdom Ginger shares:
First,

I think that it's very important to stay active in your community—and be the change that you wish to see. Given the political situation right now I think that we've slept; we've kind of been drawn to this notion that the government works the way it works, and politicians are this; there were some things you didn't like, but it all kind of conformed to a certain way of life. And now we see that it doesn't. We have someone in office [prior to the 2020 election] *who is a White supremacist, a racist, just doing stuff. So I think that being involved in your community, being sensitive to what the needs are and being civically active is very important. I may not have been an activist but I damn sure voted in every election! I think you have to be aware of that.*

Second, and perhaps most important . . .

You really have to follow your passion. I mean, I love what I do! I still love what I do. It was not a straight path. It was not like I got promoted from here to here to here to here. As I tell people, my journey took me through bramble bushes, it took me on sidetracks, and it took me through a lot of stuff. And I know it sounds kind of trite to say follow your passion, and I don't mean it that way, but if you don't do what you love, or what you enjoy doing, there's just no reason. Despite my desire to make more money, it did not influence my decision to stay the course with what I was doing. I liked what I was doing, I like the freedom, I liked the flexibility. I'm a very driven person. I know how to get up in the morning; and I don't go to bed until I'm finished with what I'm doing. I have a huge stake in any outcome. It's my reputation; it's how I work; it's my own personal brand if you will. When I say follow your passion, if you are working in a dead-end job, or a job you just don't like and you're just doing it for the money, that's great, you can have all these things; but then there's this whole side of you that's not fulfilled. What's the point in that? Because at some point it's going to smack you in the face. That's the way life works.

What's the point indeed; especially because Ginger's advice comes with few regrets about the non-traditional path she has taken since beginning her jouney in Paw Paw, Michigan.

I feel like singing that Frank Sinatra song . . . 'Regrets, I've had a few . . .' (Laughter). But I was a single mother with a small child, and there was only so much time in the day. And there is a part of me that also says that you're doing what you're supposed to all the time; so to kick yourself for those kinds of things is kind of useless. It's a waste of energy.

A waste of energy because life—what we do—as Ginger suggests, happens the way it is supposed to. For Ginger, while there may have been a few low points, she has had a lot of high points with her business and personal life; and she's done it in a way that's not traditional. Ginger has a thriving, successful business, that has allowed her to follow her passion, and is very connected to her daughter, Myko Lyric, who is on her own path to success, not in small part because of Ginger's support and sacrifices. That must be how it is supposed to be.

Finally Ginger agrees,

I don't have a lot of regrets. I have had a lot of fun. I've done some really fun, amazing things. There have been people that I have been fortunate enough to get to know by virtue of what I do; and so this is what I

was supposed to do—like I was supposed to be on the phone talking to you. I mean I've done some incredible things. I was this little girl that was raised on a farm in Michigan, so detached from the life I currently lead. That little girl has gone on a rock and roll tour, has travelled all kinds of places, met all kinds of celebrities, been in the limelight; known lots of influential people. That little girl was right in dreaming about what she wanted to do. Didn't get my Oscar or Grammy . . .

Well actually she did get to the Oscars. Myko danced with Pharrell at the Oscars when "Happy" was up for an Oscar in 2014 . . .

Follow your passion!

MICHELLE GAITHER
Coming Full Circle

M ichelle Gaither is a social worker and the mother of an autistic son. In this dual role she has personified the art of motherhood and someone with the strength and honesty to provide guidance and counseling to a population in need—first senior citizens, then veterans, and now young people in high school. Throughout her journey Michelle has possessed and developed the professional and personal characteristics to be successful in both roles. She is determined, vibrant, resilient, connected, health-conscious, educated, and intelligent. She has dedicated her life to the assistance she can provide as a social worker and, especially, to a never-ending search for the best for her son Najja.

Michelle's journey begins as a child growing up in the urban oasis which is New York, and more specifically the projects of the Northeast Bronx, New York . . . a community like any other, the nuances of which Michelle did not appreciate until she moved away as an adult.

I was born in New York in the Bronx. We lived in the housing projects. During those days I have to say it was a pretty good experience for us because we had a sense of community. It was an integrated experience where we got to learn about other cultures—not just European and Latino cultures, but even the African diaspora—we had a variety of Caribbean cultures there as well. They may have looked like us, but they had different languages and different foods; so I was exposed to Spanish and Patois dialect from Caribbean cultures early on. There were little teasings we would do using each other's languages while we were growing up, just poking fun at each other when we were kids. I didn't realize my experiences were that rich until I moved to Chicago and found out how segregated Chicago was. That's when I said, 'Wow I had a really rich background!'

The stereotype of growing up in a fatherless home applied to Michelle and her siblings; but as with most stereotypes, the reason was anything but stereotypical, but perhaps a defining moment for Michelle and her mother and three siblings. Michelle's father had a heart attack and died at the age of 27. Michelle was three. At that age Michelle was virtually unaware that her father had died.

I am the third of four children. My earliest memories were when I was about three when my dad died. I don't really remember a lot about him. But I do recall a moment being on a tricycle; and I remember him walking with me as I was riding. I

remember that vividly. I can't remember him saying anything or a picture or anything like that. I just have that visual in my head. And the only other vision I have is at his funeral. And of course, at three years old I didn't know what was going on. I remember sitting with my feet dangling from the pew. I remember my maternal grandmother just wailing, crying. I don't really remember my mother there. I know I was probably sitting beside her, but I don't visualize that. I remember seeing this large box in front of the church. I remember my two older siblings being escorted up there to look in this box; but no one took me to see the content of this box. I don't remember being sad or anything because I didn't really know what was happening. I remember riding in somebody's station wagon and all of us being huddled up.

Eventually she would come to know that her father died; but even that memory is vague.

At some point I became aware that my father had died. But I don't know when that really was. I don't remember having a conversation with anybody where they said, "You know your dad died." Because I was three. I just know he was not there for most of my life and that I relied on my mother. She was my person; she was always there. It's like when children are young things coming in and out of their lives; but you can't necessarily always put words to it.

Of the four children, there are three girls and one boy. Michelle has an older sister and brother and a younger sister who was only three months old when their dad died. Although her family was 'close-knit,' Michelle recalls feeling different.

I remember thinking that I was always different. My sisters were of a lighter complexion than I, and I remember people always saying, "You don't look like them." And although my brother is about the same complexion as I am, because he was a boy, they didn't say those kinds of things to him—as far as I know. So, I thought I was like the 'black sheep' of the family and remember people saying I was different.

The European standard of beauty—lighter skin color and long hair—was embraced and in play in the African American community in the late 50s and early 60s, when Michelle grew up. Thus, the one concession given Michelle only served to reinforce her sense of being different.

I had very long hair; and if anybody said I was attractive they'd say, "Oh well, you're pretty for a dark-skinned girl." I got that a lot. And from people on the outside I got, "You don't look like them," or "This one looks like that one," and sometimes they might say my brother and I looked alike. But sometimes they said, "They all look alike—except you." And so, I don't know if I had a complex during that time, but I know I felt some kind of way. I might have felt resentful. I never remember feeling that I wanted to be light or lighter. I was okay with me; it's just that other people weren't okay with me. My mother and I never talked about it, but I remember overhearing her talking to somebody about her complexion compared to mine and I think she was probably trying to say that a parent could be one complexion and the kids could be another but still be related. I remember being insulted by that. I remember thinking why is she saying that? Why is she making that point? I remember thinking why is that an issue; and wondering is that an issue for my mother as well?

Michelle rejected the suggestion of bleaching cream (used to lighten or even skin tone)—*I don't know if my skin was uneven or what*—which she used until she realized what it was, at which point . . .

I stopped using it. I was in my early teens and so at that point I realized what it was, and I remember thinking, 'No I'm not using this!' And I remember the whole thing with the African nose, and I remember my mother always pinching her nose and telling me I should do that as well. At first, I didn't know why she was telling me to do that either; but when I found out why I said, 'Oh I'm not doing that either.'

Despite the suggestions that she was not as pretty as her siblings, Michelle embraced those aspects of her appearance that others seemed to criticize or want to change.

I didn't have a problem with me; and in my mind I didn't know why somebody else might have a problem with me. I was never one of those kids who said I wanted to be White or I wanted to be like them. I was happy with who I was, and I just didn't understand why other people had an issue with who I was. I had African American friends and Latino friends. So, while I was friends with White kids, I never wanted to be them or be like them. That was never my thing. I just hung out with them. And as I got more Black people in my school I kind of gravitated towards them because I gravitated towards people who looked like me.

Feeling "different" also made Michelle very independent, to the point of being somewhat "estranged" from her siblings.

I was very independent. I wanted to go out and do my own thing. I don't know if that is because of my place in terms of birth order among my siblings or what. As I said, I always felt I was different; and I didn't always get along with my siblings, frequently fantasizing about being an only child. I don't know if it was because of the environment—we lived in a very small apartment, which only had two bedrooms. My mother had her own room; so, the four of us lived in the other room. When my brother got older, he moved out into the living room until he went off to college. So, we were always just on top of each other. I think I had a conflict with each one of them at different points in our lives. I couldn't always relate to them. They were my siblings, but we weren't close. We were all just kind of individually living our own lives.

Despite this seeming distance between Michelle and her siblings, her brother taught her to read at an earlier age than most of her peers.

Once my two older siblings went to school they would come home and teach me how to read—my brother perhaps more than my sister would spend a great deal of time teaching me how to read. To hear him tell it he taught me how ride a bike and basically taught me everything I know. But when he tells everybody he taught me how to read and ride a bike the running joke is that I say, 'And I taught you how to fight.' He doesn't like that part. In any event, because my brother was teaching me how to read and write I was accelerated academically when I began to attend school.

As Michelle continued to excel academically her teachers took notice. While she was rewarded by being fast-tracked from 2nd grade to 4th grade, Michelle is not certain that the reward was a good idea.

When I was in second grade, I remember my mother coming up to the school to have a meeting with my teacher. At that time, you didn't ask questions; so, I didn't know what the meeting was about—I didn't ask. But I knew I was not in trouble. There were other kids in the class whose parents were also called up to school. They came back and said they were skipping a grade. But no one had said anything to me, so I didn't think that was something that applied to me. As it turns out, at the end of school year I found out that I was also being accelerated two grades ahead. So, I never went to the third grade. And that was a defining moment for me in a lot of ways. Number one, I wanted to walk to school with my older sister, which I did while in 2nd grade. The rule was that up to the third grade we were bused to school—although it was a pretty long distance. After I was skipped to the fourth grade, I didn't have a choice; I had to walk. The other factor was that up to that point I'd always been as bright as or brighter than most of my classmates. But when I was skipped to fourth grade it was different. Third grade is when you learn multiplication. But I missed that. When I got to 4th grade my math skills suffered. For the first time I found myself academically average or below average—at least in math. I was still a good student and made good grades in all the other subjects; but math haunted me for a long time—until high school, when things turned around.

Once in high school, Michelle caught up with her classmates in all subjects—including math. Nonetheless, she also knew that she likely would not allow her children to skip grades when she became a mother. What she did not—could not—predict was that skipping grades would not be the issue that she faced as a parent.

While grades were not an issue in high school, those years were a tumultuous time in her relationship with her mother. Michelle acknowledges that part of this was because of the trauma her mother endured in losing her father at such an early point in their marriage, becoming solely responsible for taking care of Michelle and her three siblings.

We had a good mother, and I knew she loved us and cared for us. We never went without food, we always had shelter. I know she struggled with a lot of things, including my father's death; so there were times where I would see her in a vulnerable state and as a child it made me feel very insecure because I wasn't sure what that was all about and whether I could rely on her.

When I got into my teen years—where before I was more afraid of my mom because back in the day we feared our parents—I got a little ballsy and I guess I went through my teenage rebellion and I kind of stood up to her in a lot of ways. Essentially it was because I was able to see my parent and realize you're not perfect; and I think I was vocal about that.

This new "ballsyness" was different for Michelle; because as a young girl she was sensitive and prone to cry about things that bothered her or that she did not like or understand. However, the timid youngster became a bold adolescent.

As a teenager, I began to speak my mind and say what I believed and that's how my family came to know me. It may not always be pretty, and it may not always be what people want to hear, but I'm going to tell it like it is. And that included what I said to my mom. So, she and I went through very tumultuous times in my teen years. It created conflicts between us. And it was kind of a mixed bag because I love my mom so there were times when everything seemed normal and I had a natural desire to be close to her. I remember moments being the kitchen while Mom would be cooking, and we'd be looking out of the window together and we'd be just talking. We actually had good conversations about my activities and what was going on with my life. I wanted to be close to her. When we had those moments, I would cherish them.

For one reason or another—including her mother's displeasure with some of Michelle's friends—those moments often did not last—disappointingly creating even greater distance between the two. Michelle saw it as a matter of trust and began gradually holding back and not sharing everything with her mother the way she had or the way she would have liked.

I stopped disclosing very personal things to her. I would begin talking to her about things that maybe were a little bit safer or not at all. Things that I didn't feel she could really hurt me with.

Despite this push-pull between Michelle and her mother, she believes that her *teen rebellion* was actually *sort of mild compared to many others her age in my neighborhood.* While not sexually active at the time, her rebellion meant that she would go places—especially with her best friend—and not tell her mom, which caused her mom to worry. And of course, she could not always fool her mom, which would sometimes mean trouble.

One day, me and my girlfriend—my partner-in-crime—were out of school and although I never liked to lie to my mother we wanted to go to this boy's house. We were 13/14 years old in 8th grade and he was in high school—in fact, he attended the same high school as my brother. So, I called my mother and told her I was going to 3rd Avenue—a little shopping area about a 45-minute subway ride from our apartment—with my girlfriend because she was looking for some shoes. (My girlfriend apparently also told her parents she was going with me to shop for some shoes). So, my mother said okay. We got to his house around 3. His mother made finger sandwiches for us, and it was very late when we headed back. When we got to my girlfriend's house, her father said, "Your mother is looking for you." When I arrived home, my mother asked where I had been. I said I had been to 3rd Avenue, because we did have to pass 3rd Avenue to get to the train, and we had to bypass the shops, etc. She said, "you are lying," and she slapped me. Additionally, deciding my girlfriend was a bad influence on me, she refused to give me messages from her and did not want me to hang out with her anymore. But my mother's assessment of the situation was wrong. The real deal was that it was all my idea; so, I was not the one being influenced. They were usually my ideas that we go on certain adventures. Ironically, to this day that girlfriend and I are still the best friends. She lives in North Carolina and I live in Chicago; but we communicate almost every day.

⚜

Whatever their disagreements and disputes, Michelle says her mother was a great influence in her life.

Although there may have been times when she didn't know how she was going to make ends meet, she wanted us to be children and never imposed those kinds of issues or problems on us. My mother became widowed when she was 26 and she had four children. That's a lot; I can't even imagine. I had my child when I was 33. So I don't know what I would have been like having 4 kids at 26. And now you have to navigate the world on your own with these children! I feel like she didn't have time to mourn and grieve. She didn't have time to have a pity party and say, "Oh woe is me, I lost my husband." She had to make sure that these kids were raised, and their needs were met—and many of our wants.

One of the things my mother emphasized was education. There was no question about whether we would finish high school or go to college. Education was always her focus for us. I had friends who might say, "If I finish high school . . ." or "If I go to college . . ." but there was never an 'if' for us. She raised us to pursue excellence and although we were raised by a single parent in a housing project where the odds of being successful were slim, all of my mother's children graduated from high school, graduated from college, and we all have post-college graduate degrees. What are the odds of that happening?

When we were kids my mother made sure we were exposed to certain things—ballet and tap—and while I didn't like all of those things, she wanted to make sure we had exposure and then at the point where we could make a decision then we could voice that. The things we liked we could pursue and for those things we didn't like we would discontinue.

My mother always made sure she was present to support us whenever we had anything going on. She came to all of our school functions. I was always in the school chorus and she would be there for our performances. Even when getting my graduate degree at University of Chicago—my brother was graduating from Harvard Law School the day before my commencement. My mother and my siblings were in Boston for his graduation. I wanted my degree, but I wasn't all that interested in attending the ceremony, so I told her she could stay in Boston and enjoy his graduation. She said "No! I'm coming! I'm going to his graduation and then I'm coming to yours. We will just fly to Chicago." That's really the only reason I went to graduation because she wanted to come and be there and see me receive my degree.

My mother was very generous in spirit and always there for people in the neighborhood, particularly seniors in the neighborhood—but really anybody in need. We gave clothes to people who needed them. I certainly didn't know we were poor until I got to college and we were in a class discussing socioeconomic levels. I think it was important to my mother that we not be without because we didn't have a father and she didn't want us to feel that void. She never wanted us to feel like we were missing something because we were without him. So, my mom was one of the people who most influenced my life. The fact that I am a social worker and an advocate for people I think is a direct result of my mother and what I saw in her.

Michelle graduated from high school knowing she was headed for college. Her major dilemma was where she wanted to go. She knew New York and wanted to stay close to home; so she applied to state schools and colleges in and near Manhattan.

Still a good student—*everything came easy to me*—Michelle was accepted to virtually all of the schools to which she applied. And although her brother—a Cornell University graduate—wanted her to apply to Cornell, she did not. She wanted to go to Syracuse University, where she was accepted, but ended up at Fordham University, the Jesuit University of New York (Denzel Washington was there at the time) because Syracuse didn't offer her the financial aid she needed. Although she initially applied and was accepted to Fordham's Bronx campus, she was able to attend Fordham's Manhattan location, which was her preference, as *going to the Bronx campus would be like going to high school; but getting on the train going downtown was different and I felt more like a college student.*

She considered majoring in early childhood education but a high school internship at a daycare, changed her mind. Instead, Michelle chose psychology as her major.

I loved school! When I was home playing house, I was always a teacher. So, it seemed natural for me to go into Education. I always loved kids and I always loved little kids. I babysat from the time I was 13 years old. I've always been very maternal and always just loved kids; but I changed my mind working at the daycare. (She laughs) They got on my nerves—crying and snotting and sneezing . . . it was just too much! After that internship I didn't think it was going to be early childhood education; I decided I wanted to be a child psychologist instead.

To save money while in college, Michelle continued to live at home with her mother and younger sister. There were still opportunities for the now young adult Michelle to *bump heads* with her mom. In her third year in college Michelle started dating a guy more than a decade older than she—a classmate. Her mother disapproved and shared her disapproval with Michelle. Michelle says, *in the end she was probably right; but I wasn't wanting to listen at the time.*

After graduating from college and during the year she took off between college and graduate school, Michelle got a job in the City and traveled.

I graduated from Fordham with a degree in Psychology. And I was working at Catholic Charities as a counselor for kids who had dropped out of high school. Our job was to try to either get them back into school or to get their GED. That was a very good learning experience for me. I was young, probably 22, and the kids in the program were between 14 and 21; so, we were close in age, which is perhaps why I was good in the job and effective in my interactions with the kids. We had a good rapport. These were kids from all cultures—Latino, Black, and White kids.

Armed with that experience, and deciding it was finally time to leave New York and explore living elsewhere, Michelle chose the University of Chicago for graduate school.

Having lived in New York all my life I wanted to go to a place that was culturally similar to New York, that is, where I could go to the theater, I could get on a bus or a train, or walk wherever I wanted to go. I didn't want to be in the country or in the sticks like Cornell or someplace like that; and Chicago seemed to fit the bill for me. Also, I was thinking that wherever I go I might want to stay—I might not want to come back to New York, so I wanted to pick a place that I would feel comfortable in for the long term.

While in Chicago for the graduate school interview Michelle got a chance to visit different parts of the city.

I fell in love with Chicago! The Lakefront! It was cleaner than New York but it was smaller than New York, and I just liked the vibe. I decided that Chicago was perfect for me. During my interview they asked me if I could afford to attend University of Chicago. I said no, not without help—I need financial assistance. They told me they had sent a letter to my house, which I would get when I got back home, telling me that they were awarding me with a full academic scholarship. I said God wants me to go here!

On her return to New York, Michelle told her mother of her decision; and while her mother didn't necessarily believe she would go through with the move, she did not advise Michelle not to go.

My mom may have had mixed feelings about me leaving the state, but she wasn't telling me not to go. I think on some level she wanted me to go, like she wanted all of us to go and explore life for ourselves. On the other hand, of course, she may have wanted me to stay but she didn't try to talk me out of going.

And although Michelle was a bit anxious about leaving her mother alone in their home—since her younger sister went to college it had been only Michelle and her mother in the house—her siblings lived close enough for Michelle to feel comfortable that her mother would be ok.

Back in Chicago, Michelle found herself trying to navigate a whole new environment—and living on her own, having to function independently for the first time in her life.

My intent was to focus on the things I needed so that I could survive my new environment. I was too young and stupid to be scared. I would probably be more scared now. The only thing I was afraid of was running out of money and not having enough money to eat or not having a place to stay.

Michelle's initial navigation of all of this was not easy.

I was away from home for the first time, I'm in this White high-powered University with all these White folk—something I was not used to. And I was away from what I was accustomed to—my close friends, and I didn't have that in Chicago. Initially, I just had mostly superficial friendships and not people who I could go to and really confide in and let them know what I was going through.

Although my undergraduate education at Fordham was challenging academically—I had to work hard—I can actually say I enjoyed it. It was a good experience both socially and academically. The University of Chicago was different. It was less diverse culturally than Fordham, which was geared both towards somebody like me just coming out of high school and also people who were older, working full-time with families and going to school at the same time. When I came to University of Chicago, I got the sense that people were questioning whether or not I was qualified to be there. I felt it was because I am Black. That's all they knew about me; they didn't know anything else so that's the only conclusion I could draw.

Despite these obstacles, Michelle found her Chicago family in the staff at United Charities, where she had an internship during her first year of graduate school. While not necessarily connecting with her peers, the staff was a different matter.

I felt connected to the staff—the clerical and professional employees who were African American. They became my family while I was there. I was in this entrenched organization with White folk and I needed to have the ability to have some regular conversation with people I was comfortable with. I was in my New York, young, rebellious mindset and things would happen or be said that I didn't like, and I would speak my mind about it. And the staff with whom I had become comfortable would say, "We understand how you feel; we were like that when we were young too, but you need to take a chill pill." They would try to temper me and initially I would explain what I felt was wrong, and how I thought I should respond. And they'd say, "Yeah we understand," but they would try to calm me and get me to understand that there was a way to approach this so that I could stay out of harm's way. They said, "We understand you want to change the world, but not so fast." So, I went through that whole thing my first year and it was somewhat of a struggle at times.

Michelle enjoyed the work, much of which was working with the elderly, which would ultimately become the subject of her graduate thesis.

I was always interested in doing work with the very young—which is the early childhood education path that I started to take—or the elderly. This started really when I was doing the internship my first year in graduate school. We serviced the elderly population. I remember going to visit them in their homes—my aim was to develop care plans for them that would keep them in their homes living independently. I remember enjoying my conversations with them—White, Black, whatever—and learning so much from them. I was young and I was like a sponge; I just remember thinking that they were so fascinating in terms of the experiences they had and what they could share and what they could teach me. Also, what they could teach our culture and our generations, and I just thought that they were very interesting to talk with. And of course, from an economic point of view I realized that the aging population was growing and if I wanted to work in an area where the service needs would be increasing, this was it. Because of the growing elderly population, there would be greater needs for services— whether they be direct, in administration, or policy—and I wanted to pursue that niche.

Michelle graduated with an MSW from the University of Chicago School of Social Services Administration in 1983. Unsure about what direction she wanted to take in her career, her first post graduate school job was with Children and Family Services, working with children who were abused and neglected.

After completing school, as sometimes happens, career changes don't always go as planned. My graduate thesis was focused on finding services in the community that would sustain the elderly in their homes so that they wouldn't have to go to nursing homes. The idea was the elders could stay at home with their families with outside support and still live independently. My second year of grad school I opted out of an internship and instead focused fully on my academics—which was an option given to second year students.

She believes that decision prevented her from developing the networks and connections that would have culminated in a job offer at that agency or another which served the elder population.

As Michelle began her job with Children and Family Services, she was young and anxious, with a real apartment and real responsibilities—bills to pay, food to buy, and in need of a car. Living in New York all her life, where having a car was more of a burden than a necessity, Michelle did not even possess a driver's license. Initially her colleagues took her out on weekend driving lessons. When that didn't work, one of the administrators, knowing she was just out of school and didn't have any money loaned her the money to take formal driving lessons. She took lessons and got her license, although *I don't know that anybody wanted to ride with me.* Her family was also skeptical, advising her that her driving services would not be needed back in New York—or if they came to visit in Chicago.

Michelle stayed with Children and Family Services for seven years. The focus of the job was on child abuse and neglect. While it was undoubtedly stressful, Michelle appreciated what she learned.

I'm so grateful for the experience of that job because it taught me so much! It was like baptism by fire. I dealt with just about everything related to child abuse and neglect—physical medical, sexual, emotional, all of it—I've seen it, read it, heard it. I cut my social work teeth in that job.

A stint at the VA followed, where Michelle worked with veterans of all ages—including the elderly—who were in nursing homes. She was a medical social worker doing Outpatient Care—making sure the care plan which had been developed for each veteran was being followed, connecting patients to community resources, and conducting nursing home inspections. It provided Michelle with a birds-eye view of how *we as a society treat our elderly and our veterans.* The view was not a pleasant one—very few of the nursing homes were even near the requisite standards. Michelle held the position with the VA for one year, until such time as marriage, economics, and a desire to start a family caused a shift in her focus, landing her with the Chicago Public School System.

While still in graduate school, Michelle met her future husband.

I met my husband at the University of Chicago. Although he is ten years older than I am, he was in his first year when I was in my second year; and he was one of very few Black men in the program. There might have been two Ph.D. candidates who were Black males. My husband and I were not involved or dating when we were in school. We only had one or two very brief school-related encounters and did not know one another well. A few years after we'd both graduated, we had a chance encounter on public transportation. We recognized each other, but it was not until a year later when we again met on the bus and exchanged numbers. Sometime well after that second encounter, we started dating.

Dating led to a more serious relationship and eventually Michelle and Gregory got married—a major life event. A second life event occurred when Michelle decided to change her career focus—and by extension, jobs.

Gerontology took a back seat for economic reasons. It was a matter of where the jobs existed; what was available. I was married and thinking about having a family; I thought once I had a family and had children I needed to be on a different schedule with more flexibility: Summers off, spring break, and then if I had a kid in school he or she would be on the same schedule. I don't regret it. God put me where he wanted me to be. It might not have been where I would have chosen to be, but I enjoy my job, I love my students, and I have a good relationship with my them. I render a tough love—no nonsense—but compassionate approach to direct services. I give them honesty and expect it in return. I care deeply about my students and I believe most of them like me as well.

Beginning her career with the Chicago Public School System as a school social worker in elementary schools, Michelle continued in essentially that role for nearly 27 years, when in 2016 she moved into a high school environment full-time—a move she resisted for quite a while, believing it would not be the right fit. Her reaction has instead been just the opposite.

I love it! I absolutely love it! It may have something to do with the kind of high school I'm assigned to. It's a selective-enrollment school; so, it's not a chaotic environment of some urban high schools that might be exposed in the media. It's a socially positive and academically challenging experience for most of our students. We do experience our share of drama and trauma.

Her role as school social worker is to be the person to whom students can come when things are not going well—when they need to talk, to trust somebody. Michelle's office environment is designed to provide students with a sense of peace.

And although Michelle believes that she is nearing the end of her career, she believes that *this may be the best time in my career for me to be with these young people.*

In fact, after her time with Children & Family Services where there was nothing but crises—*I was always worried about placing a kid in the wrong environment and having them end up dying; so it was a really high stress level job*—the Chicago Public Schools were also a calm from the storm for Michelle. Having dealt with a number of devastating situations in her previous positions she remained cool and calm with whatever issues arose—much to the amazement of her colleagues.

I told them I had seen crises up close for many years and this is not it! They were all amazed at how I was so cool and calm, and I would just tell them I've been through the fire!

Sometimes her reaction caused conflict when she pushed back on her colleagues' inclination to be punitive, labeling, and even wanting to criminalize some student behavior, which she deemed normal behavior for children at that age even though it was not necessarily something they should be doing at school. That meant everybody did not like her, but in standing firm while explaining her position, she garnered their respect.

It was important that they see them as children, as a child, and not as a criminal or a diagnosis or a label. The same was true with Special Education kids where once again the reaction to a child's behavior was often punitive, resulting in taking away privileges. I had to help them understand that the only way to help the child was to permit him to experience things—with guidance—so that the child could begin to understand right from wrong. Sometimes I would chaperone the child myself when nobody else wanted to do that so that they would allow the child to do things that they were inclined to deny him—like going on a field trip.

Michelle's approach applied to all the children at the school, including ADHD and special needs children. She emphasized the need to support children with special needs or who had been traumatized—not to reinjure them.

Sometimes it appeared I was going against the principal of my school because I was saying no you can't do this; you can't be punitive. I was a voice for the underdog—and that was my job. I wasn't necessarily there to always side with the school or the principal but to do what was in the best interest of the child. I wasn't going to create havoc in the lives of these children.

I think my approach reflects who I am. And I think the older I get the more I am who I am. I don't really believe in the zodiac much; but I'm an Aries and Aries are born warriors and that's who I think I am.

Michelle's personality, attitude and life experiences, good and bad, prior to becoming a mother—from her sensitivity as a child, which evolved into a person who would speak her mind, her at times volatile relationship with her own mother, her choice of psychology as her major in college, obtaining an MSW at the University of Chicago, her experiences in Children and Family Services, and finally her move to the Chicago Public School system as a social worker—all prepared her for motherhood in ways that she could not have imagined as she was going through them. Just as she never imagined that the child for whom she had been preparing all her life would be autistic.

Motherhood and Najja
Michelle was looking forward to being a mother . . .

I love kids and I think I wanted to be a mother more than I wanted to be a wife.

Once Michelle was married, and having made the move to the Chicago Public School Systems, she and her husband decided the time was right. Michelle spent hours researching different aspects of raising a child—from breastfeeding, to her child's diet, learning, and so on. *[I was almost obsessed]* She felt prepared to begin the journey. Najja Malik (Naj) was born on May 4, 1993. Michelle and her husband were elated to have a healthy baby boy.

Michelle stayed home with Naj for the first year and one month of his life, then went back to work. However, the next caretaker was a *disaster,* causing Michelle to return home for the next two years of his life. Ultimately, she believes having to return home was a blessing in that she was able to observe Naj and his growth and development. All seemed normal until Naj passed his second birthday, and she and her husband noticed that their son's development was not progressing like other children his age.

I noticed some delays and took him to be evaluated when he was about two and a half years old. At the time, he was also developing a distended abdomen. We were not initially concerned because you know kids can be chubby. However, when we went to the doctor seeking an evaluation on his developmental progress the doctor noted his distended abdomen and testing found a tumor on his liver. So, we tabled the evaluation of his development and he had surgery to remove the tumor. The tumor was said to be the size of a basketball, but he recovered quickly.

The developmental testing was resumed with an unwelcomed result—a diagnosis of autism. Michelle had to take a minute.

Initially that [the autism diagnosis] was like a death sentence to me. That knocked me off my feet because I had all these hopes and dreams for his success and development. I mean I come from a family that is highly educated. I had all these hopes and dreams about my son—he was going to be all these great things. When I heard the "A" word—Autism—I was like 'oh my God!' I had a very close guy friend who had a daughter who is autistic, and I would hang out with them often when I was single. But that was my only knowledge of autism. And suddenly, I get this diagnosis and I didn't know how to handle it.

But after *crawling into my little hole* Michelle realized . . .

I don't have time for this. I must figure out what I have to do for this baby! So, I tried to get my hands on everything I could about autism. It was almost chilling because I would read stuff and then I would kind of see my son almost coming off the pages of what I was reading. I'd say that's exactly what he's doing or not doing.

By the time the tumor surgery was complete, and he had been diagnosed with autism, Naj was almost 28 months old. That was important to the autism diagnosis as there was a program available to babies who are diagnosed with autism, but it ended at age three. If you were in the program from birth to age three you received all the services that you would need. But because Najja came into the program only eight months shy of three years old, it was more difficult. Fortunately, the program administrators knew that Michelle was a social worker for the Chicago Public School System, and made sure Michelle was made aware of services and opportunities for her son. Post diagnosis, denial of the reality of Naj's condition was not an option.

Any denial about Naj was before he was diagnosed as autistic. I remember being home. The TV was on but Najja wasn't watching TV. He was laughing almost to himself. And I remember thinking, 'Why is he doing this? Is something wrong?' And I remember trying to forget about it. I didn't even tell my husband. As time went on, he was vocalizing, but he wasn't verbalizing; he was making sounds, but he wasn't saying words. I remember he said "dada" and then he stopped saying that. And then he would say hi or he would wave, and he stopped doing that.

Once it was clear that Naj was autistic, Michelle became proactive in learning about autism and doing whatever was necessary to address how it impacted her son.

I was in everything! I was in parent groups, I was in support groups, and I would drag Najja with me. At the time, my husband was working on his doctorate degree, so I took Naj wherever I went seeking information and assistance. When I discovered that the psychologist at the school to which Naj was assigned had never seen autism, a psychologist friend referred me to a psychologist in the school system so that Naj was evaluated by someone who was very familiar with autism. I knew anyone not familiar with autism might attribute symptoms to something else, resulting in a misdiagnosis. Although I was pretty much convinced that Najja was autistic—he had already been evaluated by the University of Chicago hospitals—there still had to be an evaluation by the school system psychologists.

The psychologist to whom they were referred confirmed the earlier diagnosis of autism from University of Chicago Hospitals. Michelle had to meet with the school system about what services they would provide—and this time she was on the other side. Michelle heard about the Easter Seals School, which was a private therapeutic day service. Nearly all the students in the Easter Seal program had autism. As autism is a spectrum disorder, there were kids from the lows to very high—almost Savant kids. Najja was teetering around the lower end—he was non- verbal. Thus, Michelle and her husband believed that it was a better school for Naj than the one to which he was being assigned by the school system. When she met resistance from school administration about changing schools, the school psychologist who evaluated Naj intervened and he was admitted to the Easter Seal School.

Although the Easter Seal School provided more services and Michelle and her husband had some control over how their son was treated, it was not perfect. For the first six months Michelle had not returned to work, so on some occasions when she took Naj to school she would stay for a while to observe. The school discouraged this because he needed to be able to function without her presence.

I told them that I understood that; however, Naj didn't know them nor did I know them or how the program was running. Thus, I needed to sit in periodically and see how things were going.

Michelle and her husband continued this periodic 'spot-checking' over the years, to the chagrin of some at the school.

I had to try to explain that I was my child's only advocate; and therefore, it was incumbent upon me to check in and make sure he was getting the appropriate services. I tried to get them to understand that it wasn't personal or wasn't between myself and any of the individuals. I just wanted to make sure he was getting the best services possible. Since he was non-verbal, I had to speak for him and if they were mad at me, so be it. I had a lot of battles attempting to do what was best for Najja.

Naj remains non-verbal, and his parents remain his staunchest advocates. When they realized that there was not a local autism group in the Chicagoland area, Michelle and another parent of an autistic child created the Chicago Metropolitan Autism Chapter.

We decided we were going to create a Chicago Metropolitan autism chapter. We did the paperwork, submitted it to the state, got a charter, and we had an organization. Initially it worked well.

And although she eventually stepped away from the organization to devote more time to her other obligations to Naj and her job, and to find *some peace in my life,* Michelle has never stopped looking for ways to enhance her son's life.

Michelle also stepped away from the chapter because she found herself embroiled in a fight about the direction of the organization. This was one of many fights she had, and at the time she was tired of fighting without positive result.

At a certain point it seemed like I was always fighting. Remember I said I taught my brother how to fight. And it always seemed when my siblings were in a fight I was always around to help? However, when I was fighting nobody was around. Maybe as a kid I had a lot of anger and fighting was kind of a manifestation of that. But I just always remember being a fighter and I think that was maybe part of my nature. As an adult I'm able to channel that in a more positive way—fighting for the things that I believe are important; fighting for the things that are positive and more productive and that will serve others well. I'm just a fighter by nature and that's what I do.

Because of the nature of Naj's autism—including the fact that he is now 27 years of age, Michelle and her husband are Naj's primary caregiver. Thus, an important way in which Michelle has been able to find the peace in her life has been through the support she has received from her friends and family.

There was a time when my mother would come to visit when Najja was on spring break and my husband and I were working, and she would come and take care of him. She was one of the few people who we allowed to take care of him. And then at some point my mother developed her own health problems and was unable to take care of him and so again my husband and I were his primary if not only caregivers.

Another source of tremendous support for Michelle has been her bonus daughter, whom she calls and considers to be her daughter. She is her husband's daughter born during his first marriage.

She is my daughter. She was with us at least two weekends out of the month so she's known me from a very early age. She refers to me as her second mother; she and I have a very close relationship. She is crucial in my life and I love her. And she has also taken care of Naj. She's in her thirties now and she was eight when Najja was born. She babysat for him on a number of occasions; but as he got older and stronger and she wasn't around him as much she had difficulty handling him. So my husband and I are really the only ones who can comfortably handle him at this point in his life.

One source of support that has been important throughout her journey with Naj is other parents who have autistic children.

I had a girlfriend whose son also went to the Easter Seal school, but who was about 10 years older than my son at the time. We became each other's support group. I have friends and family who love me and my son and were supportive; however, they didn't know my walk. So it was important to have another person who had gone through some of the same things I was going through to whom I could look for support. And that's what I did.

And of course, Michelle and her husband support each other.

My husband has been very supportive—especially with respect to our son. I know that when there is a special needs child involved there is usually a high rate of divorce—the man leaves the relationship because he can't bear the fact that he has a son who is not perfect. But my husband has been through his own trials and tribulations in his life and so he's a fighter; he's a warrior. He was therefore ready for the challenge; he's that kind of spirit. He saw raising our son as just another challenge in life. So, he's always been there for Najja and we share all of the responsibilities.

In fact, he now has primary responsibility for Najja because he is retired and Najja has aged out of school. Also, because he has the training, my husband is now providing him with services through a state-funded program for individuals with "other abilities" who have aged out of school. Rather than hiring somebody from the outside to come in and help or sending him to a program where he doesn't know people and can't speak for himself my husband has assumed that role. He makes sure Najja gets physical activity every day. He takes him for a walk to the track, or a park, or on the lakefront to get him out and get physical activity almost every day. Sometimes they'll invite me to go and sometimes I'll go; but most of the time I don't because I'll take that as my personal respite time to do things that I want to do. They have a great relationship. Najja loves his dad—sometimes I think he loves his dad more than he loves me! And that's o.k. too!

Seriously, I know he loves us both. As with any other family each child has his own individual relationship with each parent; and that's the case for us. So, even with his other abilities Najja has studied and learned us well. He understands his dad and knows his dad and he understands me and knows me. So he knows what he can get away with and what he can't get away with in dealing with each of us. And the fact that he has two parents allow him the best of both worlds.

Overcoming obstacles

Caring for Naj has been laden with obstacles and challenges. There have been and continue to be difficult days.

He would have bad days. He was diagnosed with seizures at 5, at some point he had asthma. He has been sick and so it's been difficult sometimes to manage all of that. I was not able to go to my maternal grandmother's funeral because Najja was hospitalized. And I think I was the only grandchild who wasn't there. At some point my cousin and I spoke during this time and she said, "You're not here and if you lived closer then somebody could be there for you." And that's when I cried. Because I realized I didn't have family here. My husband was here, and he had his family, but I didn't have my people there.

Faith and What Naj Can Do

The many challenges for Michelle and her husband in raising Naj might overwhelm many of us. Michelle has avoided being overwhelmed by her faith and how she has approached these challenges.

My spiritual connection to God has allowed me to carry through in the face of the challenges of my child's autism. My spiritual connection is my base—I'm sure of that. I don't dwell on the negative. Instead, I have a positive outlook; I see the glass as half-full, I have gratitude, which is what I preach to my clients. I don't look at what I don't have, I look at what I do have. Same thing with my son: I tell people I don't look at my son for what he cannot do I see him for what he can do.

While he was at the Easter Seal School, Channel 7 News came to interview three parents in the school, and I was one of them. One of the questions they asked was what is it that I most wanted my son to do. And I said I wanted to hear my son say, "I love you". Several days after that I went to the school to pick up Najja. And one of the aides there said, "you know what you said you wanted your son to do—to say I love you?" And I said, 'Yes.' She said, "He does that." I asked what she meant. She said, "Every time you pick him up, he hugs you and kisses you on the cheek—every day, every day. He is saying I love you in that way." 'Girlllll,' I said, 'Thank you so much for saying that because I really needed that!' And I realized what she was saying was true. He hugs and kisses me all the time. And I know people sometimes say that people with autism are detached and he can at times be detached. But he loves his mama and he loves his daddy! And he's affectionate and he laughs, and he shares laughter.

I look at the things that Najja can do. And I help him with that sometimes by telling him to do the things that he wants me to do for him. I'll say no. He will want me to put his coat on and I'll say 'No, you do that, you can do that. I'm not doing it. I'm not your maid. You do it.' I'm very direct with him. Some people are surprised about this kind of interaction with my son. I say, yeah, he has special needs, but it doesn't mean he can't do anything. I say, 'I have the same expectations of my child that you have of your child. He's not allowed to visit your home and tear things up. I don't want you to say it's o.k. because he has special needs and you feel

It's been a tough ride. We have had different issues with Najja—medically and otherwise. We faced the question of whether to medicate or not. Neither my husband nor I were inclined towards medicating Naj; however, we had to compromise because Naj was having seizures and we had to do something to help to alleviate them. We realized in certain circumstances such as his seizures that if you do not use medications they can worsen and be potentially fatal. It's definitely been a challenging and a learning experience for both of us.

There is a poem called "Holland." It's about a person who is a traveler going to Paris. They planned this trip to Paris and made all these arrangements and plans—to the Champs- Elysees and other Paris sites. They were excited. Then the pilot comes on and says that plans have changed "No, we are not going to Paris—instead, we're landing in Holland." The traveler is upset because they had saved and made plans for their entire life to go to Paris and not Holland and became highly distraught and disgruntled. And then as they are arriving in Holland they look out of the window and notice that there is beauty in Holland too—Holland has tulips, Holland has windmills, Holland has numerous attractions and places of interest. The poem is kind of representative of people like my husband and myself who have a child with special needs. It's the same thing. We had certain expectations from the beginning. We were planning a trip to one destination but landed in another. We ended up in a different place and so now we have to choose. We can focus on the possibilities of what could have been, or we can accept the beauty and reality of the destination to which we have arrived. We have arrived at a beautiful, loving, witty, perceptive, and ever-challenging place in our son called Najja.

I once spoke at an autism parent group and the poem is one of the handouts I gave to parents because when I received the poem early on, that was life changing for me. I was like "Wow that's a good way of looking at it!" It was a different stop than we had planned; but at some point, we had to say let's focus on where we are. This is not the end of the world; we can enjoy this place too. And it's consistent with the way I view life—the glass is half full not half empty. I look at Najja for what he can do, not what he can't do. And I try to let that be my focus—Najja is our Holland.

This philosophy was also helpful when Michelle was working in the school system and had to do social assessments of a wide variety of children—including children with disabilities and children with special needs.

Part of my assessment is talking to children especially those who are verbal to get their viewpoint in order to assist me in the evaluation process. I also spend time with kids who are non-verbal—also to assist me in my assessment. One of the staff members said, "You are one of the few clinicians who come and spend quality time with the kids whether they are verbal or non-verbal." But I have a special needs child as well; so I think part of my desire to do that is that I would want somebody to spend time with Naj if he were in a similar situation. So, I would rub the kids' hands and talk to them. My perspective was I'm not in that body so I don't know what they understand. I will talk to them with the knowledge that they might understand what I was saying. I will talk with him like I would talk to my son—like I would talk to any kid. And one thing I would take from that experience of working with severely special needs children is that my son can walk, my son can hug me, my son can laugh at a joke I tell. So, I am blessed. I can't go home and cry in my beer because my son has special needs because there are people who must place their children in a facility because their needs are so great. I think God puts you in certain places at certain times for certain reasons. I was working that particular job for 6 or 7 years; and I think that helps me too to realize that I don't have any reason to feel pity for myself, thinking about the parents of the children for whom I was performing the assessments and how they might feel.

How you respond in these situations has a lot to do with your attitude and your outlook on things. And then that has a lot to do with the perspective one takes on life. If I were to sit and ruminate on everything that has gone wrong or that could go wrong, then I think I would probably be under the bed unable to function. I just don't have time for that. Life is for living.

In speaking with my students I sometimes have to explain to them that rather than focusing on what you don't have you can focus on what you do have; because whatever you don't have there's always somebody who has less and would love to have your problems. So, it's important to have some balance. Sometimes we lose sight of our blessings when we focus on the dearth of our circumstances.

Self-Care

Exercise, yoga, nutrition—eating well—and finding some time to do things for herself are some of the ways that Michelle has been able to fight when she needs to fight and manage the obligations and responsibilities of Naj.

When I first start an exercise journey, I always start with yoga. It gives me a sense of peace; it gives me discipline, and it helps me to prepare my body for whatever else I'm going to do. I taught myself yoga and I also taught myself Pilates. I started the journey seriously almost 20 years ago. I followed a book that had step by step descriptions and photos. I didn't have time to go to a health club or classes; and I didn't necessarily want to, so I just taught myself using these resources. I started buying and watching tapes, reading, researching, and devouring everything on fitness. I have endless tapes, books, and magazines on fitness, nutrition, and wellness.

One other benefit of her exercise and eating routine was weight loss.

I wasn't even trying to lose weight. I was tired of being tired and I was just trying to get healthy. The place I was working had three stories and six flights of stairs; and I realized that my measure of fitness would be when I could climb up those six flights of stairs with my bag on my shoulder and not be winded. When I was able to do that, I felt successful. I went from a size 12 to a size 4-6. The weight loss was great; but I just wanted to be healthy and not tired.

People would often ask Michelle how she could do all she did with a special needs son—have time to exercise and cook and focus on nutrition and that kind of thing. Her answer was priorities.

It just depends on what you make your priority. We all have the same 24 hours in the day; it's up to us individually to choose how we spend it. And in some ways Najja was an inspiration when I realized it was important

for me to be healthy so I could be here because he needed somebody to take care of him. As he was growing and getting taller people were asking, "What are you going to do when he gets taller?" My response was, 'I'm going to be his mother.' But particularly because I was healthy and strong myself, I knew that he would not be any kind of challenge that I couldn't meet. I wanted to be able to take care of myself not having to rely on any-body else, not relying on medication or physical assistance or anything like that. And if I could take care of myself then I would be able to take care of Naj. As long as God says that I'm going to be here then I want to be able to take care of my son.

As a result of her physical metamorphosis and focus on nutrition and wellness, Michelle has developed a few philosophies about health and the importance of taking care of ourselves. First,

God has given you one body and if you betray it, it will betray you.

A second philosophy that Michelle has developed during her jaunt through this life is an important one:

One lesson I learned on my journey was you have to put yourself first. You can't give from a point of depletion. There was a point in my life that I was somewhat resentful because I felt like I was giving of myself to ev-erything and everybody else and I got the leftovers—the crumbs. So, I de-termined that I had to put myself first. If anyone accuses me of thinking selfishly, I consider that a compliment. I'm glad I've been able to reach that point in my life. I have to make sure I get my needs met first and then I can give to others from a place of fulfillment and not resentment.

We, as African American women tend to take care of everybody else at our own expense; and that's why we're sick and unhealthy. The stress is kill-ing us. That is a very important message for us to hear and learn.

Taking care of herself means Michelle finds time to do things that give her joy. She works around the obstacles that present themselves and is deliberate in finding her own time.

When my husband is unavailable, I don't have somebody to say, 'Can you come sit with Najja?' So I have to find respite in my own way. One of the things I do (she laughs) . . . I'm a crossword puzzle fanatic. And it's also important to me to stay connected with friends and family members, so I do reach out and talk to people to have some social connection. Most often it might be via telephone. When Najja was in school and I was off

I would take that time to connect with friends, go to lunch, go to doctor's appointments, go to the grocery store, that kind of thing. And then as I said sometimes my husband would take him out to the park, so I have a few hours. Unfortunately, Najja does not always sleep well, which means I'm up sometimes when I should be asleep. When he does sleep, sometimes I might get up and do things that give me relaxation.

And although she no longer writes poetry as she once did as a teenager, she turns to writing when she needs to.

I do write—just not poetry. And every now and then if I think that I'm not going to communicate effectively with somebody in person or by phone then I'll write a letter. And I've been known to write some very profound letters! But that's kind of the extent of my writing, except what I write for work.

Michelle, who was 59 at the time of this interview, came to these realizations—these philosophies—in her mid-forties *after things were not going as they should.* Once she started making sure she was in a good space, it enhanced her ability to work through all the other issues—expected and unexpected—that accompanying raising a child—now man—with special needs.

Major Triumphs:

The fact that she is surviving on this journey with her son without letting it overwhelm her, the positive relationship with her network of family and friends, and her health are Michelle's major triumphs to this point. About each she says . . .

Surviving. *I did not let it get to me to the point I couldn't function anymore. I can get up in the morning and open my eyes and say, 'Hey it's a new day!' even in the midst of some of the worst stuff I experienced with my son. Sometimes I might go to bed and think I don't know if I can do this tomorrow. Then I sleep and wake in the morning and I'm happy to see a new day. God gave me grace and mercy to do this all over again; and I have to do it differently and hopefully better today.*

Family and Friends. *I have a good network of family and friends whom I consider to be close and dear. They are people who are loyal to me, they care about me, they care about my well-being and I feel very rich and blessed in the sense that I know I have people I can reach out to and talk to them about thoughts, dreams, experiences and just plain life-sharing. The fact that I've been able to have that in my life is of great importance to me.*

Health. *My journey of trying to eat better and balance my weight has taken me to a level where I am able to inspire others and to let others know what I've done and help encourage them through their own individual journey as well. I obtained a certification in health and wellness. My philosophy on health and wellness becomes incorporated into my service provisions with my students and my role as a social worker. I remember one of my social work professors saying that "social work is the conscious use of self," meaning that if you're going to be a good therapist, a good social worker, you must bring yourself into the mix. You can't take the position where I'm the clinician and you're the patient and you have this distance. My students, and whoever I work with, they get a piece of me—so they know who I am. I give them excerpts and anecdotes of my life to let them know that I've been through some stuff too, where things didn't always work out either. So, they get to know me and get to see me and see my vulnerability. And so even when I'm telling people about health and whatever they see my human flaws not just their own. I have the similar story; I went down the similar path. I think I'm very relatable to others. I think people relate to me because I am real and never pretentious. I don't look at others as less than. We are all just on different legs of our respective journeys.*

Evolution:

In my teens I was very flighty as most teens are—trying to figure out who I was. That might change on any given week or month depending on what internal or external influence was winning out. Today I am very grounded. I know who I am and I'm happy with who this person Michelle is. Today, I have strong convictions. I have a strong belief system, my walk with Christ has helped me because I have seen my faith manifest itself. I know that there are things that have happened to me in my life that make me know that there is a higher power that has gotten me through those tough times, those periods in my life. So that helps me when I'm going through stuff. I look back on those things and say, 'God got you through that, so he'll get you through the next thing.' I have this sign on my office door that says, "You've survived 100% of everything in your life so far, so there's a pretty good chance that you'll survive whatever is next."

I've been through trials and I've been through tribulations and I'll go through more, but I look at them as learning experiences. I know I must get something out of it; I have got to learn something from it. So that I don't see things as 'Oh God why is this happening?' Instead, I say, 'What is it you want me to learn? There's something you want me to learn.' And I believe that everything God is taking me through is because of something he wants me to learn or something he wants to teach me at that point. And it's up to me to figure out which one it is. And I need to go from there. And that's helped ground me.

In addition, I'm older, more mature. Don't think for one minute I know everything, and I got it all down; because I'm still growing and I'm still learning, and I'll continue to 'til I take my last breath. What I'm saying is that I am at a greater comfort level in myself now than perhaps I was 20 or 30 years ago. A lot of people probably can say that—maybe some can and maybe some can't. But I think when I was younger, I was in a place where I was wishy-washy and not sure of myself—of what I believed or where I stood. But I got it now. I know what I believe. I know what I feel. I can say no to people in a comfortable way. I can say no and be okay with saying no, I'm not doing that. No that's not going to happen. When I was 20 or 30, I'd say okay I'll do this without really wanting to.

Michelle recalls one such example when she was younger, involving her efforts to help a friend with a young child who did not have a car by taking her to the grocery store. Giving her a ride to the store was not in itself the problem. It was that her friend wanted to shop for hours; and the fact that Michelle accommodated her, although in doing so she and Naj would not get home until very late—taking them both out of their schedule.

I felt like I should do that. As I got older and I started dealing with Naj's issues I realized I had to say no and I started to do so and do so without feeling stressed and without guilt I had to realize that my life is not like hers; my life was not like my friend's life. They had freedoms to do things that I didn't because of Najja's needs and the things we needed to do to move his life along. I realized I had to take into consideration my family and my son and what our needs were. When people would invite Najja and me to places that were crowded I would have to say no because I knew he did not do well in crowds. The more I said no I became more comfortable with that. I knew that Najja does better with just me or my husband because he wants our attention. It was difficult for some friends to understand, but most do now.

My husband helped me with that because he said, "Your circumstances are different than everybody else's. Your life is different so you can't do everything that others might want you to do." But that's true for all of us. We all have to look at our individual situations and that of our families and make decisions that are best for us and not base our decision upon the needs of others. You have to see where that fits into your schedule. And I think that's a good rule to follow whomever you are.

The other critical aspect of Michelle's life that has guided her during the good and bad times of her life is her faith. Like most African Americans our roots are in the church. Michelle recalls going to Sunday School and church as a young child—often unwillingly. It was something she had to do, but not something she took seriously, in terms of understanding the concept of faith. In high school, she joined the church choir, as a suggestion from friends who liked her singing voice. She only sang in the choir twice a month and didn't join the church. Until one particular Sunday.

I don't remember the day, nor the topic. The pastor was talking, and I just remember for the first time I was listening, and his sermon spoke to me, to my life.

The result was Michelle's decision to be baptized. She was 16 at the time; and began attending church regularly. When she got to college (*I think I was dating a guy who was more atheist than Christian*), she pulled away from the church—but not her belief in God.

It wasn't that I didn't believe, I never stopped believing. But I just stopped going to church.

A friend she met in graduate school—*who was saved*—and eventually attending her husband's family church, where his uncle was a pastor, returned her closely to her faith.

At that point in time I again began really listening to the Word and hearing it and feeling like it was speaking to me. I was inundated with the Message—reading the Word, reading scripture, and reading the Bible. And that's when things really came full cycle. Because as a teenager I still didn't quite get it; but as an adult with a husband and a child and having gone through some things in life now it all gave me a different outlook and had a different impact. That's when I really committed my life to Christ. And it's pretty much been that way ever since.

It means I'm living a conscious life, which means that I'm realizing that God is in everything and every aspect of my life. And I realize that in all things I must seek God in prayer.

I believe in the scripture that says, 'pray unceasingly', constant prayer, pray about everything no matter what's going on. And I have to stop and think and take the time out to spend with Him and talk with Him, and check with Him, 'Am I doing this right, or should I be doing something else?' I'm more conscious than I was back then when I was 16. Now it's a part of my walk. It's part of my relationships, it's part of my conversation.

Mistakes

While Michelle acknowledges the mistakes she has made in her journey thus far, those mistakes are part of the journey; therefore, she has no regrets.

I know I've made mistakes; probably made some yesterday and I have already made some today. But I can't speak to regret in that sense because I think everything happens for a reason. And I believe there's supposed to be a lesson in everything. And part of the experiences in life—the good, the bad, the mistakes, the triumphs, the successes—is learning. You have to learn from stuff. That's why we're here to learn and grow; and so, if I looked back on all the mistakes I've made and regretted them, then I wouldn't be where I am now—I wouldn't be Me. I think I'm here because of some of those mistakes and that I had to make those mistakes in order to learn and do things differently and maybe even better. And as a result of those mistakes I have a story to tell and can be a blessing to others. As I continue on and make new mistakes, I hope those mistakes result in new growth experiences for myself and my tribe. Making new mistakes will be new learning experiences. I can prosper from that and move on and move forward. Where you are at a particular time in life, even if you're making a mistake, that's where God wanted you to be for some reason; and it's my job to figure it out—figure out the reason.

Included in Michelle's takeaways from her life so far is the importance of *knowing yourself—knowing who you are:*

That's a journey because you're constantly evolving into who you are as you get older. But it's important to be consciously trying to figure it out— who you are and what you are—because that informs in terms of the decisions that you make. Am I making this decision because somebody else made it or am I making this decision because these are my values? What are my values? Where is my line in the sand that I draw? Asking 'who am I?' defines for yourself what is acceptable to you that does not compromise your moral compass. That certainly evolves as you get older because it changes. But what I would say to young people is to be on that constant journey of trying to figure out who you are and what you are and what you believe in. Knowing what you stand for or what you don't stand for is important but something young people don't always think about. Instead they often find themselves following whatever is trending.

Moderating that criticism is her acknowledgement that . . .

. . . it's hard for young people today and I often say to my friends that I'm so glad I didn't grow up in this day and time. We didn't have all these distractions. We didn't have social media, cable television and were not exposed to explicit sexuality. We were genuinely kids. And if we saw any of that stuff it was accidental. It was like giggle giggle because we knew we weren't supposed to see it. These days kids are exposed to it, they think they're supposed to be exposed to it, they will do it in front of you, and if you say something, they look at you like, "What's wrong with you, did you come from Mars?"

While technological advances have their place, with all of the access to social media, Michelle believes that the human element is missing, causing greater stress and more isolation than is healthy.

It looks like they [young people] are more advanced than we were, but I don't think so. In fact, it has stunted them in a lot of ways—emotionally and socially. Because of social media they don't know how to interact and have social relationships. They interact more so in isolation.

There is a comic strip: Pearls Before Swine (animal caricatures), which I have on my office wall. In the strip several people are texting each other on their phones. First person: "I feel so lonely all the time." The next person is saying, "I do too." The third person says, "Well at least we have social media." The next person says, "Yeah it's such a real cruel world; gives me a lot of hope." The next person says, "Right; like we have a community." The next person says, "Yeah instead of always being surrounded by strangers." The next person says, "Yeah just like the Cafe I go to, no one even talks to me." The other one says, "Mine too." Everybody agrees with the same thought. Then they look up and realize they're all in the same Cafe.

And even when her students acknowledge the rightness of Michelle's approach, she is realistic about her efforts because of the 'culture' of social media.

While my students get it, they hear me, it's so imbedded in the culture. So as soon as they leave my office, and somebody starts texting them it takes them right back to where they were in the beginning. It's like back in the sixties you didn't wear long skirts because everybody wore miniskirts. Today its technology and the phone thing. That's what everybody does. Everybody's using technology so you use technology too. That's what the culture is.

Michelle believes the effects of the culture are sobering.

It actually kind of frightens me. I see it just getting worse because technology is always evolving; and perhaps taking us to another level and moving away from social contact and relationships.

Despite this realization, Michelle is undeterred in her efforts to affect the lives of her students. She says, *if there is breath and life there is always hope.*

The Evolution of Michelle

Today, Michelle Gaither—caregiver, mother, wife, health/wellness advocate and social worker has evolved from her younger self. Her jaunt from outspoken rebel at 15 to the person she sees in the mirror at 60 is both different and the same. She is no longer the family's nonconformist, but she is also not hesitant to have her say. Moreover, whatever insecurities she may have had along the way have been supplanted with a confidence and self-assuredness that embraces the person that she has become, not in spite of but because of the trials and tribulations of her journey.

I don't consider myself to be the rebel or the black sheep of the family. What they all know about me is that I'm going to speak up and say whatever it is I need to say. Although I suppose that I am still a rebel to the extent that I do things my way, I'm not a shrinking violet by any stretch of the imagination. But I guess they accept it, realizing that it doesn't mean that she's against us or doesn't like us, it's just her personality. So, no, I don't consider myself to be the black sheep of the family anymore. Maybe it's someone else's role now, but it's not mine. (She laughs)

And . . .

I know who I am, I know I'm a likeable person, I know I'm a lovable person and if somebody gets to know me and they see the sincerity of who I am they are going to like me. I like who I am. I like myself. I like who I've become—I don't know that I always did; but I do now. I feel my personality has come full circle and I know who I am now. I am confident of who I am now; and so, when I have a belief and a belief system, and it's been tried and true and tested nobody can move me off of that. And that's my foundation. So maybe my major triumph is that I finally know who I am, and I like myself and I feel comfortable with myself and I like who I've become. I'm not trying to be anything else or anybody else and I'm not trying to be a people pleaser. Often my interactions depend on who it is and what you can handle. Sometimes I'm very blunt and straightforward. Sometimes people can't handle that; but people who know me and know who I am just say, "There she goes again." Those are the people who call me Micki or Michelle. They know that I might say something to them that at times might come out harsh or crass, but I hope they know it's rooted in love. It's all love here.

MARILYN ROBINSON
Resistance & Resilience

Rejection is like a slap in the face but is often far more painful. The sting of the slap will subside; however, the stinging pain of rejection, especially for a child, can linger—sometimes for a lifetime. Overcoming that rejection—in addition to many other challenges and obstacles—and moving forward in life, which itself will have roadblocks and obstacles, is the challenge. Meet Marilyn Robinson—an ordained Lutheran minister.

Marilyn spent the first seven years of her life in New Orleans in the care of her grandparents, and thereafter in Chicago with her mother and three siblings. Her journey to the pastorate has included navigating gangs and violence as a teenager in Chicago, time as a member of the Black Panther Party, drug abuse, college, sexual assault, marriage to a military man and life in Germany with two children, divorce, homelessness, overcoming total blindness, family discord, graduating from the seminary, and finally finding her path as a minister.

Born in New Orleans, Louisiana at Charity Hospital, Marilyn Scott—nicknamed Lynn—and her cousin Teddy spent their early childhood with their grandparents. Lynn especially remembers her grandmother.

I know what it is to be loved and cared for because of those first seven years with my grandmother. My grandmother lived in the 9th Ward on Flood Street. She had a huge property there and created a wonderful environment for my cousin and me. We had the best backyard in the world with fig and berry trees! We didn't want for anything and my grandmother took care of us. It was a significant piece of my life. That corner house on Flood Street became the "starter" that leavened my entire life; always providing sustenance and ample memories to feed upon during lean times.

Grandfather

As close as Marilyn was to her grandmother, it was different with her grandfather. She believes that the foundation of her fear of rejection was watching and being a part of the way in which her grandfather rejected her mother when her mother got pregnant.

I was born out of wedlock, which deepened an already great chasm between my mother and her stepfather whom everyone called Mr. James. He did not spend much time with pretense and just instructed me to call him Uncle James rather than grandfather. He did not spend a great deal of time with me; and when he did so it was to give me instructions on how to sit or not sit, where to go or not go, what to do or not do.

My Mother

Marilyn's mother was 17 and unmarried when she got pregnant, and her grandfather did not accept Marilyn's father. So, after her birth, Marilyn's grandparents decided to raise her, while she believes putting her mother out of the house.

She was just not in their home anymore. I'm not sure when I knew she was my mother, but my first recollection of her was when she was standing in the doorway in my grandparents' house during one of her visits. My grandfather was yelling at her and she was weeping. Although I recall my grandmother being there, my grandfather was clearly in control. And my mother just walked out the door.

Despite this incessantly cold reception—at least from her father— Marilyn's mother still came to visit. And when Marilyn was school age she went to live with her mother.

When it was time for me to go into the first grade my mother came to get me. We went to live in a house on Bayou Road—also in the Ninth Ward— and I got a new dog named Queenie.

Bayou Street

Initially excited about this new adventure—living with her mother, exploring her new neighborhood, learning how to skate, and meeting new playmates—one incident changed Marilyn's excitement to pain and discomfort, solidifying her fear of rejection.

Shortly after my mother and I moved in a bunch of other children and I had gathered on our block to take turns riding a new bike. Everybody was getting a ride; and I said, 'when am I'm going to get a turn?' The girl who owned the bike said "Never; you can't ever have a ride." I don't know if I even asked why. I don't hear myself asking why. But I remember just sitting there. Eventually, I just removed myself from the group and walked home.

The rejection that young Lynn felt was transformative.

As I was taking those steps up to our house, I literally felt the life leave me; and the Lynn that was before that incident no longer lived. A different Lynn was there, whom I've been struggling with all of my life.

Although the internal pain was palpable, Marilyn made every attempt to hide it.

The human psyche is profound in that I still did everything I was supposed to do. I'm very good at covering. I didn't tell my mother or anyone. I set a perimeter of safety where I would skate when I was outside. I did not venture past it or even look in the direction of the place that harbored so much pain. My neighborhood became me, my mother, my dog Queenie— with the occasional visit from the neighborhood fruit man.

Except for school, Lynn's only connection with other children was on visits she and her mother took to see family or friends who had children.

Although she was a smart student, even in grade school, Marilyn's anxiety about rejection persisted. When chosen to narrate the school play in the first grade young Marilyn was *terrified*. She was not afraid of *messing up;* rather . . .

. . . *my fear was that someone might reject me again without reason; someone might say s/he didn't like my performance. It would come to be the thread that was always weaving in and out of my life.*

Although Marilyn's role as narrator of the school play went off without a hitch, her fears did not abate. These fears were perhaps compounded by the absence of her biological father—a man she never met and whom she never sought out, although she felt his loss.

Not knowing my dad was a very big loss for me. As a child, I attached myself to other men who had been a father figure to me. I would give them Father's Day cards. I think I wanted to feel like I had a father or something. I have now reconciled myself to the fact that I will never know my father, and I appreciate the things that I see and admire in men who exhibit what I think would be fatherly traits. But I no longer need to give them a Father's Day card to recognize it.

Marilyn got a reprieve from the constant reminder of the incident in her neighborhood, and perhaps a brief respite from her fear of rejection when she and her mother moved to a new neighborhood on S Prieur Street in New Orleans. The move came with the opportunity for having a father-figure in her life.

New Family on S. Prieur Street
While Marilyn was living with her grandmother, her brother Michael Joseph was born. When she and her mother moved to S Prieur St. she was introduced to her baby brother and his father, Warren JaLuke, who would however briefly take on the role of the father Marilyn never met.

After we moved to S. Prieur Street, my sisters Jacqueline Ellen and Gwendolyn Anita were born. They were all Warren's children. Warren's relationship with my mom was on and off—they did not get married—but Warren became kind of my dad. He shucked oysters and would take me with him out into the country to check his oyster traps. I'd wait in the truck away from the gators while he checked his traps. Eventually, he would come back with these big burlap bags full of oysters and sometimes crabs.

Warren would be the only father Marilyn knew, but their relationship was short-lived because of the rocky nature of his relationship with her mother, and the fact that a few years after the move to S Prieur Street Marilyn's mother moved she and her siblings to Chicago.

Chicago

When Marilyn's family moved to Chicago they stayed with Teddy and his mom—Marilyn's Aunt Rosalie—who had moved to the West Side of Chicago ahead of them. For Marilyn, it was a glorious reunion with her cousin. They would go through fourth and fifth grade together—leaning on each other as they navigated school and all of its promises and perils.

Teddy and I ran through gauntlets in order to get in the school. There were gang members lined up by the fence. And their job was just to take our lunch money. We would have to give them our lunch or give them our money every day. And finally, I said to Teddy, 'we're not giving up our money.' And I actually stood there and told the gang member, 'We're not paying today.' And he looked at me and you know threatened me and I said, 'You can kill us, but we're not going to pay you anything.' And Teddy is standing  *there like, "I don't really want to die over some change, we can eat when we get home." I said no. And the Grace of God, the gang guy looked at me and said, "Girl go head," and he never bothered us again. We just always got through.*

Then Marilyn and her family moved to the South side of Chicago.

While the West and South sides of Chicago had things in common— gangs, urban danger, and urban poverty—to go from the West Side to the South Side of Chicago was like being in two different worlds. To live in Cabrini Green (south side) you have to talk and behave in a certain way if you want to be safe and live in Cabrini Green. Same thing if you are going to live on the West Side of Chicago—you have got to know what is expected. We learned what to do in both environments.

After this last move it would be fifty years before she and Teddy would see each other again.

Suppressed Memory

When Marilyn was still relatively young, she was the victim of sexual assault.

It was a family friend and he assaulted us regularly when he babysat. I remember I told my grandmother that we were playing with Uncle Frank. The color drained out of her face—which was difficult for her since her skin was white. She didn't say anything. He was caught in the act and that's how it stopped. Once it stopped, I forgot all about it. In fact, I suppressed the memory of what happened until I was 16 and started having bad dreams— dreams of sexual assault, of seeing a man's face, and seeing myself lying in a coffin. One day I told my mom about the dreams and I asked her had I been sexually assaulted as a child. I thought that she was going to pass out. She just sat down. I think all this time she believed we had gotten past that and were safe. She was just undone.

Reflections on My Mother

To a great extent Marilyn's environment in New Orleans, and certainly in Chicago, reflected decisions her mother made for she and her siblings. Those decisions seemed to make life more or less difficult for the family and were therefore not always easy for Marilyn to understand or accept.

I think my sisters think that I didn't love my mother; that I loved my grandmother more than my mother. And I think my mother thought I loved my grandmother more, but I know that was probably guilt talking on her part. My relationship with my grandmother was developed during those formative, young years; and I never understood my mother. My mother came in my life when I was growing up and didn't understand things. I didn't understand why she kept having children. She was not married! That became a source of shame and embarrassment to me. My mother drank beer and all I remember is the smell of the morning after when people have been up all night drinking beer—that foul nasty smell of beer and cigarette smoke. But for my mom . . . it's just complicated. I mean I think I loved her, cared for her, and stood by her. But a lot of times I did not understand her behavior. It was illogical. 'Mom if you do A it leads to B; but Mom if you don't do A and jump to G it just doesn't make sense. We're hurting here because you're not doing the right thing!' That's the kind of way I thought, and I'd look at her and I'd think these things. But I know she cared for me—she would come and get me out of trouble.

And there was a time as Marilyn grew older when she was in plenty of trouble.

Evolution
Somewhere between navigating the gangs on the West Side of Chicago, her home environment, and going to a private Catholic school on the South Side of Chicago, a somewhat rebellious teenage Marilyn found her way to the Black Panther Party; then to partying, drugs, rehab, college, and marriage.

Wild Child/Rebellion

It was like I was a bystander watching Marilyn be stupid doing all kinds of crazy things during this period. I didn't believe it was what I was made to do or should be doing but I was just doing it. I even tried to cut my wrist a couple of times. Although the cuts were not fatal, they were real. I remember the painful sound of my grandmother's voice when she and my mother found me on the bathroom floor. Both were devastated, and together they took care of me. My mom was devastated and physically weakened by the event. She was never physically strong. My grandmother took care of her and me that night. I fell asleep that night with my grandmother holding my hand and praying.

Looking for a way to express herself more positively, and because of her admiration of Angela Davis, Marilyn joined the Black Panther Party.

Around the same time, I joined the Black Panthers. It wasn't just part of my rebellion; I was committed! I listened to the Last Poets and embraced the ideas and concepts furthered by the Panthers. Angela Davis was my hero; I love her! Although I was seemingly not the person who would embrace Angela Davis, liberation ideology, and become a card carrying member of the Black Panther party, at the time all of those things defined me, both intellectually and physically: I began wearing dashikis, natural hair, and hoop earrings. Substantively, I was as disruptive and confrontational as a well-educated person could be.

Despite what might be characterized as a more constructive, albeit militant aspect of her rebellion, a destructive side of Marilyn's rebellion, brought on by the return of suppressed memories remained.

Once my mother acknowledged that I had been sexually assaulted I didn't know what to think about myself. Even with the difficulties with my mother, I was living in a pretty good environment and I felt secure. But on the inside, I felt differently. I felt like I was damaged so what the heck, I would just go out and do whatever I wanted to do. I was just not myself anymore. I began being wild and crazy. I went out with guys, I did drugs, I put myself in danger.

Marilyn was so heavily into drugs in fact that she entered into a drug rehab program while still in high school. While there, counselors tried to help her with her drug habit and also dissuade her from the militant ideology of the Black Panthers. These latter efforts were to no avail.

But her trials with drugs and rehab convinced Marilyn of the power of prayer.

For me I think it was just the grace of God that kept me alive. I shot up heroin and did all kinds of drugs that took down or killed other people. I traded drugs for sex and did things that jeopardized my very survival. God bless the church mothers that pray for everybody!

In the midst of everything else, Marilyn was baptized. While she continued with her destructive behavior, she started going to church and searching the Bible for answers. At the same time, she started dating a member of the church who was more than twenty years her senior. That relationship caught the attention of her mother and the pastor of the church.

After I graduated from high school, I started out at Malcolm X College in Chicago, but transferred to Anderson University in Anderson, Indiana after my first semester—actually I was sent there by the church. This was probably post Panthers. My mother and the pastor got together and I think for a number of reasons—including a car accident because I was running the streets, and dating this older guy (he was around 40) who was a church member—they shipped me to Anderson, Indiana and put me in a Church of God Bible College and told me I would be watched. The school had a no smoking and no drinking policy, which did not stop me from doing either. Marijuana was also popular.

Eventually, Marilyn got past being forced to go to Anderson and focused her attention on a teaching career.

I determined that I wanted to be a seminarian professor. I wanted to teach the Word—that was my ultimate goal. I knew I understood the Word that was gifted from God, which I needed in order to do something with in my life and which is why I wanted to be a professor. And I was also interested in special education and working with kids.

Ultimately, Marilyn's path to becoming a seminary professor was thwarted in part because of the bad acts of a professor at Anderson. She would, however, fulfill her interest with working with children after she was married.

Dale

Marilyn first met her future husband Dale when both were students at Anderson. Their initial bond was based in a shared trauma.

I think what we had in common at that age is that we had both been sexually assaulted. We were feeling pretty badly about it but on the other hand, trying to live through it and be brave. His father had been a merchant marine; and the family was living pretty well in Washington, D.C. when his father died. Dale had something akin to a nervous breakdown when his father died. His family—Dale, his mother, and brother—moved to a less safe neighborhood in Washington DC. It resulted in a pretty horrific childhood. When he was in elementary school walking home by himself, he was accosted and sexually assaulted. The assaults continued for some time.

Marilyn's experience with her babysitter was different, but it was no less traumatizing. And these traumas are what Marilyn and Dale shared. It was the foundation of their relationship. They believed it could also be the path to love and a better, shared life.

Because of what happened to each of us we thought that we had a better understanding of what it meant to care and to take care of and love someone. We wanted to love one another and we wanted to be authentic and real. We thought our past experiences had put us in a position where we were going to be in love in a good and positive way because that's what we really wanted.

In hopes of ensuring the success of their union Dale and Marilyn went to counseling before they got married to work through issues associated with their childhoods and to address Marilyn's fear of being touched by or intimate with her future husband.

Even though I had been through all that I had been through I needed to talk about my fears. Sexual abuse is traumatic and has post traumatic symptoms that can control and influence your actions and your emotions. The lifelong effect of sexual abuse is like walking around in wet clothes; you can't help but feel the weight of them because they are waterlogged, but there is nothing you can do about it. So, it was weird to me, my fear of sexual intimacy in a marital setting after so much promiscuity. But it was real.

The counseling was especially important because one of Marilyn's college advisors told her not to marry Dale, cautioning her that she and Dale were too different. And while Marilyn does not believe that she loved Dale . . .

I was the great cause' person and believed that I could not only make the relationship work but help Dale move forward in his life. In addition, I don't like being told what not to do. The word 'no' from my advisor was like a 'yes' in my mind. That is how arrogant I was. It turns out that the advisor was correct—Dale and I were at odds on a number of issues. I don't think either of us knew enough about ourselves or each other or love to love each other. I think we had some fantasy about what love was and that's what we were striving for.

Nonetheless, Marilyn and Dale got married; Son Kenneth was born two years later. Two years thereafter, Marilyn was pregnant with their second child. In her sixth month Marilyn miscarried their son Jonathan. The miscarriage was devastating to Marilyn and Dale. Eventually, Dale would return to work, while Marilyn remained home to take care of Kenneth.

The miscarriage was difficult for Marilyn both emotionally and spiritually.

I had nightmares and would wake up screaming and crying trying to understand why my child died. It was hard to believe God had not answered my prayers. I felt for the first time as if God had said 'No' to me.

Friends helped.

A chaplain friend told me, "I haven't a clue what to say to you, and I understand that you are struggling emotionally and mentally. You could sit here and lose your mind and not recover, but I don't want you to do that. I want you to try as hard as you can to hold on to whatever reality that is not painful right now. Hold on to that."

Two others—Angie and Robin—helped her turn the corner. Her friend Angie showed up unannounced in her red Corvette, saying, "You take care of everybody else and I'm here to take care of you!"

I let her help.

Perhaps the person with the greatest impact was someone from church, whom Marilyn did not know very well.

I had gone back to church. I was moving on. But I had developed this twitch and my arm was jerking. This lady—Robin—came over to me and said, "I see you have stopped crying." My first instinct was to put up my guard, so I acted like I didn't know what she was talking about. Then she said, "I see you're twitching; don't do that." She asked me to walk out with her and I did and she told me her story. She had eight pregnancies and all but the last ended in miscarriages. What resonated with me was that she described everything I was feeling—there was someone whom I didn't know but whom I could relate to in every way about the miscarriage. I could feel my defenses dropping. She was very gentle, personable. It was so good to hear an echo of what was going on in my head. It helped me focus. She was the first to say, "You're very angry with God. Is this your first no from God?" I told her that I was devastated and mad at God, but resisting being angry because it was not the Christian thing to do; it was not authorized. She was a tremendous help.

Germany

Working through her heartache and trying to take care of herself became Marilyn's focus for a while. Daughter Janai was born a year after her miscarriage. By this time Dale had enlisted in the military and was stationed in Germany, where Marilyn and their children joined him. Marilyn began working at a Child Development center—*something I loved*—in Germany. Both Marilyn and Dale were ministers, and there was a positive outlook for their future.

It did not last.

I began to feel like I should leave Dale when it became apparent that in order to please him I had to stop being me. We were both lay ministers at a non-denominational chapel service on post; however, our gifts in ministry were different and did not complement one another professionally and personally. What we lived at home and how others saw us as we ministered was different. I really felt this was one of the most inauthentic times in my life; someone like me, masquerading as me, trying to fly under the radar in order to make my husband happy and keep up appearances. We are taught the husband is the leader in the home. Thus, in following him, I gave up so much of what I was educated and trained to do, including what I had inherited from the strong women of faith in my family.

And working at the Child Development Center in Germany—where she ultimately became director—was not enough to compensate for what Marilyn had given up. She knew something had to change.

Something did change. Marilyn's life-changing moment is indelibly etched in her memory.

I was in Germany at a Sunday service and we were up tarrying (waiting to be filled) for the Spirit; and I received the baptism of the Holy Spirit. That's how we say it: full of power. I was filled with the Holy Spirit and began speaking in tongues. That was my breakthrough, that was my freedom, that was my liberty. That was my in-touch moment about who Marilyn can be—and really is in spite of her baggage. When it happened, I talked about the shame, and I talked about the damage, and I talked about the rejection and I experienced something right in the pit of my belly that was different and greater and better and so powerful and different and refreshing and renewing than that other feeling—rejection—because that is all I ever knew. But this was different. And I liked it. And it enables me to press through. I am not the same, I am not what I ought to be, but I keep pushing and pressing because of that experience; and it is kind of a divine function and thing that has helped me to be sitting here, standing here, to be present right now in the world. That became very important to me—particularly at the time. It helped my marriage—helping to dissolve the wedge that broke my husband and I up. Dale experienced the same thing at the altar that same day.

Because she and her husband experienced a similar renewal, Marilyn believed there was hope for their marriage.

As I was not the same, I tried to love and honor and respect him. I spoke directly to him. I told him I could not go on the same way because if I did it would be a negative outcome. I told him if he would try, we could maybe make it. He wanted to try; he liked the idea of being given another chance. He thought it would be an advantage to him as I would change. But while I did not yell at him anymore or get angry anymore, the new person was not the person he was looking for or hoped for. In the end he did not like the new person. He became resentful and it became very difficult for him.

Marilyn continued to try to stay in her marriage.

It took an additional 10 years for me to leave because when I talked to the wife of one of the pastors and told her I was leaving Dale she said if I walked out it would cause others to stumble. I was a role model to them. So, I stayed. I was also thinking about my kids—although perhaps not realistically about how they perceived things.

And then a second life-changing moment may have made what had been difficult—ending her marriage—possible.

In 1994 at the age of 41, Marilyn went blind. She had a genetically triggered retinal detachment. Her eye problems—which her son Kenneth would inherit in high school ending a promising football career—began when Marilyn was in grade school. A trip to the eye doctor resulted in a dire diagnosis—Marilyn would eventually go blind because of the shape of her eyes—they should have been oval, and they were almost flat. The problem was in both eyes.

Each time they attempted to repair the problem I would see less in each eye until at about the 10th repair in one eye, I became totally blind. That was 1994.

Losing her eyesight was life-changing not just because she could not see, but Marilyn believes it was the catalyst for Dale's leaving.

The first words from my husband when I first lost my sight and couldn't work anymore were, "You are now going to know what the rest of us live.

You always thought you were all of this but now you are going to see how the rest of us live." For me, there it was again—that rejection.

Certainly, part of it was the strength and courage that he thought that I had; but also, that I was always too smart for myself. He just didn't like how I operated and how I carried myself, and what I did and didn't do. We were still in Germany; and by now I was a director for the military's Child Development Service. I had a GS job and he was out of the service. He did not have to be, but he chose to be. So for a while I was the only one working. Then, I got him a job working in one of the child development centers, although he was not getting paid what I was getting paid. And I guess that was problematic for him.

When he said that, I thought, "Wow! I knew you had issues but you would rather me be blind and what does that mean? I'm going to be dependent on you and going to be like everybody else." Anyway, it was a real slap in the face for me to hear him say that rather than, " God this is so painful; I'm here for you." Not empathy but disdain—and something akin to a happiness that ". . . now you're going to know how the rest of us feel." What he said was extremely harsh. It was another rejection in my mind—and an issue of trust.

Despite her sense of rejection, intellectually Marilyn knew it was not really about her, nor was it her fault.

I knew my husband; but I did not know the degree to which he had this lack of empathy. I understood, 'This really isn't about me; it is about you.' But it's hard not to feel that rejection when the timing sucked and your daughter and I are here, I can't see, and you're going to walk out. That doesn't make any sense. I do like details and I do think things through—perhaps too much sometimes. And sometimes I know more than I care to know; assess things quicker than I probably want to. But I don't see that I should be punished for that, and I don't see that I should be rejected for that. I certainly don't mean any harm by it. It's probably safer and better to not be authentically who I am, or I'll end up feeling like I need to apologize for being who I am. Because inevitably someone is going to get tired of me being me; and they're going to attack me and they're going to say, "No we don't want to play with you anymore. No, we don't want you to come around." That is how I felt when he eventually left the home saying, "I just can't take it anymore; you're blind, you're this, you're that."

When Dale left, their children blamed Marilyn.

Because I was there and they felt I had not done the right thing causing Dale to leave. Both kids. Dale spent lots of time with them and was successful in getting them to empathize with him and blame me.

Part of the children's angst—especially her son—was likely a residual from being taken from their parents and placed in other homes for a time after Marilyn lost her sight and Dale voluntarily left the military

Janai went to one family—a German missionary home—and Kenneth went to a US military family. He hated it. We couldn't take care of them or pay our rent; so, for a year they were gone. Dale was no longer in the service. Finally, things got better and we had them come back. Janai did ok because she was young. But Kenneth was 6 years older and not taking it that way. Part of his resentment perhaps of us both; but both kids had a hard time resenting their dad—because they saw him as weak or less strong so it couldn't be his fault.

The children returned as Kenneth was in the last years of high school. Marilyn had been given some hope of her eyesight returning if she had surgery back in the states. So when Kenneth went to college, Marilyn flew to the US to have eye surgery. Janai remained in Germany with Dale awaiting Marilyn's post-surgery return. Plans changed and rather than Marilyn returning to Germany, Dale and Janai flew to the states, where the family was again reunited. However, within two years, Dale left. He had started a relationship with the woman who was living in the home to help with Janai because Marilyn was still completely blind.

With the exception of her miscarriage, Marilyn counts her failed marriage as her biggest disappointment.

I was raised Catholic and thought God would save my marriage as I was committed to it. I felt guilty about wanting to leave—like I was giving up on God. But when it just collapsed—Dale walked out and didn't look back—it was disappointing. It didn't take very long, Dale divorced me and I didn't know he had. He hadn't been paying the rent. The landlord came and told me that the rent wasn't paid. I was blind and on disability at the time. Dale was telling me that he paid the rent but he was actually only paying a portion of the rent. The landlord 'graciously' allowed us time to gather what we could put in two suitcases before putting us out. I had to leave all my furniture, my red crystal, all of the kids' photos and albums, everything we had collected over the years living in Germany.

Even in this dark moment, Marilyn found her strength.

As much a part of my life as I sometimes allow this feeling of rejection to motivate or dictate what I do and don't do, there's something greater in me—resistance, resiliency—that will not allow me to acquiesce to it in a way that's been detrimental. It doesn't predominate because sometimes what is required is greater than what I'm afraid of or the possibility of rejection. I have to act; I have to respond, and so that's what I do—I take care of my kids; I take care of negative situations. I stand and fight because that's what I have to do. I can't let a thing go if it's a source of injustice or someone's being wronged or anything like that. I have to speak up.

Marilyn did not acquiesce. Believing her blindness to be permanent, she returned to Chicago with her daughter, who stayed with her aunt, while Marilyn went to a school for the blind for a year, learning braille and how to navigate her life with a cane. Her life and that of her daughter's had to go on despite her blindness. Thus she was preparing herself.

Then in 2000, six years after she lost her sight, Marilyn regained much of it—especially in her left eye. While her depth perception did not return—she cannot drive at night, and macular degeneration in her good eye is a problem—she is able to see and drive during the day.

With much of her eyesight restored, a middle-aged Marilyn realized the time was ripe to pursue the rest of her life's work—in the ministry. So, in 2008 she went to seminary school.

It's what I always wanted to do. Going into the seminary would allow me to speak to the religious structures here that are more in line with civil, cultural worship that is more a form of godliness. I wanted to ensure I had access to authentic platforms, like seminaries, in which to teach the Bible. I wanted to learn the languages of the Bible—Hebrew and Greek—and to just bask in an area of service that would allow me to continue my first love, reading, followed closely by history and ancient texts; to study the development and responses of human beings spiritually as they collided with one another and the planet. You can become engaged in all of this when you make a commitment to teach the "Bible", especially to the ones who are pursuing a "call" to ministry. I just knew this is what I am called to do. It fit me. I believed in hindsight it was the catalyst wherein I learned how to self-differentiate and allow myself to self-differentiate; to recognize the need

for human beings to journey towards that freedom of identity without apology. It makes a difference in how people engage with society at large when they enter it with a foundational understanding of who they are. The "Bible" or developing a faith in God will facilitate and direct us as we navigate the waters that lead to our "isness" in Christ Jesus. We are less afraid! Empowered! Compassionate!

Before she completed the seminary, Marilyn took on the responsibilities of a hospital chaplain. She was known as 'Chaplain Mo, the Singing Chaplain' because when she would see patients Marilyn would sing to them.

I love to sing.

In fact, singing was one of Marilyn's first loves—she once had visions of becoming an opera singer.

I think of Jessye Norman, Kathleen Battle, and Marian Anderson; all of those people have or had such beautiful operatic voices. I love to hear them and would like to have joined them.

Although opera was not her destiny, coming from a family of singers who started singing in church choirs—*my sisters are beautiful singers and have beautiful voices*—Chaplain Mo took a singing approach to her chaplain duties to lift the spirits of the hospital's patients, while also focused on finishing seminary.

There was a second health scare to overcome before she would complete the seminary. In 2009 Chaplain Marilyn had a stroke.

I was working as chaplain at Nebraska Medical Center. On one particular day, I was getting ready to go home, but not feeling well. My boss got a wheelchair and took me to the emergency room. I was having a stroke. I passed out; however, they gave me the necessary medicine immediately, and although I lost some function I got lots better quicker because of the medicine.

While she still has some residual impairment both with her eyes and physically from the stroke, when all the dust cleared from childhood trauma, teenage misadventure, marriage, children, life in Germany, blindness, and a stroke, Pastor Marilyn finished the seminary in 2012. It was and remains a major accomplishment for her.

Direction of the Church

Her first pastoral assignment was a three-year stint at Ascension Luther-an Church in Tulsa, Oklahoma, This was followed by serving two years as interim pastor for a trio of Lutheran churches—Redeemer, Ascension, and St. Marks—which had entered into a shared pastor arrangement in Oklahoma City. Her third assignment since she completed the seminary was with Resurrection Lutheran Church in Saginaw, Michigan, which be-gan in 2018.

These last eight years in the ministry have provided her with ex-perience and insight giving rise to her thoughts about the direction of the church—all churches—as places of worship, direction, prayer, and comfort.

Direction of the Church: Getting out of the Sin Business

We have to get out of the sin business; although it's profitable for church-es because guilt is very lucrative—it keeps the pews full and keeps people coming and keeps people off-balance. And as long as people are off balance and looking to another human being to tell them what only God can tell them then they—churches—are going to continue to hold humanity hostage to moral certitude as the goal rather than acceptance of the "good" that God has already pronounced upon us in the "finished" work of Christ, the death of Christ on the cross, and his resurrection, actively working on our behalf to reconcile all of humanity back to God's self—the Cosmos—every living thing.

God is love. God is not the author of confusion and God does not need our fear! God's love is the hardest thing to believe about God: we want and resist it all at the same time. "No one can love me that much," is the inner struggle and so we experience a relationship with God or knowing God as a "relapse" more than as a constant life-giving faith and relationship.

My Hope is that the church will radically change, die, be born again with an understanding that God is now; that God's presence now in us and with us is the key to envisioning the outcome of "exercising" faith or belief that will lead to the development of values—values that will generate a spiritual prowess enabling humanity to "see" and "do" good to one another because it is the just thing to do. The church should be helping the world to see through the eyes of God the "commonality" of our humanity that contributes to our sustainability while creating just communities focused on life and not death.

Reflections on her journey

My Mom

As Marilyn grew older, became a mother herself, and a minister she has been able to better understand her mother.

I saw that my mother was very vulnerable, a very broken woman. She easily loved; easily trusted. I felt badly for her sometimes for that; while sometimes I resented it because inevitably it caused her so much pain. Then she became ineffective, she couldn't function because she was caught up in some crap that somebody said to her.

This realization about her mother informed Marilyn's life in some ways.

I like to exercise care. I don't make assumptions about anything, and I like to take my time with people and situations; I almost wait for the honeymoon to be over. And then I begin to determine what kind of relationship this is or what's going to really happen. Then the real part of being together starts. That means I start a relationship assuming it's not going to work out and then see how it evolves.

Future

In considering her journey thus far and wondering where she is headed Pastor Marilyn turns to God for direction. A brief conflict with a small portion of her last congregation was resolved, but left her asking *is this the task for me to always be fighting . . . to be in a situation where there is crisis and conflict?*

Not believing herself—or perhaps wanting herself—to be the one called to take on such a challenge, Pastor Marilyn also acknowledges that *in the midst of conflict I do preach the Word and I do know that it is the most important thing.* Nonetheless, she is left to wonder.

How long will it take for this to change? In the meantime, there is a prophetic call on my life to do what I'm doing. I couldn't do anything else. And the life of a prophet is never one of peace and is never guaranteed safety. But it is a very hard thing to be and do. So, whether I stay in Saginaw* or not the

*Marilyn is no longer pastor at the Saginaw church.

situation is not going to change and all I can do is continue to be the person that God wants me to be—and stand firm and be strong and courageous. And to preach the Word and teach the Word and live the Word. And that in itself sometimes is terribly painful and a heavy burden. But I wouldn't know what else to do with myself. When I think of myself outside of this, I can't think of myself anywhere else; so, there's nowhere else for me to be.

Pastor Marilyn finds solace in difficult times in the song *For the Good of Them* as sung by Rev. Milton Brunson and taken from *Romans 8:28*: "*. . . things will work out for the good of them who Love the Lord.*"

That is just true. And without that faith that God will see you through it will crush you.

The takeaway from Pastor Marilyn Robinson's journey so far is a mini-sermon about the continuum of life, based on the message in Isaiah 55:11, which says:

So will the words that come out of my mouth not come back empty-handed. They'll do the work I sent them to do, they'll complete the assignment I gave them.

Believing! *I believe the presence of God in my life is continuous; an ongoing ever-deepening relationship, facilitated by the continuous action and content of God's Word, impacting my life, moving in me, enlightening me as I become the light that I am called to be in the world on behalf of others. This continuous action of God's Word at work in me, Incarnate God, and God's work in Christ on behalf of the world is important because it forces me to look to God and forces those who would want to make the focus all about me or themselves to see God rather than seeing me or themselves.*

The Prophet! *God's word always works and accomplishes what it is sent out to do! In this present darkness, the prophetic preaching of the Word of God is therefore vital. "Thus saith the Lord . . ." should be the emphasis of our preaching. Our work today as ministers of God cannot be politically or emotionally impaired. We cannot allow ourselves to be held hostage by the world's understanding of God, God's love, and how God acts and thinks about humanity.*

God is Love! *God's word always accomplishes what it is sent out to do. God, the Word, sent God's love into the world in Christ Jesus. That Word/ God's Love is immutable! It is continuous. We are engaged, as always, in* *the daily human struggle for power, position, and praise. We continue to marginalize, ostracize, oppress, impoverish, wage war, and victimize on behalf of these three pinnacles (power, position, and praise). Whole cultures and peoples are demonized and dehumanized in order to ensure that only a specific clientele has access to the three "p's".*

But God! Hallelujah! But God so loved the world that he sent his only son into the world, to die a violent death so that the world, through that life, death and resurrection could experience resurrected living in God's love.

This is the Good News that strengthens me, forms, and establishes continuity in my life; when all else fails, the power of God's love is more than sufficient; it is the Love that liberates the one so that the one can preach liberation to the many. No power on earth can stop God's love from being experienced; no power on earth can stop God's love from achieving justice and annihilating the crooked and rough places (this includes the three-"p's") on behalf of everyone. I preach and live in the reality of this Love, God's Love that breaks every enslaving yoke.

Did Lynn, Marilyn, Pastor Marilyn ever figure out why that young girl so many years ago would not let her ride the bike? She still is not certain.

Even when I sat in the counseling chair and I told this story and I was asked whether I had come to grips with this, I never really had an answer.

And the absence of an answer has meant that Marilyn remains cautious. She is careful in her relationships; not letting her guard down and acknowledging that she makes conscious efforts to present herself in a way that would avoid rejection.

When I talk about my persona or that I have many layers to how I represent or present to people, that is what I did. And if I have to do that and that is what it took or takes to keep people off and to keep someone from saying "no you can't have a ride" or to not face rejection that's what I did.

Thus, in 2018 as she transitioned to a new pastorship in Michigan her excitement about a new adventure was tempered.

When people ask me [about the new position in Michigan], "What do you think about going forward; are you getting excited?" I usually say 'No, not really. I'm not. I wait. Will I enjoy it? I don't know. I'm careful with myself, which means that I take care about whether, when, how, and not to let my guard down. If I let my guard down, I can never get a [bicycle] ride.

The caution and uncertainty that remains with Marilyn Robinson today is real. However, it also cannot—should not—obscure the triumph of her journey thus far. Pastor Robinson's triumph is not only what she has overcome, but also her ability to keep moving forward in spite of the obstacles placed in her path throughout her life. And we celebrate her with the knowledge that she will continue to do so!

STEPHANIE BROOKS

Family, Community, Our Mental Health
A Lot to Do

Black women have a lot to do. We take care of our husbands, our children, other people's children, our parents, grandparents, and anyone else who might need care. At the same time, we work—whether for minimum wage or a lot of money—to supplement our families' income or because we are our families' only income.

In our role as caretakers we are also advocates for change—whether physically taking on a challenge as Harriet Tubman did, repeatedly risking her life to help Black folk escape from slavery, or as Stacey Abrams has done by inserting herself into the political arena, both by running for governor of Georgia, and then after a questionable loss, not giving up, but fighting against voter suppression. Even before Stacey was born, however, Shirley Chisolm knew that the interests of Black people and particularly Black women had not been and were not going to be on the top of anybody's list, so she was the first Black woman to run for president. Aretha was our Queen of Soul, but she also posted bail for Angela Davis. Katherine Johnson was a quiet mathematician in a closed White male space program who provided the calculations for John Glenn to circle the earth. All of these women had 'other stuff' going on in their lives—but they went beyond that 'other stuff' to help change the world.

Often, our choice of profession is based upon our recognition of issues within our community that need to be addressed. For instance, the African American community has been slow to talk about or think about issues associated with mental health. In fact, until recently it has long been a shared belief that Black people don't do psychologists—and certainly not psychiatrists. We believe we can handle our own problems, which are nobody else's business—especially not a stranger. In fact, we think going to a "shrink" means you are either crazy or too weak to do what you need to do. Unfortunately, it has meant that we sometimes languish in our mess!

Stephanie Brooks, a 50 something African American woman is all of the above: caretaker, advocate, and a clinical psychotherapist, intent upon doing what so many African American women do with their lives—uplifting our community in her own special way.

Families, finances, children, marriages, divorces, careers, communities. There are many challenges with which African American women are faced, many burdens which we must shoulder—with our families, in our jobs, and our communities. We don't climb onto a platform waving a sign that says, look at all I am doing and have to do!" Instead, we just do. In exploring the journey of Dr. Stephanie Brooks, we see all of this 'stuff' and find out how she has been able to navigate challenges, support the people in her life, and practice her profession while continuing to pursue, find and implement opportunities to help others.

Herstory
Born and raised in Newark, New Jersey to parents from New York and North Carolina, the story of Stephanie Brooks' parents meeting contains a bit of intrigue of its own.

My father, the oldest of nine, was born in Harlem. He was in the Air Force when my parents met. My mother is an only child from Gibson, North Carolina, a small town literally about 100 steps from the South Carolina line. She was born in McColl, South Carolina. When she was about 22 years old my mom migrated north to stay with relatives—primarily because her boyfriend had moved to New York. They planned to settle down and move forward with their lives, but she got pregnant and they didn't get married. My dad met my mother at a house party hosted by his aunt in Newark two months after my older brother Ricky was born. The story is that my father said to my great aunt, "I'm going to marry that woman," referring to my mother. That sounds just like my father. He would make a declarative statement and then go about making it his business to make it his project—to make it happen. My mother said that when she met my father, she "liked him a lot." He was tall—six-three—and he charmed her (my father would always tell me "don't let nobody charm you"). Soon after meeting, and although he was stationed in Texas, they began dating and were married within a year—on Christmas Day. Shortly thereafter my father legally adopted my brother.

Porch Ladies—and Family Secrets

Families will sometimes keep secrets; Stephanie's was no different. Stephanie was born nearly 2 ½ years after her parents married. Neither she nor her brother knew that they had different fathers until Stephanie was nearly 12 years old. Their parents were not the source of the information—it was the little ladies on the porch down south.

We would go down south every summer and stay with my grandparents in Gibson. During one of our visits my grandmother and her sister, Aunt Annie, were on the porch rocking back and forth. We were playing with our cousins and I heard them talking. One of them was saying something like, "He sho' does look like his daddy, uh huh."

Ricky heard it too, and at this point, he did not know he had a different father. My dad was always working—he worked two jobs—and would take Ricky with him in the evenings and on the weekends so that he could spend time with him. He didn't treat him any different and there was no reason whatsoever to think my dad was not Ricky's biological father.

When we got back home that summer Ricky and I—and this is one of the things that pains me because sometimes I used to feel like I shouldn't have participated, but when you're a kid—started looking through paperwork, and that's how we discovered it. When we asked my parents about it, they were very forthcoming with Ricky. My mother and Ricky's dad agreed that he would not see Ricky until he was 18. And at 18—I was with my brother— he met his father John and his sisters and brothers down south.

After all of this came to light, stuff started to make sense to me—so much attention from all these little old ladies. And John's siblings all knew. Every- one knew, even my second cousins knew, but no one said anything. It wasn't till we overheard them gossiping on the porch and rocking back and forth— maybe they thought it was time to spill the beans.

Second Born—Double Standards

As Stephanie grew older two things became apparent—there were double standards around gender lines for she and her brother; and despite being the youngest, she was the responsible sibling.

I used to get upset with what I felt was a double standard—Ricky used to get away with so much because he was a boy and he was the oldest. The real- ity was that I was the responsible one. When we were at a party, he was sup- posed to watch out for me. But I'm the one who would say, 'It is time for us to go.' I didn't have a language then to call it what it was—privileges. Some of it was privilege based on gender and some of it was privilege because he was the firstborn. It was evident later on when it came to education. My

parents were pro-education for all of us; but because he was a Black male in Newark, he went to a private boy's prep school. I was fortunate enough that I had some talent and was accepted into the Arts High School which was the performing arts school. But I had to test in and audition and the whole thing. My parents' explanation was that Ricky needed to get the best education because he was going to be responsible for our family. That was sort of a double message for me because my father always told me that I could do anything I wanted to do. So, I was like, 'What?'

The gender-based double standard about which Stephanie was confused persisted with her other three siblings—two sisters and a brother.

Cynthia who is four and a half years younger than I am attended a science high school—she had to test in and everything. My younger brother Norman went to the same school Ricky went to; and then Sharonda, my youngest sister, wound up going into a vocational high school in the area. I understood it intellectually, but my sisters and I didn't like it one bit– it didn't seem fair!

Fair or not, Stephanie understood—understood the plight of Black boys for whom care is not taken to enhance their opportunities for success.

Adoption and Foster Kids

Stephanie's last two siblings—Norman and Sharonda—came to the family through adoption: first Norman and then Sharonda.

At some point, my parents decided to be foster parents; and they planned this out to make it happen. Along the way, they also decided they wanted another child. At that point, there were three of us: Ricky, myself, and my sister Cynthia, who for all this time had been the baby. Then Norman came into the family when he was four months old. At the time they used to keep babies who were to be adopted at the hospital in the nursery before they placed them. So, ours was his first family. His parents decided that they couldn't raise him. After Norman had been with us for nearly two years, my parents adopted him. So now they had two boys and two girls.

Referring to her mother as *the first social worker I knew*, Stephanie recalls that the family of six lived in a three-story, two-family home that had lots of room and thereafter also became an emergency shelter and foster home for many children. That is how Stephanie's last sibling—Sharonda joined the family.

Sharonda came to our house when she was five days old. Her mother was 14 and was living with her older sister who had her own kids and couldn't take care of everybody. The plan was to return Sharonda to her mother when her mom was older and more responsible.

Sharonda was never returned to her biological mother; instead becoming a permanent member of Stephanie's family. Both family tragedy and the state's *auction block* approach to adoption delayed the family's formal adoption of Sharonda.

About a year after my father died the state decided they were going to terminate Sharonda's mother's rights because she never showed up for a visitation. But the state also started 'shopping' Sharonda for adoption. Sharonda had been a pretty happy kid; but after they started trying to 'shop' her, Sharonda was noticeably upset and stopped doing well at school, My mother was really torn about whether she wanted to adopt her because she was getting older and my father had died.

Stephanie offered a solution.

I was 20 and in my last year of college. I couldn't imagine Sharonda with another family. So, I told my mother that if something happened to her, I would make sure Sharonda was okay. With that, my mother went ahead and adopted Sharonda. As soon as Sharonda knew my mother was adopting her she was once again fine. She felt the stability come back; she was no longer being shopped all over New Jersey. When they take those kids on this 'show and tell' I get really political. This is like being on the auction block.

There was almost a sixth child in their household. Corey was four months old when Stephanie's parents assumed responsibility for him as a foster child. His family successfully petitioned the court for his return when he was about three years old.

. . . which broke my mother's heart because she bonded with Corey as she had done with different kids that stayed with us. But I think with Corey she saw his sadness. He was such a cute baby and so sweet, but there was something about him that even at two months old seemed sad.

Four years later the state took Corey from his biological family again. Although he did not return to Stephanie's family, he stayed in touch—especially with Stephanie's mother. In fact, he helped the family to take care of Stephanie's mother during the final stages of her illness.

Corey moved back to New Jersey from Fayetteville, North Carolina to help with my mother. She was diabetic and on dialysis and had so many doctors' appointments. Her condition just spiraled out of control. Corey was there for about ten months, participating and taking care of her while she was home and back and forth to the doctor and the hospital, cooking and doing whatever he could to help out. My mother's reaction: 'I got all my kids' home!" She was very contented with it.

Tragically, Corey lost his 19-year-old son to a drive-by shooting in Fayetteville three years ago, and in the final sad twist, after returning to New Jersey, Corey died in December 2019 of a drug overdose, while celebrating his birthday in his bedroom at Stephanie's mom's home. Sharonda found him.

Stephanie's one-word reaction to Corey's final plight seems appropriate: *Terrible!*

Daycare

There was a point at which Stephanie's mother left her job outside their home and opened a daycare. As the oldest girl, some of the responsibility for providing daycare for the foster kids and her younger siblings fell on Stephanie.

I grew up always taking care of kids. We were constantly changing diapers, changing clothes, making sure the children were where they were supposed to be—doctors' appointments, and so forth. Some of these kids were immediately placed somewhere else and some of them stayed with us for a few years. There were also the emergency kids who stayed with us before parental rights were terminated—as had happened with Sharonda.

For the most part, Stephanie was a trooper—she did not mind doing what was necessary—an attitude that has stayed with her throughout her adult life—because *I felt like I was helping my mom.*

Although occasionally she might have felt the burden—*why y'all got me doing all of this?*—she says in retrospect it never really interfered with what she wanted to do.

If I said I wanted to go somewhere or had to do something, I don't ever remember my parents telling me that I had to stay home and babysit the kids. We knew we had to look after each other because they were working, and we were latchkey kids; so, one of them would say, "I'm going to call the phone and let it ring two times," or "Don't answer the doorbell." However, I don't remember it really getting in the way of band rehearsals or going to church or feeling burdened by it.

College

Through a series of circumstances, including the fact that Stephanie had skipped a few grades, she and Ricky graduated from high school at the same time, and both were accepted at William Patterson College in New Jersey in 1978. Because her father was ill, family friends drove the two of them to school in their station wagon filled with Stephanie and Ricky's belongings.

My dad was sick—he had some cardiac problems. So, he wasn't with us, but he surely had gone shopping with both of us to get everything for our dorm rooms.

The move did not go quite as planned.

I was 16 and really clear about what I was going to do; so, they moved me into my dorm room. But when we went to move my brother into his dorm he said, "I'm not going to college." And so, I just looked like, 'Oooh you're in trouble!' Nonetheless, after Ricky's pronouncement, he went home, and my parents struck some deal with him to go to vocational school. He worked, but he was always getting retooled because the jobs were not long term. They were closing factories in our area all the time. Thus, at times Ricky struggled because of his decision.

While Stephanie was not conflicted about going to college, when her father died in December 1979, less than a year after she entered William Patterson, at her father's funeral Stephanie announced she was not going to go back to school but would stay home and work. Her mother disagreed.

She said, "That's not happening." So, I took my little butt back to school.

But she still sought to lessen her mother's burden.

I was a Resident Assistant in the dorms, and I had a nursing home job as a result of my mother's connections. So, I came home on the weekends, was changing diapers and beds and sheets, and so forth.

Family

My Mother
Her mother's influence on Stephanie's life has been profound.

I've watched her and learned what to do and what not to do. I watched her work her butt off and I even talked to her about it so that although I have felt this great responsibility to give back and to give to others, I also learned and understood from her that I needed to have a life outside focused on the things that I like to do.

There are some behaviors Stephanie learned from her mother designed to help her survive that have allowed her to learn and grow.

My mother taught me to be in control, not to show vulnerability. There are positives and negatives that grow out of that. The negative piece is something that I wish she had worked on more before she died because I think it would have freed her up to set boundaries with people. So often she would do things that she really didn't want to do. I would sometimes tell her that I thought people were taking advantage of her because they knew she would do what they asked even if she should not.

It was not until 1986-87 when I was in the midst of my postgraduate study when I began to disclose how scary it was for me to be vulnerable and admit that I was sometimes not in control. So, I've had to learn how to set boundaries around some things and really think about when people make requests. I ask myself, 'Am I doing this because I want to or am I doing this because I feel like I should do it?' My mother taught me that without really knowing it. But she also gave me a big capacity to care for people. I'm glad I was around her to watch that. There was just no end to what this woman would do for people, and that was incredible!

Stephanie's mother died in 2016. Coming to terms with her mother's death has been quite a challenge.

I think that the hardest thing for me has been my mother's death. We all know that people are going to die, but I still haven't wrapped my brain around it. I think about her every day. And I know that things get better, but there is a void. I remember the first week: usually, when I leave my practice, I would call her on the phone while I was in the car and talk to her while I was driving home. It was hard to get her off the phone, so, by calling her then I could listen to everything that she had to say without rushing off and having her say, "Well you don't want to talk to me." The first week after she died, on my way home I dialed her number. Her voicemail came on and I realized, 'Oh shit! She's not there!' You know, it hit me. That's just been hard. And what's more difficult is that I think about what it might be like for my own daughters, and I can't make it better. There's nothing I can do to make it better. There's nothing I can do in the event that I die for them not to hurt. And I know how much it's going to hurt them. It's just one of those things that you just have to be with because you can't force any kind of resolution. I don't think there is a resolution. Going down to her gravesite helps sometimes.

Stephanie's grief over her mother's death was all the more difficult because it was delayed. She was responsible for all of the arrangements—they had a service in Newark but took her back to North Carolina to be buried with her parents—and helping her siblings. Trips to North Carolina since have helped.

I'm still grieving because I haven't been able to just be. So, every once in a while, I get restless and I will say to my boyfriend, 'I need to take a trip because I need to have a conversation with Dorothy.' We will drive to North Carolina because I know when I get restless and thinking about things and anxious that I need to make that trip. Sometimes it will be about the circumstances of the property and my siblings. And I'll say to her, 'Well you see what's going on.' [She laughs]. My boyfriend understands it now, but the first time I did it he kind of looked at me strange and wondered what was going on. But we've done it a couple of times now and sometimes I do it over a weekend. I just say I'm not going to go into work on Friday so we can drive down on Friday. Sometimes I won't even stay at the house with my other relatives. I just check into a hotel. That Saturday I'll go to the cemetery, I'll clean the grave, and do whatever I need to do and come back home on Sunday. In that way, I have time to do what I need to do; and he [my boyfriend] lets me do that. Dealing with the loss of my mother is still a work-in-progress. I don't know if I will ever get over it.

Because she is a psychotherapist, Stephanie thinks that her grieving process is *a little bit better* because of her knowledge and experience with others around grieving or conflict and problem-solving. But . . .

. . . I find myself getting stuck because sometimes you don't see your own blind spots. They truly are just that: blind spots. And so, I embrace that I have my blind spots—and that I need help.

My friends who are therapists understand even if I don't. On the other hand, my boyfriend tells me he doesn't know why I'm struggling with this. He says, "You always figure these things out." But I tell him 'I need to talk this through so just listen and nod your head occasionally. Work with me.' [She laughs] And he does.

My previous narrative has been I don't need any help. And that is not a helpful narrative. I need help. And I can say that now; otherwise, I don't have permission to reach out. I know my family thinks I'm strong—the stalwart. But that is not always the case and they need to understand that.

My Father

The relationship between fathers and their daughters is important, can be complicated, and usually has a lasting impact. Stephanie bonded with her father both intellectually and musically.

My father read a lot. And I love to read, so I now know that everything was an intellectual exercise with him. He would say, "Here, read this book, I think you will like it." And it wasn't a textbook and it wasn't a book about Paris. It might be a fictional novel, that on occasion might be a little inappropriate for me to be reading. Then he would ask me questions about it. And we would get into little debates. He would really stretch me by asking, "Well, what's your rationale for that?" I would be right there in the moment with him about it. It was our private time—usually because he was drinking tea and up reading. It was usually early—I'm a morning person and both my parents were as well. So that was my time with my dad.

The musical connection . . .

My father played bass and I played flute and sax, which is how I ended up at the performing arts school. So, my father and I had that connection.

That musical connection between Stephanie and her father seems to have been passed on to her daughters.

Alexis plays upright bass and the piano and Simone plays acoustic and electric guitar.

Stephanie says that her father taught her how to protect herself in a different way—but it was confusing.

And this is where I was confused about what was going on with the boys—are boys allowed to do some things that girls are not? My father used to have these talks with me saying "Don't let any man tell you what you can and cannot do," which was the confusing part because I would say to him, "But you won't let me go to work with you. How come I can't go to work with you?" He said, "You don't need to go to work with me; your brother needs to go to work. He needs to learn how to work." And so it still didn't make sense to me. I would say, 'I remember the conversation that no one's supposed to have sex, but you give him condoms; what's that about?' It just didn't make sense. At which point my mother would say to me, "It will never make sense; just leave it alone." And that just kind of shut it down.

Both Parents

Despite the passing of both of her parents, Stephanie continues to feel their presence.

Spiritually, I very much feel that both my parents are alive and present in me. There have been times where my mother or my unconscious or whatever you want to call it is in my dreams. I always dream but sometimes I have dreams about her on consecutive nights. I'm like, 'Okay, what's up? What do I need to do that I'm not doing? What am I missing here because she is trying to tell me something? She's bugging me. She won't let me sleep.' Typically, that makes it better. I grew up in a family that was very spiritual around these kinds of things. So for me, it feels like a natural extension that when people come to you in dreams and things happen that you need to pay attention to the signs; so, I pay attention.

Preserving Their Blood, Sweat, and Tears

In addition to dealing with the personal trauma of losing her parents, and most recently her mother, Stephanie's role as Executrix of her mother's estate has presented another set of challenges. The property represents her parents' sacrifices. Although it might be easier to just sell the property and distribute the proceeds, she continues to keep and manage the property as well as other matters related to her mother's estate. It has not been easy.

I would like to be able to hold on to both of these houses. I know how hard they worked for them. We lived in a second-floor apartment there in one of the houses; and, then my parents moved out and bought their own house—the second house. Thus, I know that their generation worked hard for that house.

Despite these challenges, Stephanie believes that her mother made her executrix of her estate for a specific reason.

Because she knew I could handle it. She knew I can set boundaries—firm boundaries—but she also knows that I have a softness that people don't see all the time. I hold my brothers accountable when necessary. I try to keep the peace among all of us when necessary.

Understanding that the peace might not always hold, Stephanie's mother gave her alternative instructions for handling her role as Executrix.

My mother gave me my clear direction before she died. She said, "Don't make yourself crazy; this is not worth dying over. Continue to do what you need to do with the property, but if they get on your nerves, sell the property, and give everybody their portion of their money and tell them to go away."

But Stephanie has not done that. She sees the sacrifices her parents made to acquire the property and wants it to remain in the family. Again, it has not been easy.

My parents worked hard to buy this house using the GI Bill. And it survived the riots. It makes no sense whatsoever to lose this house. It's not so

much how much they paid to buy the house, but every dollar they paid on it was blood, sweat and tears.

Thus, keeping the property in the family—and managing her siblings who reside in them—is important to Stephanie. For her, it represents her parents' legacy.

I love my brothers and sisters, but I view what I'm doing as my payback to my parents because I know what it took for my mother to keep me in school.

She and her sisters share a 'do what needs to be done' attitude; which is not necessarily the same attitude shared by their brothers, who sometimes require some not so gentle prodding to participate in the maintenance of their parents' home, which they also inhabit.

I don't understand why they don't have the same hustle—because my sisters and I all have the same hustle attitude. We can always work.

Her daughters are not sympathetic to their uncles. Stephanie draws on her daughters' reactions as a source of support, but also sees the situation as a teaching moment.

My daughters say, "Really? So you all are going to take care of them?" I said, 'I'm just gonna figure it all out. We'll work it all out.' I also say to my daughters, 'If your sister was out there and didn't have a place to go and you

have any money and you have two houses, what would you do?' They tell me they get what I am saying but they also see the stress [that all of this is causing me] and I understand that is their concern.

Stephanie's property management skills also extend to her grandparents' home in North Carolina. Thus, her mother's admonition about being made crazy by all of her responsibilities is real, although Stephanie believes that she has been—is becoming—*kind of* successful at following that advice.

Triumph: Stephanie's Daughters

African American women with children seem most often to be mothers first, which simply means that when asked about their greatest triumph, they respond "my kids!" Stephanie Brooks is no different.

My kids are my greatest triumph! Given as much time as I spend working and doing everything else, I just feel really blessed that my kids turned out okay. They will have challenges down the road, but they just have been a gift!

Initially though, by the time she reached college Stephanie had decided against having kids, believing that it was *way too much work.* Her mother seemed troubled by that decision, periodically asking if she really was never having kids. Stephanie seemed certain about her decision until she was in her early 30s and received a medical diagnosis that might have prevented her from having children.

I knew I loved kids and worked well with them, but at the time I really wasn't sure what I was going to do—until I was in my early 30s and I was diagnosed with lupus. I started thinking about it—I might not have any kids, and I wasn't happy with that possibility. Long story short, I didn't have lupus; but it scared the mess out of me for three years.

After she got married, Stephanie decided that she wanted children despite the perceived perils. The result: Stephanie has two adult daughters—Simone and Alexis—whom she and her ex-husband Erik helped navigate through childhood, puberty, and college.

I had Simone in the blizzard of 1996. It was considered a high-risk pregnancy because this was during the time that they thought I had lupus.

Thankfully, there was nothing wrong with me and nothing wrong with her. But because the doctors believed my pregnancy was high risk, they scheduled me for a C-section. It turned out to be scheduled on the day of the blizzard. My doctor called to say he was not going to the hospital and neither should I. Although I was not in imminent danger of being in labor, listening to the sirens from fire engines, I became a little bit concerned about what if I go into labor and I was stuck in the house in the snow.

Stephanie did not go into labor that snowy night; and when she did a few days later, a healthy eight-plus pound Simone was born without incident.

When Stephanie needed to go back to work but did not want her new baby subjected to the winter elements, her recently relocated grandmother volunteered for babysitting duties.

She said, "I'll come down and help with my great-grandbaby." She's stayed for about a month—watching Simone and incessantly talking to my mother on the phone—who was still working—and just gossiping. It was nice for her to have the time with Simone. Although Simone was only two and a half when she died, she remembers her great-grandmother.

Her grandmother's availability to help with Simone was possible after Stephanie's grandparents' reluctant relocation to New Jersey (my whole family trekked down to North Carolina to move them) a few years before Simone's birth. Neither grandparent was happy about the move, but they ultimately acquiesced.

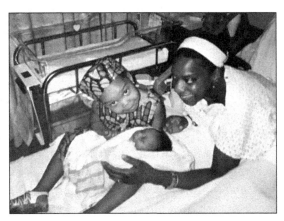

It was really hard to get my grandfather to move. He was all tearful and not wanting to move. But he couldn't take care of himself or my grandmother. He still tried to drive my grandmother to the supermarket because that was his job and his pride would not let him ask anyone else. But he really couldn't do those things anymore. We didn't want to take over but there was no other alternative . . . they just don't make men like that anymore.

A few years after her grandparents' move, Stephanie's grandfather died, prompting her grandmother to want to move back to North Carolina. Ultimately, she returned to North Carolina for visits but not to live. Thus, she was also in New Jersey for the birth of Stephanie's second daughter, Alexis. Sadly, Alexis was still a baby when her great grandmother died.

My grandmother was holding and playing with Alexis before she went into the hospital. I worried that she might be getting tired and asked her if she wanted to rest. She said, "I'm playing with the baby. Be quiet!"

Today, Stephanie is intent upon supporting her daughters to whatever extent she can as they move forward in life, without *getting too much in their business.*

Divorced in 2003, Stephanie and ex-husband Erik lived together for three years post-divorce.

No one knew. We decided that it was important for us to make sure that the girls had stability, so, we just sort of did what we had to do.

Stephanie gives her ex-husband his props.

Erik always shows up for the event. That is why he gets a pass from me all the time—after I tell him off. He's always showed up. He talks to [our daughters] almost every day.

Nonetheless, Stephanie has always been the custodial parent and primarily responsible for her daughters, financially and otherwise. She is not burdened by that fact and very proud of them.

Just raising them and watching them grow up and become adult women who are responsible and socially conscious and political—I'm just . . . [without words in her pride]. I try to listen to what they're tuning in to. And they are engaged in all kinds of things—on and off social media.

Both daughters decided on Drexel University in Philadelphia for college, benefiting from tuition waivers courtesy of Stephanie. Simone has graduated, with a degree in fashion design. She already has two lines of clothing—one for *curvy girls* like herself and the other is a men's clothing line. *She loves it and she's good at it.* Alexis has two more years before graduating with a degree in biology. She has expressed a desire to do hard science brain research. Stephanie would like to see her continue to graduate school for an MD Ph.D. *I think that would be awesome and give her more of an edge. She's saying maybe.*

Like most parents, even though her daughters are now young adults, Stephanie worries about them but tries to do so at a distance so as not to invade their space or transfer her worry to them.

Despite her worries, ultimately, she trusts them, saying . . .

. . . you have to trust that whatever decisions they make are going to be the right decisions.

Life's Work

Dr. Stephanie Brooks is Senior Associate Dean for Health Professions and Faculty Affairs and a clinical professor in the College of Nursing & Health Professions at Drexel University. She is a licensed couple and family therapist, clinical social worker, and Clinical Fellow and Senior Program Consultant for the American Association for Marriage and Family Therapy (AAMFT). In addition, Dr. Brooks has a private practice as a clinical psychotherapist.

Wow!

The path to her current professional status started with her concern for social justice in her community.

Social Justice—Something Felt Wrong to Me

Perhaps because of her tendency to watch, observe and ask questions, Stephanie's chosen professions as social worker, counselor, and psychotherapist were always her destiny. Yet, it was really her social consciousness—her sense that *something felt wrong*—that led her on a path toward social justice that culminated in her professional choices.

From the time I was catching buses—because there were no school buses in Newark, I had to take public transportation downtown—I was sort of watching folks. On Sundays, on our way to church, we walked past the Youth House, which I discovered was the juvenile detention center. What struck me as I was walking past there and listening to the yelling from the windows was that they were babies in there, just young babies. How did they get in the Youth House? Sharonda's mother had been put in the Youth House for fighting. Something just felt wrong to me about that. There was probably some other place she needed to be. The Youth House was just punishment.

Thus, for Stephanie, choosing psychology as a major in college was key after recognizing the need for Black folk to seek and obtain help for mental health issues even if it was just to work through problems and issues of everyday life.

I was drawn to psychology because I saw people all around me hurting in a variety of ways and people not acknowledging it. You didn't spend a lot of time emoting; you just handled your business.

Social Work

Stephanie graduated from college when she was 20, intending to immediately enroll in a Psychology Ph.D. program. However, her paternal aunt who possessed several degrees suggested she take some time off. Stephanie heeded her aunt's advice and took two years off. She believes on reflection that it was good advice because it allowed her to slow down. After first working in a job at an insurance company to just catch her breath, Stephanie found a job working in a psychotherapy clinic in Newark focused on working with families.

I made home visits to people who didn't show up for therapy. They had more pressing needs—sometimes it was raining in their apartments while I was sitting there. I would connect them to resources and talk to them about what to do. But I could only do so much because I didn't have a degree. It was there that I discovered that I wanted to get a degree in social work. I realized that social workers did therapy and they worked with people who looked more like me. In the literature during that time anyone that was Brown or Black was in the abnormal psychology book, but I decided that everybody I knew can't be crazy!

Stephanie's plan for her professional life really started as a graduate student at the University of Pennsylvania seeking her Masters in Social Work (MSW). And she intended to return to the clinic once she had her degree. A few years later she planned to open her own agency.

One proposed name for the agency was 'The Four C's.' It was something about community and culture and I remember saying I'm having a full-scale social service agency because I knew I would need to offer a wide array of services. There had to be some kind of recreational human service component and community component if I wanted to get people into therapy.

The idea of an agency ruminates in her head even today, periodically causing Stephanie to have some regret for not moving forward. However, as she begins to think of next steps in her professional and personal life, she realizes it's not too late. Besides that, Stephanie believes that the alternate path she took was the right one at the time.

In my last year in grad school for my MSW, I was preparing to take the position at the psychotherapy clinic in Newark. Instead, I accepted a position as a social worker in both the Brain Behavior and the General Psychiatry Units at the University of Pennsylvania. I was intrigued by the work. When I told them about the position to which I was committed at the clinic, my interviewers countered with the benefits package and a promise to pay for my further education. While it was a hard phone call to the clinic to tell them I was taking another job, I made the call. I knew that the position at UPenn was what I needed.

Stephanie's decision to take the position at the University of Pennsylvania was her best move for a number of reasons. Aside from the fact that UPenn paid for her post master's education, it provided her with opportunities that were not available at the clinic.

I had a great deal of autonomy with a lot of room to start looking at program development and policy. It was a wonderful experience and my first position in leadership as the clinical director, which was unheard of for a non-medical person—especially someone so young. I was a baby in my late 20s.

University of Pennsylvania's Social Work Program was pivotal for Stephanie's educational development because of its emphasis on *eradicating "isms"*.

There was something about the Penn program that spoke to me, and it was the only program that I saw pictures of any faculty of color in its brochure. I tell people in my department, 'You have to do more than just say it, you have got to have pictures and you need to have curriculum because students of color are looking for those things.'

Because of time spent in her position at the University of Pennsylvania, Stephanie seriously considered going to medical school, specializing in Psychiatry.

If I had a mentor—if someone had pointed me in the right direction, I probably would have gone to medical school and gone into psychiatry; but at the time I had no idea where to even start. I was pretty good in science—I was one of those nerdy kids who read stuff about neurology for the house/

office. I was just obviously really curious. I didn't think about myself as being bright and was very anxious all the time because I was fully aware that I was having classes with everyone older than I was. In my head, I knew I had to work hard to make sure that nothing happened because everyone expected me to be able to do well. I didn't feel like I had any room to fail whatsoever—particularly since my brother had stayed back a couple of years. All along that is why I used to think, I gotta get this right! It was a lot of pressure.

Psychology

Drawn to psychology because *I saw people all around me hurting and people not acknowledging it*, Stephanie didn't fully understand what she saw until she was in her 20s and in graduate school. Her awakening was stunted by her community experience.

In my neighborhood and community, you didn't spend a lot of time emoting, you just handled your business. I watched people have these tragedies and traumas in their lives and they would just keep pushing. I didn't understand and wondered, 'How are these people dealing with this?' I saw people who were seemingly perfectly fine, and they would get into addictions and then you watch their lives spiral out of control. These are people I went to school with, people in the neighborhood. The neighborhood was pretty stable when I grew up. White people moved out because we moved in, and for many years this was a stable block of Black families and Black people. Watching these people change when I was young, I wondered what happened?

Her personal family experiences gave Stephanie further insight.

It was that kind of stuff all around me because the neighborhood was starting to change, and I would see people and families and people dealing with death and accidents. But what clinched it was probably what happened to Ricky when he was 14. As a result of a freak accident, Ricky lost his eye. I don't think Ricky ever really dealt with that. I don't remember him crying or him complaining, He was wearing glasses immediately. He got his license and began driving; he ran track; and so it certainly didn't inhibit him in the way that he had talent. But I know that it must have had a profound impact on him. And I think that there were some messages that he probably received that he wasn't allowed to grieve what had happened—that was that. I recall getting that same message when my dad died: this is sad but gotta keep moving.

Professional Challenge

The path to and through many professions can be challenging, rife with unavoidable obstacles. For African American women, compounding those obstacles is the now-acknowledged glass ceiling designed to sty-mie/undermine our advancement beyond a certain point. Being able to get through those tough spots—despite sometimes incredible unfairness and bias—is the difference between moving forward and staying stuck; between staying sane or going off the deep end. Few of us are immune from this challenge—including Dr. Brooks. She recalled a specific profes-sional challenge she faced more than a decade ago.

In 2010, the chair of her department—who had hired Stephanie and had been a mentor—decided to step down as chair and program director. Stephanie had by this time completed her course work for her Ph.D. and was finishing her dissertation. As she had worked closely with the chair, Stephanie was the clear heir apparent. Nonetheless, disgruntled faculty members convinced the Associate Dean to do an outside search with a job description that required a Ph.D. An angry Stephanie decided it was time for a job change. Nevertheless, utilizing a bit of mother-wit strategy, she submitted her application for the open position anyway, creating a co-nundrum for the search committee. After being invited for an interview, she withdrew her application. After an unsuccessful search, the Commit-tee asked Stephanie to become the interim chair. After much thought and introspection, Stephanie agreed to become Interim Chair until the com-mittee selected a chair. After the second failed search Stephanie was asked whether she would consider being chair of the department.

I sat with it [the offer to become chair] for about three months before I said I would, and I negotiated the terms. But that was probably the hardest moment for me professionally. I felt like I had worked my butt off for years only to have this roadblock. I would have been cool with folks coming to me if they were straight about it, but that's not what was going on. This was a bunch of cloak and dagger bs. And I was not going to participate in it as though I didn't have any power at all. I was not going to make it easy for them to move in this direction.

Next Steps

Stephanie Brooks knows there will be next steps beyond academia. Although, at this point, she is not certain what the next step is going to be as early retirement is not an option—*I'm gonna be working forever.* Thus, she believes that in ten years she will be *somewhere else doing something else.* There are aspects of her current work that she enjoys and would like to continue—particularly her consultant work with the AAMFT Minority Fellowship Program.

I get a lot of pleasure from that position because I have the opportunity to do program development. And I am training or contributing to the training of clinicians and researchers and policymakers to work with folks who need it—people who are on the margins, and families. That is very satisfying.

Dr. Brooks' work with the AAMFT Minority Fellowship Program has also been impactful. So much so, that the students whom she has mentored and with whom she has worked during her five years (2015-2020) as Executive Program Consultant for the MFP program expressed their heartfelt appreciation for Stephanie in a video entitled, *The Legendary, Dr. Stephanie Brooks.*[7]

And for now, she will be able to continue that work.

This is when I know the ancestors and God are looking out for me. They re-upped the consultant contract for another three years thank God. They had a lot of turnover and personnel issues there and I've been the only constant really. I agreed to stay for the three years. I enjoy the work. I'm developing additional training for Master's level family therapists and Doctoral level family therapists to prepare them to either do clinical work with underserved marginalized populations or research regarding underserved, marginalized populations.

It is work similar to what she envisioned when she planned on creating and running her own social welfare agency.

Part of my mission with the agency I envisioned was to create something where people felt welcome and where we were very intentional and culturally focused, Here, I have been able to develop educational counseling

---

7. The Legendary Dr. Stephanie Brooks, MFP Executive Program Consultant (2015-2020), AAMFT Foundation—YouTube

programs that have a social justice orientation for students with a similar focus and orientation. I hope that what students take from these courses will allow them to have an impact in our communities.

The consultant work she does is an extension of those goals and what she sees as part of her future *ideal world* where Dr. Brooks would continue to do some of that kind of work in developing programs and helping people and going into agencies and helping the agencies.

That would be a great job for me to do.

Recent budget cuts create a bit more pressure on Stephanie to decide her future. As a newly appointed Associate Dean at the time of the cuts she was able to save some programs—small programs with a social justice focus—that were at risk. She acknowledges, however, that the uncertainty of who might next be affected by budget cuts means that the pressure to decide her next step persists.

She has determined it is not full-time private practice.

I'm keeping my practice. If I get fired, I can ramp that up. It is something that I could do to make money, but it's not something that I want to be doing full time. It's lonely doing practice full time. You see clients in and out all day unless you join a group practice, but even that is lonely. Your job is still seeing clients.

Stephanie knows what she wants to do. It's a matter of carving out a position in a way that meets her need to be stimulated and energized:

I need to feel stimulated and energized by different kinds of things. It is one of the reasons I like doing a little bit of administration, some policy program development, and direct service because I can shift during the course of the day. I know what I want to do it's a matter of carving the job out in a way that will work for me and what I want to do.

On Being a Black Woman

Invisible . . . People Don't Show up for Black Women!
In April 2018, two African American men were in a Starbucks in Philadelphia waiting on someone to join them. When they refused to leave when asked, the police were called, and they were arrested. The whole incident caused a huge public outcry culminating in apologies and promises to do better from Starbucks CEO.

In stark contrast, similar and more egregious mistreatment of four Black women—two at separate Waffle House locations in Alabama—in a four-week period in April 2018 garnered little notice in the media and no apologies or promises to do better from anybody.

These incidents emphasize the invisibility of Black women to the rest of society. And whether we talk about it or object to it, Black women are keenly aware of our invisibility because we live it daily.

It's hard being a Black woman in this world. People don't always show up for Black women. And so, everybody knew about Starbucks; but the Waffle House incident in Alabama involving Black woman, received little notice and even less outrage. I tell Simone and Alexis that they have to be there for each other and for their friends because everyone is not there.

Professionally, I used to get upset about these microaggressions. I am an Associate Dean of Health Professions in the College of Nursing. In that role, I have nine academic departments for which I am responsible. There is an Associate Dean for Nursing. He's a White male. He's cool. But it's interesting to watch how people will email him about the entire college and, or if we're all sitting in a meeting, someone will say, "I want to sit down with Al and really work out our plan for growth for the next three years." I sit there thinking, 'How are you going to do that when I have the other half of the college—as if I don't exist—and I'm sitting there for 90 minutes.' The Associate Dean of Nursing was smart enough to say, "Well if you really want to talk about this, I think you need to have Stephanie who is Associate Dean . . ." But the fact that I have to say 'Hello, remember me? I've only been here 26 years.' These kinds of responses come from some White males and ironically some White females.

And of course, it's not just on the professional level.

That kind of back and forth—whether it be double standards or invisibility—is tiring. I remember when I was a young student in social work school in Philadelphia. I liked to shop. Inevitably at some point during a number of my shopping excursions, I would realize that I was being followed by some store detective—profiled. I would think, 'Why are you looking me up and down and following and tracking me in the store?' Then I always said something to whoever was following me. I was ready to fight! I usually relayed my experiences to my peers. Finally, one of my colleagues said to me, "You have got to learn how to calm down or you're gonna have a heart attack! You have to decide when you want to fight and what you want to do and when you just want to dismiss people yourself." That observation stuck with me over the years causing me to ask myself in these situations, 'Is this something I need to take on here and now or something to take on at another level.'

Having to take it on at any level is sometimes the problem.

Importantly, one of the ways in which Stephanie has addressed many of these concerns is in her professional capacity as Associate Dean of Health Professions, which has enabled her to both shine a light on faculty of color—particularly hiring a number of African American women—and share with them what she has learned in her own interview and negotiation process so that if the candidate accepts the position s/he has negotiated a package that will allow him/her to be successful.

I've watched the injustice. I've seen young faculty come from institutions, say a Latino woman and a White male with the same mentor, and he's prepared and she's not. It makes me wonder, what happened? Well, I know what happened. So, that is one of the ways I try to use some of what I experienced and learned.

Dr. Brooks nonetheless recognizes that there continues to be a problem with the professional staff being recognized for their knowledge and expertise. Too often, the acknowledgment comes late and is laced with incredulity.

Then there is the professional staff that we have here that people treat them as though they don't exist. These folks have master's degrees and they're like daily on the front line dealing with compliance and so forth, but they are ignored until they have a problem they need to help with, and then I hear, "I didn't know Kelly knew all that stuff."

Despite these persistent issues for faculty and staff of color, Dr. Brooks is cautiously optimistic that things will change.

Diversity has been a challenge for this and other universities. Yet, after 26 years I am allegedly more visible (laughs), and I have some hope that things may change a bit more for maybe the generation of women who might be 10 years behind me. There could be a shift because there's more awareness and discussion and movement to be more inclusive.

Finding Our Voice

In the process of her professional and personal journey, Stephanie Brooks has learned quite a bit that informs how she proceeds and what others may do to successfully navigate the paths they travel. Whenever possible she shares those bits of wisdom and hopes to continue to do so in her next steps. Thus, for both professional and personal growth and development, Dr. Brooks asserts that it is essential that young African American women and girls find and use their voices—even when to do so may seem risky.

One of the things I want to say to girls is to begin to tune into the voice that's in them. Because one of the lessons that I learned over the years is that I wasn't aware of the ways in which I silenced my voice. For example, I would feel like this is something that I probably shouldn't do, or maybe in a particular situation I believed that I should say something in that moment or say something about what's just happened here, and I would edit myself; I would silence that voice. Or I really want to do this; it's going to make me happy, but everyone else is doing this and so I would go off and do this and then find my way right back to that always. Or it can be as simple as I like this color paint, get it! Why the hell are you thinking about a neutral color? Because you think that's the right thing, right? You have to really find a way to start to listen to your own voice when it speaks to you—and trust it! Realizing this internal dynamic is so important for everyone but particularly for girls because they/we are often told to be silent in different ways. Because Conversely, what I find is when I listen to my voice, I'm usually spot on and I'm happy and I feel like I made the right decisions. I've been true to myself.

Black Women at Church

In addition to the influences of her parents and grandparents, there was another specific group that influenced her growing up—Black women at church and in her community.

As children, we were immersed in church—choir, junior usher board. I was also in Girl Scouts. What was for me helpful, what I internalized, was watching these different church women constantly teaching kids. Some of them were more traveled than others; some of them worked in business, some of them were educated. It was there in church that I discovered the Delta Sigma Theta sorority, which I later pledged. And watching all these women, I liked what they were doing—volunteering and working with the community. I would ask these women questions about what they were doing and why they were doing it, and they would talk about it. I liked the kind of

impact they were having—and I wanted to be a part of it. There was some-
thing about what they were doing that resonated for me. I thought, 'Okay,
this is something that I can do' because I was looking for ways to change
things. I had watched depression—mental and economic—daily in Newark.
Some of the decisions I made about graduate school relate back to these
women I observed. I was committed to undoing things in communities and
policies that impact people who were oppressed.

Spirituality/Faith

The memory of what she loved about church and the ladies she met and
observed there may contribute to Stephanie's current effort to find her
way back to a more formal religious experience. Although it was a place
she once enjoyed, she drifted away when religion became less about fellowship and spirituality and more politicized.

I'm spiritual and I pray, but I've been trying to find my way back to that
church experience I enjoyed and whose influence helped me along the way.
I found it to be energizing, a place I would go to refuel. I want that again.
I want it to be a cheerful space and not one where I feel like I have to be
politically savvy. I really enjoy the fellowship, but I also don't want to feel I
have to participate—now they get you to do all kinds of things. I feel more
comfortable saying no, I can't. I deserve this. Why can't I just come and en-
joy it the way I want to enjoy it?

Change

Me Time

Stephanie Brooks has been a working woman for her entire adult life.
Beginning as a social worker and then getting her Ph.D. in Couple and
Family Therapy at the age of 45, Stephanie recognizes that she is in a better place than her mother and hopes her daughters will be able to say the
same. But her work life is still substantial; something she would like to
change in the next few years by working less professionally and more on
herself—whether through home renovation or rekindling relationships.

I think that I am in a different place than my mother because I have
more options than she had just in terms of being able to make money. But I
would like to be working less. I am working on my kitchen. I thought about

hiring a company to do it all at once but decided I would do it in pieces. It's starting to look great, but it's much more inconvenient than doing it all at one time. And the only reason I'm not doing that because I'm putting my money in other places.

I love to cook. I love having people over—people with whom I have close relationships and who are in my inner circle, I need to have some sanctuary. My home is the only place I can have that sanctuary because I have control. You can't have control over here. You can't have control on the streets. So, I'm starting to get back to rekindling some of the relationships and finding a certain resultant joy.

At this stage in her life, another motivator to become at least a bit more self-focused and to find that 'next step' is Stephanie's realization that mortality appears to also be in the mix—

I'm 56. When I think about my friends, they are now like late 50s to 70. What happened? It was just yesterday!? I graduated from high school in 1978, and we are having a reunion. It's the first one I'm going to go to. I said, 'well, I don't know if we'll make the next one, so I should probably go the way people are dropping off. So, I will make it my business to go to this one.' It's in June and I will get a chance to see the folks who are still with us.

Despite this jolt of reality, she's still young enough to think about what else she wants to do. With a social justice consciousness developed as a child, Stephanie fervently believes there is more for her to do. She is searching . . .

I've been trying to figure out what is the one big thing on which I would really love to have an impact? I feel like there is something big that I have left to do; that there is more for me to do.

Having reached all of the professional goals that she set for herself in her twenties—and many she had not even imagined—Dr. Stephanie Brooks is certainly at that point in her life where she is trying to decide on her future. Her decision is, however, less about personal benefit and more about honoring how she was raised and what she learned from her mother.

I have worked for everything that I have, but I've had opportunities that other people have not had. And so figuring out how I can just continue to use my privilege in a way that I can make a difference on multiple levels is what I want to do. I've been trying to figure out what is the one big thing I would really love to have an impact on? I feel like there is something big that I have left to do. I feel like there's more for me to do; something at a larger level. I just have to find it. Sometimes, it finds you. And so perhaps it will present itself. It could come to me; I hope it does.

One interesting aspect of growth and maturity—aging—is that it allows us to change so that we can finally relax. No longer bounded by worries about what we should do we realize that we can place a greater focus and emphasis on what we want to do—personally and professionally—to find contentment, our "Chi" our essence, our soul, our inner-self. For those of us who reach that point, it can be liberating. It is sort of like the Exhale in Waiting to Exhale. We don't have to wait any longer. Stephanie Brooks is in the process of that change and embracing it.

I am so much more flexible than I was as a young woman. I was pretty rigid and controlling. I had a lot of rules about what I could and could not do, when and why I was doing it. But it was my desire to have control and try to manage my space. But I was really dogmatic about it. Sometimes my mom would say, "You just don't care how you hurt people's feelings." I'd say, "No, I just said no, that's all I said." Now, I'm a lot more diplomatic than I used to be. I still say no and mean it and won't bend around some things, but I'm more thoughtful than I used to be.

Before I respond to people I try to think and reflect on my response and what impact it might have on them. Similarly, if I'm going to do something, I try to think about it on a larger scale—if I do this, what is this going to mean? I wouldn't do that when I was younger. I was like, 'I'm going to do X,' and I'd jump into it. And there is something to be said for that way of thinking. Because you just get in and deal with whatever the issue is. But I find that now I'm much more like that softer side of me. I'm more vulnerable now than I've ever been. And I actually like this part of my personality. It certainly has made me a better parent. I think it has made me a better therapist. When I think about my work over the years: my clinical work from my 20s and my 30s; and then in my 40s and 50s, when I started to not be afraid of myself and what I feel accepting all my own flaws, things got easier.

Most people who come into therapy are critiquing themselves about what they should and shouldn't do: "I should be this way", "I should have been doing that," "I should have thought about this," I should abide by that." And part of the battle is accepting your own imperfections. That makes you—you. So I'm definitely at a place where I have accepted my own imperfections around lots of things and I'm not predictable—and I think it's a great thing. People are constantly surprised by some of my choices, and I say I do this because it makes me happy or this person is in my life because they make me happy.

So, what makes Stephanie Brooks happy?

What makes me happy has changed. I think I'm much more purposeful about making decisions about where I'm going to put my time and what I want to do. And I consider how something I do is going to further help me with my mission: if I do this, how is this going to help? What is it? What does it mean? And if I realize it's going to take me too far off the rails I'm saying no, because it's going to require a lot of energy.

It's definitely maturity and experience. If someone called me today and said I want you to come into our agency and do a one-day cultural diversity workshop I would say no because one day is not enough time. Years ago, I would have said yes. Today I will say one day is not enough time. Early on, I knew that inside and I knew it from my experience, but I would not have said it. And so now, if you pose the same question, although I'm not really invested in doing the work, I will be clear that if you are really committed, this is what I think it needs to look like. And if you want me this is what you need to do. I'm much more comfortable in my skin than I used to be around that kind of thing. I am more confident and comfortable with that and also telling you that if you want to have an impact on racism it isn't happening in eight hours.

Stephanie Brooks has had a lot to do . . . And now in her own way and in a way that makes her happy, she keeps on doing it!

NEXT TIME:

**ORDINARY EXTRAORDINARY
AFRICAN AMERICAN WOMEN:
THE MILLENIALS**

Coming in 2022 . . .

We continue our celebration of African American women in our next book, *Ordinary Extraordinary African American Women: The Millennials*. Our subjects are women between the ages of 25 and 44. Their journeys are so very different from each other and those we have celebrated in our first two books. Their common bond as African American women is their uniqueness, commitment to excellence, and their ability to overcome obstacles and persevere in our community, country and in our world.

Join us!

ACKNOWLEDGMENTS

Thank you, God, for the Grace of my parents, Winfred & Granville Colbert, and the Blessing of my siblings, Winfred, Wynell, Jordiene & Jonathan. All of them allow me to do what I do. God is good—all the time!

Thank you to my editors, Alexis, Ms. Vina, Joy, Wynell, and all of those who allowed me to talk through the writing process. If I don't mention you, it is only because I am at that age of forgetfulness; but my thanks are no less heartfelt. Thank you to Wendy for always checking on me and my book progress. I'm waiting to return the favor. Thank you to friend and confidant Norma June Wilson Davis, who is the inspiration for this series of books, an Elder we celebrated in the first book, and a special person to me. Thank you to retired Professor of Chemistry at the University of Iowa Dr. Leodis Davis—who is also a fabulous artist—for your friendship and encouragement. Thank you to Venise Berry, Felicia Hall Allen, and June Davis for your support, and belief in this project through your words. To Sherry and Tony Roberts and the Roberts Group for creating a wonderful book that we are proud to share. Thank you to Ginger Campbell and SNAP Productions, Inc. for your innovation, creativity, persistence, and marketing prowess. Thank you to Brian Sanders & Agent Hi5 Productions for your much-needed social media expertise at a time when the book industry has to be very open to alternatives. Thank you to Beverly Holmes Smith—Journalism and Education in action! Thank you to my sister Wynell for your love and for keeping me grounded in this project and in life—when I did not want to be, but absolutely needed to be. A special thank you the author of the Foreword, who happens to be my sister,

Jordiene J. Colbert Petitt. Joy's nickname is perfect as she is my absolute Joy! She has been thoughtful, patient, and loving as my confidant, editor, sounding board, recipient of my rants when I get frustrated, who would also tell me to, "settle down; bring it down a notch." She is my friend and just so dear to me. I could not have done this without you Joy! Finally, a warm and heartfelt thank you to the women we celebrate here—for your willingness to bare your souls and share your stories with all of us. On behalf of our families, friends, community, nation, and the world, thank you for the contributions you have made in the lives you have touched and the lives which will be touched in reading your stories.

In Memoriam

In Memory of the Elders we celebrated in our first book who we lost:

Leola Bradford 1927–2017

Donna Y. Brown 1937–2018

Mary Lou Miles 1921–2019